D1070863

CRUSADER

General Donn Starry and the Army of His Times

MIKE GUARDIA

CASEMATE

Philadelphia & Oxford

Published in the United States of America and Great Britain in 2018 by
CASEMATE PUBLISHERS
1950 Lawrence Road, Havertown, PA 19083, USA
and
The Old Music Hall, 106–108 Cowley Road, Oxford OX4 1JE, UK

Hardcover Edition: ISBN 978-1-61200-544-7
Digital Edition: ISBN 978-1-61200-545-4

A CIP record for this book is available from the British Library

Printed and bound in the United States of America

For a complete list of Casemate titles, please contact:

CASEMATE PUBLISHERS (US)
Telephone (610) 853-9131
Fax (610) 853-9146
Email: casemate@casematepublishers.com
www.casematepublishers.com

CASEMATE PUBLISHERS (UK)
Telephone (01865) 241249
Email: casemate-uk@casematepublishers.co.uk
www.casematepublishers.co.uk

For Marie and Melanie

Also by Mike Guardia:

American Guerrilla

Shadow Commander

Hal Moore

The Fires of Babylon

Contents

Foreword

I first met Donn Starry in 1973. I was a young West Point cadet on summer training at Fort Knox. He was the 2-star Commanding General of the US Army Armor Center. If I had any doubts about whether I would remain at West Point, and any doubts about whether I wanted to be an infantryman, artilleryman, or a cavalryman when I graduated, he erased them. General Donn Starry was a courageous warrior, a once-in-a-generation thinker, a gifted writer and speaker, and uncommonly engaging with senior and junior soldiers alike. He was, quite simply, the officer I wanted to emulate in my own career.

Mike Guardia chronicles the career of this superb, transformative leader. Drawing on a wealth of both serious and amusing anecdotes, he captures the essence of Donn Starry's leadership over the course of his long and illustrious career.

In 1981, I met Donn Starry again. Due in no small part to his inspiration, I had remained in the Army, and I was serving in a cavalry squadron in Colorado. He was the 4-star Commanding General of US Army Training and Doctrine Command. It was a perfect fit for this warrior-scholar. He had come to Fort Carson to introduce the Army's new doctrine—AirLand Battle. Ever the thinker, ever the teacher, he was almost single-handedly changing the way the Army thought about maneuver warfare.

Mike Guardia's story is especially persuasive on this point. Donn Starry redefined modern, maneuver warfare and set the Army on a path of rigorous and relevant training and education, many elements of which persist today.

The last time I met General Starry was in 2010. I had become the 4-star Commanding General of US Army Training and Doctrine Command. He had agreed to visit and to compare the challenges he faced in Training and Doctrine Command post-Vietnam to the challenges I faced as the wars in Iraq and Afghanistan began to slow down and other challenges in Europe and Asia began to emerge. He was impressive, as always, and helped me see things with his rich and thoughtful historical perspective, a perspective that contributed to changes we would eventually make in our leader development model. He died a year later, a leader of consequence to the end.

In the course of US military history, the greatest accolades go to the Generals and Admirals who are victorious in the decisive battles on land, at sea, and in the air. It is ironic that those who take on the harder task of preparing our military for war during time of peace are often forgotten. It is my hope that Mike Guardia's *Crusader: General Donn Starry and the Army of His Times* will ensure that this great military leader is not forgotten.

General Martin E. Dempsey (USA, ret)
18th Chairman of the Joint Chiefs of Staff
37th Chief of Staff of the Army

Introduction

May 1970: Increasingly frustrated by the Communist incursions into South Vietnam, the US launched a full-scale attack against the enemy's strongholds in southern Cambodia. At the tip of the spear was Colonel Donn A. Starry, commander of the 11th Armored Cavalry Regiment. Mounted atop their M48 Main Battle Tanks and M113 Armored Cavalry Assault Vehicles, Starry's regiment squared off against several thousand North Vietnamese and Viet Cong operating in the Cambodian border-lands. Although critically wounded on the front lines, Starry rallied his men to a decisive victory that captured the largest enemy cache in the region. For his audacious leadership and courage under fire, Starry was awarded both the Silver Star and Bronze Star Medals.

A 1948 West Point graduate, Starry entered the officer ranks during the inaugural years of the Cold War. Although he missed combat in World War II and Korea, Donn Starry became one of the most influential commanders of the Vietnam War. In a conflict dominated by airmobile infantry, Starry was a leading advocate for tank warfare in Vietnam. As a member of the Mechanized and Armor Combat Operations in Vietnam (MACOV) study group, his recommendations helped shape the contours for the use of American armor in Southeast Asia.

Following his tour of duty in Vietnam, Starry took command of the US V Corps, forward-stationed in West Germany. At the time, the US Army had shifted its doctrinal focus away from counterinsurgency and back towards the conventional defense of Western Europe. However, Starry noticed that the current doctrine for defending Europe—a plan known as "Active Defense"—was fundamentally flawed. In response, he created a new doctrine known as "AirLand Battle," which emphasized small-unit initiative, synchronization of air–ground assets, and striking at the enemy's rear echelons before he had a chance to mobilize them. Codified in the 1982 edition of Field Manual (FM) 100-5 *Operations*, AirLand Battle paved the way for the US Army's decisive victory during Operation *Desert Storm*. Starry retired as a four-star general in 1983.

Like most battlefield commanders from the Vietnam era, Starry's legacy is often overshadowed by the controversy of the war itself and the turmoil of the immediate postwar Army. However, with the development of AirLand Battle, it is hard to imagine anyone who has had a greater impact on modern maneuver warfare.

The idea for *Crusader* began in the summer of 2010 when I was a young armor officer in the US Army. Starry remains highly revered within the armor community and I learned much about him during my time at the Armor Officer Basic Course. When I began researching this project, Starry was still living but had been suffering from a rare form of cancer. Although his family gave me their blessing to pursue the biography, they politely declined my request to interview the elder Starry given the precarious nature of his health. Nevertheless, each member of the family selflessly gave their time and energy piecing together the information needed for this book. Donn Starry tragically lost his battle with cancer on August 26, 2011. He was 86 years old.

Throughout his career, Donn Starry was a prolific author. During my time as a junior officer, I read many of his works on armored warfare. His seminal text, *Mounted Combat in Vietnam*, explored the use of American armor in a war dominated by light and airmobile infantry. *Mounted Combat in Vietnam* was the last installment of the 13-part *Vietnam Studies* series commissioned by the Army Center of Military History. Starry's book, however, was the only one in the series to be completed *after* the war, thereby offering a full account of armor and mechanized operations while the other installments covered their respective topics up until about 1971. Together with historian George F. Hoffman, Starry also wrote and edited *From Camp Colt to Desert Storm*, a complete history of American armor operations from the World War I-era Tank Corps to the Gulf War tank battles at 73 Easting and Medina Ridge. Other works by Starry include his numerous articles written for *Military Review* and *Armor Magazine*.

However, the best primary resources for this book were "The Donn A. Starry Papers" and "The Donn Starry Photo Collection," both located at the Military History Institute's (MHI) archives in Carlisle Barracks, Pennsylvania. MHI's collection contained various letters, position papers, command documents, oral history interviews, and more than 300 photographs of Starry during his time as chief of the Army's Training and Doctrine Command (TRADOC). In 2009, the Combat Studies Institute (the professional publications arm of the Army's Command and General Staff College) privately published these papers under the title *Press On! The Collected Works of General Donn A. Starry.*

Government documents, including the 11th Armored Cavalry's "After-Action Reports," provided a wealth of information for this book. Since Starry was no longer living, his surviving family graciously gave me their time for numerous interviews. They also sent me an abundance of Donn Starry's personal and professional papers that remained in their possession.[1]

I give special thanks to Donn Starry's children (Mike, Paul, Melanie, and Melissa) for their kindness and hospitality. Without their collective help, this book may never have been written. I would also like to thank the courteous and attentive staff at the Military History Institute, the TRADOC Archives, and the Copyright Clearance Center for their assistance during my research. Finally, I would like to thank the editorial/production team at Casemate Publishers for their patience and professional support.

The reader must bear in mind that this is a book about Donn Starry. His life is the driving force behind the narrative. Therefore, the reader will not find many detailed discussions on the broader aspects of the Cold War, Vietnam, or the evolution of modern Army doctrine. While I have included *some* discussion of these aspects for the sake of context, they are discussed largely inasmuch as Starry participated in them. In a career that spanned more than 30 years, Donn Starry proved himself to be an innovative leader and a visionary of modern maneuver warfare. *Crusader* is his story.

CHAPTER I

Call of Duty

The story of Donn Albert Starry begins, in earnest, during the Gilded Age of American history. His father was born Don Albert Lacock near Cedar Rapids, Iowa, in 1897. Orphaned at the tender age of six, the young Don Lacock was taken in by the widow Emma J. Starry. Madam Starry had lost her own daughter several years earlier. "So the townsfolk, as was the custom in country farm communities in those days, took in the kids. Some of them were old enough to fend for themselves. The younger ones they just took in and raised as members of their own family." Thus, the elderly widow formally adopted Don Albert Lacock and changed his surname to Starry.

For most of her young ward's formative years, it was a time of peace and prosperity—both at home and abroad. The US had emerged victorious from the Spanish–American War and had become a superpower on the world stage. With new overseas territories in the Caribbean and the Pacific, the US now had easy access to foreign markets. Acquisition of the Panama Canal in 1901 further solidified America's dominance in the Western hemisphere. Under the steady hand of President Theodore Roosevelt, "Big Stick Diplomacy" and "Trust-busting" became the rule of the day. Europe, for the first time in nearly two centuries, was at peace and the Industrial Revolution had improved the quality of life for Europeans of every stripe.

For Don Albert Starry (formerly Lacock), however, there was little concern beyond finishing his studies at Cornell College and starting a nuclear family, the likes of which he had never known while growing up.

But as the elder Starry enjoyed the stable, idyllic life of the Roosevelt–Taft era, a storm was brewing on mainland Europe. Indeed, the political geography of the continent, and the fate of two generations, were about to change.

In August 1914, after years of ethnic tension, a young Serb named Gavrilo Princip assassinated the heir to the Austro-Hungarian Empire, Archduke Franz Ferdinand. A series of war declarations followed as Austria-Hungary mobilized against Serbia. The ensuing Great War took the brutality of combat to a new level. It was a war where bomber aircraft and tactical fighter planes made their debut. Machine guns provided a deadly, rapid fire capability to infantrymen in the field. It was also the first war that harnessed the destructive power of chemical weapons, including phosgene and mustard gas. Meanwhile, the opposing sides had dug themselves into a network of trenches and made minor advances against the other in what quickly became a stalemate along the Western Front. The most innovative killing machine, however, was the tank.

> The story of Sir Ernest Swinton's invention, the tank … began in World War I [said Starry]. Born independently in both the British and French armies, tanks became the subject of considerable debate regarding design, development, and employment. In the United Kingdom a coterie of single-minded tank and mobility enthusiasts persisted in developing concepts for mobile, all-arms warfare built around tank-led striking forces. In France, Col. Jean Estienne, with the backing of industrialist Louis Rheault, was able to convince the General Staff of the potential worth of light tanks employed in mass to break the trench-bound stalemate and restore maneuver to the battlefield.

Still, many Americans were confident that the war in Europe would run its course without their involvement. Those hopes were dashed, however, in the wake of German aggression on the high seas and their pernicious behavior on the diplomatic front. When America finally entered the war in 1917, some 14,000 men of the American Expeditionary Force were mobilized to join the fight in Western Europe. A year later, however, nearly 2,000,000 men had been deployed to the European battlefront.

> My father enlisted in the Tank Corps out of college. The Tank Corps and the Air Service [which later became the Army Air Corps] were the premier branches of the time. Recruiters from both services worked college campuses of the nation, seeking to enlist the brightest and most active young men into these

elite organizations rather than rely on conscripted forces. They also sought—at least in places like rural Iowa, where my Dad went to college—young men from the farms, men who had at least some experience with engines and the running gears of machinery. Some soldiers of the day enjoyed basic soldier training at Camp Colt, a site now buried in the town or on the battlefield at Gettysburg, Pennsylvania.

Such was the case for the elder Starry, who took a liking to the soldier lifestyle. As a young corporal, his promotion orders to sergeant were signed by none other than Captain Dwight D. Eisenhower, the camp commander. Eisenhower would, of course, go on to become the Supreme Allied Commander in Europe during World War II and serve two terms as the 34th President of the United States.

"Since but a single tank was available for training at Camp Colt, Sergeant Starry and some of his buddies were trained in their tanks— French-made Renaults—at the Tank Corps School at Langres, France." The commandant of the Tank Corps School was the young Lieutenant Colonel George S. Patton Jr. Even during his formative years as an officer, Patton had a reputation for his hard-charging, "piss-and-vinegar" approach to combat leadership. During the Battle of Saint Mihiel and the Meuse Argonnes Offensive, Patton stormed through the barbed-wired, trench-laden fields *on foot* as he accompanied his tanks into battle.

For the young Sergeant Starry, life in the Tank Corps was nearly too much of a whirlwind to recount. The Camp Colt-based units arrived in France during the latter months of the war. Essentially, "they deployed to France, then turned around and came right back home." Indeed, neither Starry nor any of his immediate comrades from Camp Colt saw action along the Western Front. Barely a few months after the Armistice was signed in November 1918, the US Military demobilized in a manner more helter-skelter than its 1917 buildup. Thus, "after rushing to the colors, undergoing partial training in the United States and France, and hustling off to combat," Sergeant Starry took a brief respite to the casino resorts of Monaco before returning to the hinterlands from which he had come. Many of Starry's comrades would eventually go to war again. "But in 1919, such a possibility was so remote as to be unthinkable to the men of C Company, 329th Battalion, Tank Corps, AEF."

That spring, the elder Starry returned to the United States to pick up where his civilian life had left off. He returned home with back pay and bonuses totaling $81.53 ($1,295.88 in 2016 dollars). The pell-mell demobilization, meanwhile, continued and by November 1919, more than 3,000,000 soldiers had been mustered out. But despite this downsizing, and his own discharge, Sergeant Starry's life in the military was far from over.

As "Return to Normalcy" became the rule of the day, Don Albert Starry married his college sweetheart, Edith Sorter, and took a job in New York City at what is now the Kraft Food Company. Among these concrete jungles, his only son—Donn Albert Starry—was born on May 31, 1925. Originally, the scion's name was identical to his father's. But, for reasons unknown, the elder Starry later decided that he did not want his son to be a "Junior"—and thus amended the birth certificate to read "Donn," spelt with the double "n."

Before making the family's home in New York, however, Sergeant Starry taught secondary school in Iowa for a year. "I guess he thought that [teaching] wasn't for him," said the younger Starry, "and was lured off to Boston by a Tank Corps buddy named Bill Helms, who was the son of an earlier Helms, the founder of Goodwill Industries of America. The idea was that my dad and Bill Helms were going to work in Goodwill Industries, which Dr. Helms was just starting. My dad went to Kansas City and married my mother … and took her off to the East Coast with him. Eventually, he decided he didn't want to stay with the Helms organization and went to work, first for Marshall Fields, then as the Export Manager for Kraft." Shortly after their son's birth, however, the Starrys decided that New York City was not the ideal place to raise a child, and moved to rural Kansas. Once there, young Donn enjoyed a childhood that was typical of most boys growing up in small-town America.

In many ways, Donn Starry was a product of his time. His was the so-called "Greatest Generation," raised on the harrowing tales of the Great War, the prosperity of the Roaring Twenties, and the hardships of the Great Depression. The Starry family, though not untouched by the economic turmoil, still fared better than most. Kansas was at the farthest edge of the Dust Bowl, and the Starry siblings recalled the faint traces of sand and soil that blew into Kansas City—the dying strands of the dust storms that had destroyed lives and communities elsewhere in the Great Plains. The Starrys also recalled that it was a time of transient labor—a time when men roamed from town to town looking for any means of employment they could find. It was not uncommon for itinerant workers (victims of the Great Depression) to show up in a strange town and go door-to-door, asking to cut lawns, prune gardens, or chop wood in exchange for a meal or even a few cents of pocket change.

A good portion of Starry's childhood, however, revolved around his father's membership in the Kansas National Guard. "I think he always regretted, really, that he never stayed in the Army or accepted a commission during World War I," said the younger Starry, "because he had an affinity for the military." Thus, shortly after the family's arrival in Kansas City, the elder Starry accepted a commission in the local National Guard armory. In his civilian career, many of his business colleagues were National Guardsmen; it was they who probably persuaded him to accept an officer's commission. With the stroke of a pen, the former Sergeant Starry became First Lieutenant Starry, commander of Headquarters Company, 2d Battalion, 137th Infantry Regiment, 35th Division, Kansas National Guard. "Of course, there was no longer a Tank Corps … [and] for reasons now lost he elected to join the infantry."

Shortly after his father's appointment to command Headquarters Company came the younger Starry's own appointment as Brevet First Lieutenant in the Kansas National Guard. In other words, "I was the company mascot," Starry said.

> I suppose that was what started my interest and whetted my appetite for military service. The year was 1929 and I was four years and some months of age when Governor Clyde M. Reed "assigned" me to my father for quarters, rations, discipline, and for such other duties as might be assigned by the company commander. Those included, as it turned out, periodic drills at the local armory—first located in an abandoned movie house and later a more substantial building—and attendance at all or part of an annual two-week summer camp at nearby Fort Riley.
>
> It was a terribly lean Army. The National Guard was pretty much a reflection of the Regular Army. Although Headquarters Company was authorized several high-frequency radio sets, there was but one on hand. Radio operators and crews took turns operating this lone radio. Ammunition boxes salvaged from summer

camp were painted to look like the real thing, complete with wooden knobs and dials and hand-painted scales. Operators and crews for whom there were not enough radios would go through the motions on their wooden mock-ups as the crew picked to operate the real radio practiced.

One older model Ford stake-and-platform truck was assigned to the Kansas City garrison. Companies assigned took turns using it for weekend field exercises. At night it was necessary to park the truck headed downhill for an easy, clutch-assisted start in the morning. It was easier than pushing.

Thus was the condition of the country's defense preparedness for whatever national security challenges might come next. It assured that there would be a reiteration of the mobilization frenzy of World War I.

Indeed it did.

For by 1940, as Donn Starry was coming of age, the political climate was much different than it had been during the late 1920s. Isolationism still rang high in the halls of Congress, but that ideology was quickly losing steam as Nazi Germany—which had initiated another European war on September 1, 1939—advanced on all fronts. From these developments, the US government authorized a full-scale increase in military spending. Meanwhile, across the pond, the British relied heavily on American logistics in their life-and-death struggle against the *Luftwaffe* and the *Kriegsmarine*. The Empire of Japan, however, was of little concern to anyone. Despite their recent aggressions on the Chinese mainland, everyone knew that the Japanese could *never* challenge the US military.

But as the situation in Europe and the Pacific went from bad to worse, Donn Starry tended to his studies and excelled in all areas of his high-school career. "I played football for two years," he said, "I swam for three years and lettered in both sports. I played football, not very well, on a team that had some awfully good football players. Good crew, super coach, and a good bunch of guys, but they were out of my league." Nevertheless, his skills as a player were such to earn him a place on the varsity team. He was also active in student government and displayed remarkable skills as an amateur photographer, even going so far as to build a darkroom in his family's basement.

His favorite subject in school, however, was the young Leatrice Gibbs. "Letty," as she was called, lived down the street from Starry and had been the object of his affection since they were young children. Letty was a year older than Donn but the age difference (an unspoken taboo in the realm of adolescent dating) didn't dissuade him from pursuing her.

And pursue her he did.

By the end of their high-school years, Letty and Donn were a regular sight at the local movie houses and soda fountains—enjoying the blissful life of a teenage couple.

Meanwhile, as Donn outgrew his childhood role of Brevet First Lieutenant for the Kansas National Guard, he took on more practical jobs within the community. For several summers, he hauled samples of wheat from a silo at a local farm. It was a half-day's work, and good pay for a Depression-era job, but it left Starry with a debilitating allergy from the grain. During these long, allergy-inducing wheat hauls, Starry acquired a red handkerchief as the only means of relief from the constant congestion. That red handkerchief became his unofficial calling card as he kept it with him for the rest of his life. And although he eventually shed the role of the Headquarters Company "mascot," he still accompanied his father to their monthly drills, taking every opportunity that he could to feed his appetite for all things military.

"Somewhere along the line," he said, "someone described West Point to me and I decided I wanted to go there." Indeed, Starry was fascinated by West Point's legacy of leadership. Its graduates included military legends such as Ulysses S. Grant, Robert E. Lee, Stonewall Jackson, and John J. Pershing. Since its founding in 1802, West Point had been the nation's premiere military academy and the primary source of commissioned officers for the US Army. A rockbound citadel ensconced on the banks of the Hudson River, West Point lay some 50 miles north of New York City. The school was renowned for its uncompromising standards of honor and discipline, and the Gothic architecture of the campus complemented its reputation as one of the most rigorous schools in America.

Gaining admission to West Point, however, was no easy task. The applicant files read like a "Who's Who" of America's best young scholars. Valedictorians, National Merit Scholars, and Eagle Scouts were among the many who sought to join the Long Gray Line. Admission to the Academy was further restricted by a Congressional nomination process.

About the time I was a freshman in high school I started taking the Civil Service Commission examinations that members of the Congress could use to select appointees to West Point. There were no college entrance exams to use as a standard, so the Civil Service Commission created these exams and then Congressmen—a lot of them just to avoid the image of political favoritism—would give the examination, and then allege, of course, that they were giving the appointments out on the basis of who did best on the exams. They were tough and comprehensive examinations and, if you didn't have some experience in taking that kind of exam, you were apt not to do well. So, most of us … took the exams several times before we actually took them for record. I wasn't even old enough to go to West Point when I took it the first time.

Donn Starry took the test twice more before he took it "for record." In the midst of preparing for his test however, his fortunes changed in the wake of the Pearl Harbor attack.

On the morning of December 7, 1941, the Imperial Japanese Navy launched a surprise attack on the US naval base at Pearl Harbor, Hawaii. Like everyone else in America, Donn Starry was shocked and dumbfounded. No one had anticipated a first strike against Hawaii, much less from the Japanese. To this point, nearly everyone had dismissed the Japanese military as a second-rate fighting force. Now the US had been thrown into to melee alongside the ailing Allied powers as they tried to beat back the onslaught of Nazi Germany and Imperial Japan. The following day, President Franklin D. Roosevelt declared war on the Axis powers and signed legislation increasing the number of cadets to the federal service academies.

Riding the tide of good fortune, Starry sought an appointment from Senator Art Capper (Kansas) in the spring of 1943. Having earned a passing score on the Civil Service exam, Donn was elated to hear that Senator Capper would grant him an appointment. That appointment, however, was to the US Naval Academy at Annapolis. "Somebody beat me out for the West Point appointment," he said, "but I was the second man on the senator's scoring list, so he offered me an appointment to Annapolis. *I didn't want to go to Annapolis.* So, I called the guy who had the West Point appointment … and found out that he wanted to go to Annapolis."

A few days later, the pair walked into Senator Capper's office whereupon Starry said: "Have we got a deal for you." With the senator's curiosity piqued, Starry explained that his comrade wanted to attend

Annapolis and that they wanted to swap their appointments. Impressed by the young men's initiative, Capper granted the request and Starry left the office that day with an appointment to West Point.

By now, however, it was the summer of 1943 and Donn Starry, having graduated from high school and reached his 18th birthday, had to register with the local draft board. Consequently, he was inducted into the US Army as a buck private on August 13, 1943. It was soon discovered, however, that he had taken the Civil Service examination and had earned a Congressional appointment to West Point. "I joined the Army at Fort Leavenworth in August of 1943," he recalled, "and before we could complete any substantial amount of basic training, it was decided that all of the folks who were going to go to the military academies needed to be sequestered from the Army as a whole. So, they organized training units at Lafayette, Cornell, and Amherst [colleges] so that we could get out of the military training environment and study for the entrance exams"—because after a prospective cadet had passed the Civil Service exam for his Congressional nomination, he had to pass an *additional* entrance exam authored by the Academy.

"The entrance exams," Starry recalled, "were far more difficult than the appointment exams. As a matter of fact, it's a good thing they let us study because I don't think any of us would have passed the entrance exam had we been doing something else … particularly something as rigorous as military training in those days, getting ready for war. It was a real good opportunity. So I went to Lafayette College in Easton, Pennsylvania, and spent the winter of 1943–44 there." Thus, as a young private, Starry recalled the preparatory program as one where they took Basic Training in their spare time: "the bulk of the exercise was to go to class and get yourself ready to pass the entrance exam." Starry took the exam and passed it in April 1944. "Those of us who didn't pass the entrance exams, for whatever reason, went back to the ranks of the Army." After a few weeks of well-earned leave, Starry and his cohorts received orders to report to West Point on July 1, 1944.

Although they were excited to be attending their dream school, Starry and his comrades often wondered if the war would last long enough for them to get through West Point. After some initial setbacks in the Pacific and North Africa campaigns, Allied forces had regained the initiative by summer 1943. Not surprisingly, many of Starry's comrades either turned down their appointments or eventually resigned from West Point to fight on the front lines of Europe or the Pacific. In fact, one of Starry's Jewish friends had passed the entrance exam but refused his appointment, saying: "I'm Jewish, so I can't appear to be shirking"—obviously aware of Nazi Germany's contempt for all things Hebrew. "So, he went off to war. Tragically, he was killed in the winter of 1944 in the Ardennes Offensive. And there were several people like that."

From Donn Starry's point of view, however, West Point was a long-term, strategic investment:

> It was not easy to see in 1943 where and when the war was going to end. There was certainly no perception that it was going to end in 1945, and I thought to myself: "You've got to go to some kind of [officer] training. This isn't exactly OCS [Officer Candidate School]. It's better than OCS," and I really wanted to be a *career* Army officer. So, I had the problem of how I was going to be a career Army officer if I didn't go to West Point—which was where all the career Army officers come from, or so I thought at the time … in those days the perception was that's where they all came from.

Starry found that several of classmates saw West Point the same way. They, too, wanted to be career officers and saw the Academy as the most likely conduit to that end.

Donn Starry arrived at West Point on July 1, 1944, initially as a member of the wartime Class of 1947. To meet the manpower needs of World War II, the Academy's curriculum had been accelerated to three years instead of four. The cadets' first day at West Point was called Reception Day, or "R-Day." It marked the beginning of a strenuous indoctrination known as Cadet Basic Training, or "Beast Barracks" as it was commonly known. Although exclusively for West Point cadets, Beast Barracks largely resembled the Basic Training program of the Regular Army.

Most West Point graduates remember their R-Day as a blur of savage put-downs, dreadful stares, close calls with heat exhaustion, and the constant reminder that "I *wanted* to come to West Point." For Donn Starry, R-Day certainly lived up to its chaotic reputation.

Scurrying off the train at the West Point depot, Starry disembarked with several hundred other new cadets, all eager to begin their journey into the officer ranks. His classmates came from all over the country, most of them from small towns he had never heard of: Berryville, Virginia; Aberdeen, South Dakota; and Lakewood, Ohio, among others. They represented nearly every walk of life. Some were fresh out of high school while others, like Starry, were graduates of the "cram schools." Some had had a few years of college under their belts. Some had given up trade careers in carpentry, machinery, and electrical work to try their hand at soldiering. Others were enlisted men who abruptly traded their chevrons for cadet gray. Whatever their background, they all came with the aspiration to become officers and fight the Axis powers.

Every summer during Beast Barracks, the junior and senior-year cadets assumed the role of drill sergeants, instructing the new cadets in military matters. Upon meeting his cadet instructors, the strenuous journey of Beast Barracks began. All at once, Donn's new name was "Mister"—Mister "Dumbjohn," "Dumbcrot," "Dumbwilly," or occasionally, his last name.

"Slap on a brace, Mister Dumbjohn."[2]

"Get those shoulders back, Mister!"

"Hey Mister, quit looking around!"

"Move out, Mister!"

Then came the seemingly endless drill and marching commands: "Attention! Left Face! Right Face! Forward March! At Ease!"—and very little of the latter. Soon thereafter, Starry learned the sacred "Four Responses" which every new cadet had to use whenever he was addressed by an upperclassman. A new cadet's responses were limited to: "Yes sir," "No sir," "No excuse, sir," and "Sir, I do not understand."

Starry also discovered that the cadets were not referred to as freshmen, sophomores, juniors, and seniors. Instead, they were referred to, respectively, as Fourth Class, Third Class, Second Class, and First Class cadets. Traditionally, the Fourth Classmen were known as "Plebes," a derivative of the word *Plebian*, referring to the lowest class of Roman society. Third Classmen were called "Yearlings," a term used to describe a year-old farm animal. The Second Classmen were "Cows," but the origin of that term remains obscure. The most likely explanation was that, in years past, the cadets had no leave until after Yearling year. Thus, when the rising Second Classmen returned from their summer furlough, it was heralded as "the cows coming home." The First Classmen's nickname was merely an abbreviation: "Firstie."

Throughout Beast Barracks, Starry learned the fundamentals of soldiering: rifle marksmanship, patrolling, hand grenades, and the proper technique of shining shoes. As expected, every block of instruction had been tailored to the current threats in Europe and the Pacific. There were regular classes on the tactics and organization of the *Wehrmacht* and the Imperial Japanese Army. Beast Barracks culminated with the so-called "Plebe Maneuvers" at Pine Camp (present-day Fort Drum) near Watertown, New York. It was a weeklong field exercise that introduced Plebes to the art of bivouacking and how to maneuver at the squad and platoon level. Upon their return to West Point, Starry and his fellow Plebes we regrouped into their academic year companies. Starry thus found himself assigned to Company L-2 (L Company, 2d Regiment).

> Of course, the [West Point] curriculum today bears no resemblance to the curriculum when I went there, which is probably a good thing. It was an engineering school in those days, which was a hangover from the 19th century when somebody said West Point produced more railroad company presidents than it did generals, or words to that effect. The engineering culture continued, and I guess it does to this day to some extent. But it was strictly an engineering school. The first liberalization of the curriculum came after World War II, and I guess that's why I enjoyed my last two years there as much as I did—because it was not strictly engineering. The social sciences got started.
>
> West Point's problem, to me, then, and has been ever since, is, in a word, relevance. West Point is only useful to the Army if it can be relevant to the Army's problems and to the challenge of providing leaders for the Army. And if it doesn't do that … then you have to wonder why you have the place. I've always maintained that, particularly in recent years, a young man who goes to a good college, that has a good curriculum and a good Professor of Military Science, in today's world has an awful lot better chance of coping with the world in which he or she finds themselves when they join the Army than does a West Point graduate.
>
> And the place has always been isolated. They [cadets] don't see soldiers except when they go out in the summertime. Many of them have said to me that they have a hard time relating the world of soldiers to the world at West Point.

Indeed, for many years after his graduation, Starry believed that West Point was in what he called a "state of crisis"—a crisis of relevance:

Should we disband it and abandon it? I don't think so, but at the same time, to the extent that we preserve that isolation, which is so easy to do up there, to the extent that we let the Academic Board and its overbearing influence on the kids' presence up there deprive it of its relevance to the rest of the Army, then we're doing ourselves a great disservice. I've been a critic of the place for years. It's not that I'm critical of West Point or the purpose of it or anything else. I'm critical of the fact that it's lost its relevance, by and large.

Nevertheless, Donn Starry excelled in his cadet life. While keeping up with his studies, the young cadet also proved himself on the Academy's swimming team. In fact, the sport dominated so much of his leisure time that his classmates began calling him "Fish." He also sought refuge at the weekly Catholic Mass—even though he was Episcopalian. Since the Protestant service was so early on Sundays—and Sunday morning provided cadets their only opportunity to sleep in—Starry identified himself as a "Brevet Catholic" and attended Mass, which conveniently started later in the day.

By the end of Starry's first semester, he was fortunate to have remained "proficient" in academic standing. Meanwhile, the Allied offensive in Europe had stalled under the Germans' counterattack in the Ardennes forest of France. History would call it the Battle of the Bulge. Soon, however, the Allied offensive was back on track and by February 1945, the Allies had penetrated deep into the Fatherland. With the Americans closing in from the west, and the Soviets from the east, a frantic Adolf Hitler committed suicide on April 30, 1945. One week later, the German Army surrendered and the news of V-E Day rang throughout the world.

Meanwhile, in the Pacific, the enemy strongholds on Tarawa, Saipan, and Iwo Jima began to collapse under the fury of Allied offensives. In June 1945, the Imperial Japanese Army fought its last losing battle on the island of Okinawa. But even as the Allies closed in on the main archipelago, the Japanese refused to surrender. Wanting to bring this destructive conflict to an end, and well aware of the bloodbath that would follow an invasion of the Japanese homeland, President Harry Truman made a difficult decision: the atomic bomb would make its debut on the Empire of Japan.

Following the nuclear devastation of Hiroshima and Nagasaki, the Japanese government finally lost its will to fight. On August 14, 1945, Emperor Hirohito broadcasted a pre-recorded radio speech announcing Japan's unconditional surrender. He instructed all Imperial troops to lay down their arms and to cooperate with the newly arriving occupation force. Finally, on September 2, in a ceremony held aboard the USS *Missouri*, a Japanese delegation signed the official document of surrender. With the stroke of a pen, World War II had finally come to an end.

Now that the war had ended, West Point resumed its normal four-year schedule. To accommodate this change, the Class of 1947 was split. "At Annapolis, they simply split the class by academic order of merit," said Starry. "They took the top half and graduated them in 1947, and took the bottom half and graduated them in 1948. At West Point, they wanted an even split but they didn't want to do it as it was done at Annapolis ... there would always be that perception of the 'dumb guys of 1948.' That still hangs over that Annapolis class, incidentally." Thus, to entice cadets of 1947 to stay on for another year, West Point offered a number of incentives. In exchange for reverting to the Class of 1948, cadets were offered flight training, amphibious training, and numerous non-engineering electives at a reduced course load. "So, the last two years were really, from a lot of standpoints, pretty enjoyable," Starry recalled. "I had a lot of time to read, and do a lot of things that I would never have done otherwise, in a curriculum where the workload was spaced out. I really enjoyed that."

During his final two years at the Academy, the Army Air Forces (still referred to, colloquially, as the Army Air Corps) separated to become the United States Air Force. Subsequently, many of Donn's classmates commissioned into the Air Force. At the same time, Starry also saw the racial desegregation of the US armed forces. To this point, blacks had served in segregated units often led by white officers. Nevertheless, black cadets had been attending West Point and Annapolis alongside their white counterparts for decades. A black cadet's tenure at the Academy, however, was no simple feat. Often, cadets of color were shunned, harassed, or became the victims of unrelenting "gotcha games."

Starry recalled one black cadet in his company, Joe Kiernan, who was a frequent target:

They treated him like shit. I never could figure that out, because he was good guy. They tried to get him in trouble. They accused him one time of a violation of the Honor Code, which you just knew they ginned up on their own. They were trying to get rid of him. We had a bunch of hard core southerners. I never could understand, first of all, why the other cadets put up with that. We had a number who treated him decently, but they were passive about it, whereas those who didn't treat him decently were *active* about it, and I could never understand why the passive ones—who were, in fact, in charge of the organization as cadets—weren't more active in trying to prevent the things that these guys were obviously doing to this fellow. He was a good man and graduated in the Air Force as a fighter pilot.

Seizing the opportunity for flight training and a lighter workload, Donn Starry opted to stay with the Class of 1948. All things considered, the flight training had influenced his decision. At some point during his cadet career, he decided that the pilot culture appealed to him and that he should pursue a commission in the Air Force. While he has happy with his decision to stay for an additional year of military electives, the decision did not go well with his sweetheart, Letty. Being a year older than Donn, she had already graduated from the University of Kansas and was counting on him to have graduated in 1947. "I had to strike a deal with her that it was all right to wait another year," he said. That deal, as it were, had Letty moving to Highland Falls, New York—the town directly outside the gates of West Point. Serendipitously, she found a job with the Army Athletic Association and later as a secretary at the Holy Trinity Catholic Church at West Point. Soon thereafter, the couple announced their engagement and set their wedding date for June 15, 1948.

Meanwhile, the flight instructors at nearby Stewart Field took on the cadets of 1948 for extensive flight training. Previously, these Air Corps instructors had taught a select group of cadets with every class. Traditionally, during a cadet's second year at West Point, he had the option of becoming an "Air Cadet," and the remainder of his summer military training would occur at Stewart Field among other air bases. Now, however, the Class of 1948 was scheduled to take flight training *en masse* even if they had no intention of commissioning into the Air Force. "We spent a whole summer up there [Stewart Field] in what would have amounted, I suppose, to the equivalent of primary training

in the Air Corps. In the end we got a check ride and a flight physical."
Based on that flight physical and check ride, cadets who were deemed
eligible for service in the United States Air Force were placed on the
Air Cadet list. Starry passed his initial physical and his check ride
aboard a T-6 fighter-trainer. "I was among those who were going to
graduate and be commissioned in the Air Force. That was two years
away from graduation, and in those two years no one thought anything
more about the matter. We were eligible, and we all went along with
the idea in mind that we were going to be commissioned in the Air
Force if we were on that list." Unfortunately for Donn Starry, that
would not be the case.

As the spring of 1948 came along, Starry and his classmates had to
begin the process of branch selection. "They passed out a list asking
what branch we wanted to be in," he said. "You listed them in order of
preference." The Ground Cadets had the greatest variety from which to
choose: Infantry, Field Artillery, Combat Engineers, and the like. For
the Air Cadets, however, their branch selection seemed obvious—they
would simply enroll in the United States Air Force. Still, the latter-day
Air Cadets were encouraged to select a ground-based Army branch in the
event they were not selected for the Air Force. However, when Starry
received his branch selection form, he admitted that: "I wrote down Air
Force in the first three blanks and left the rest of them blank because I
was going to be in the Air Force according to the previous work that
we had done"—or so he thought.

> I took the flight physical again, and about two weeks before Graduation, I
> received a notice that I had been *disqualified* for flight training based on a piece
> of cartilage out of place in my nose [a deviated septum]—the result of a high-
> school football injury. So we had a squabble between doctors. One doctor said,
> "It is disqualifying," and the other doctor said, "It is *not* disqualifying." While
> the doctors were squabbling, the administration at the Academy made out its list
> about who was going to graduate into what branch, and they'd taken those of
> us who were foolish enough to do what I had done and just put us in branches
> to fill the quotas.

These leftover Army branches were typically the less glamorous fields
that nobody wanted—Quartermaster, Transportation, Coast Artillery,
and Adjutant General (Personnel).

By the time the doctors got through with their squabbling and said, "Okay, I guess it's all right for him to go in the Air Force," the Adjutant at West Point—a tough lieutenant colonel—had made up his list, and said to me, "I'm not going to change my list just for some cadet like you. You're going to graduate in the *Transportation Corps*." They also decided that those who were going to serve in [noncombat] branches needed some combat arms training, so you spent two years in combat arms [infantry, cavalry, artillery, etc.], then you reverted to your basic branch, went to that branch school, and served in that branch. So I said, "Okay, I'll take the cavalry/armor as a two-year assignment," and then immediately began trying to figure out how I was going to get transferred, because I *really* didn't want to serve in the Transportation Corps.

Starry was mortified, to say the least. Among West Point lieutenants, there was almost no lower form of existence than a truck commander. West Point's culture glorified service in the infantry, cavalry, and artillery—the so-called "Big Three"—and most of its graduates served in one of these career fields. Those who fell beyond the spectrum of combat arms were derided as being "desk jockeys" who purposely shunned the fieldwork of soldiering. It was a bitter pill for Starry to swallow, but he nevertheless chose to make the best of it. "I decided that dream [of being in the Air Force] was gone—there was no sense in me going to fly airplanes now. What I had to do was get a branch of the service that I wanted to serve in and see what I could do with that."

At this point, Starry had at least a passing familiarity with the modern armor force. Being the son of a World War I Tank Corps veteran, he remembered well his father's stories of the French-built mechanical beasts. From his daily readings of the *New York Times*, Starry had learned of General Patton's armored exploits on the European mainland. He also marveled at the courage of the Sherman tank crews as they took on the vastly superior Tiger and Panzer tanks of the Wehrmacht and Waffen SS. Indeed, the M4 Sherman had been the workhorse of American tank units throughout the war. Although it was still in service, it was slowly being phased out in favor of the M26 Pershing and the forthcoming M46 Patton. Armor units, as they were, still fell under the traditional cavalry branch, as they were a mechanical extension of the traditional mounted mobility provided by horsemen and dragoons.[3] Come what may, Starry preferred the rough-and-tumble world of armored warfare to that of a truck tender.

On June 8, 1948, Donn Starry graduated from the United States Military Academy. "We were the first class to graduate after the National Security Act of 1947 created a National Military Establishment with a Secretary of Defense and Departments of Army, Navy, and Air Force instead of War and Navy Departments." They were also the first West Point class to be commissioned into the Army and Air Force as separate services. Handing out their diplomas was the first ever Secretary of Defense, James V. Forrestal.

"We were 301 at graduation. Some 188 of us were commissioned in the Army, 111 in the Air Force." Three of Starry's classmates later transferred from the Army to the Air Force. One classmate, Joe Seymore, transferred from Army to Air Force and then back to Army. He was the only member of the Class of 1948 to fight in Korea as both a fighter pilot *and* an infantryman. Among Starry's more notable classmates were Sid Berry, who would return to serve as West Point's Superintendent from 1974 to 1977. Another classmate was James Van Fleet, Jr., whose father had commanded the US III Corps during World War II and later commanded UN forces in Korea. The younger Van Fleet commissioned into the Air Force and was assigned to the 13th Bomber Squadron during the Korean War. Tragically, Van Fleet, Jr. and the crew of his B-26 disappeared on a night intruder mission near Haeju, North Korea, on April 5, 1952. Neither Van Fleet nor his crewmen were ever found. Among Starry's classmates who remained with the original Class of 1947 were Alexander Haig and Brent Scowcroft. Haig served with distinction in Korea and would later serve as Secretary of State under President Ronald Reagan. Scowcroft would later become the National Security Advisor under Presidents Gerald Ford and George H. W. Bush.

Now second lieutenants, Starry and his classmates sallied forth to take on the world. The war against the Axis powers was over but the new "Cold War" had now emerged. It was to be fought not necessarily with bombs and bullets, but with words and ideas. The "hot" battles would be fought largely by proxy at the farthest corners of the earth. Words like "Mutual Assured Destruction," "Nuclear Holocaust," and "Balance of Power" would steer foreign policy for the next 40-plus years. Donn Starry and his classmates would be on the front lines.

CHAPTER 2

The Cold Warrior

"After almost two months of Graduation Leave, and a number of marriages, the 188 of us commissioned into the Army assembled in August at Fort Riley, Kansas, for our branch-immaterial Ground General School. This was our first active-duty assignment, and although we were still students, albeit 'officer-students,' Fort Riley had real soldiers for us to see. There, we integrated with contemporaries also commissioned in the Regular Army in 1948." These Ground General School contemporaries included college ROTC graduates and OCS graduates—some of whom had previously been enlisted men during the war.

The Ground General School itself was a relatively new concept. As Starry described it, the Fort Riley course was "an opportunity to bring together all newly commissioned second lieutenants in the Army and put them through a common course of schooling, since they had come from a variety of commissioning sources—OCS, West Point, and college ROTC programs." As fate would have it, the assistant commandant of the Ground General School was Colonel Oscar Koch, who had been a lifelong friend of the Starry family. Donn remembered that Koch had been "the Regular Army advisor to my dad's National Guard Company for a long, long time during the 1930s." In fact, Colonel Koch went on to serve as General Patton's chief intelligence officer during World War II. Koch later earned a modicum of fame when he published his memoirs of the conflict, *G-2 Intelligence of Patton*.

Still, Donn was mildly bristled about having lost his chance to commission in the Air Force. "I even had wedding invitations printed,

'Lieutenant, United States Air Force,'" he recalled. Years later, however, Starry admitted that he was glad that he didn't become a pilot:

> In the Air Force, the officers do all the fighting. The airmen are technicians. It's a different world. It's one of the things that's hard to explain … when you explain the difference between the Army and the Air Force. The soldiers fight in the Army and the officers lead. The officers fight in the Air Force and the soldiers support the officers. I don't think, certainly in retrospect, that I would have been nearly as gratified with a career in the Air Force as I have been with my career in the Army. I have a feeling of comradeship with the soldier ranks and the noncommissioned officer ranks of the Army, largely because I grew up with them, I suppose. You can't do that in the Air Force.

In the summer of 1949, however, the more pressing issue on Starry's mind was how to stave off his enrollment into the Transportation Corps.

"Virtually all of us were assigned overseas," as the Army still had a large occupation footprint in Europe and Japan. Naturally, most went to Germany, Japan, and Okinawa—but a lucky few landed in Panama or Hawaii. Those assigned to Hawaii, Europe, or Panama enjoyed "accompanied travel" with their wives, while those assigned to the Far East had to wait a year before family housing would be available. "Thus, we came to know the terms 'geographical bachelors and widows.'"

Arriving in West Germany in August 1949, Donn received orders to the 63d Tank Battalion, attached to the 1st Infantry Division. "The 63d Tank Battalion was an interesting organization," he said. During World War II, there had been no tank units organic to the infantry divisions. Instead, the Army had taken its corps-level tank battalions and attached them to the divisions. Consequently, "the battalion that was attached to the 1st Infantry Division was the 745th Tank Battalion." After the war, however, the Army created a new Table of Organization for its divisions, including one organic tank battalion and separate regimental tank companies. Thus, in 1948 the Army activated the 63d Tank Battalion under the 1st Infantry Division, bearing the lineage and honors of the original 745th Battalion.

As Starry recalled, these tank battalions were "in the context of the time, heavy organizations; that is, the companies had four platoons, five tanks each, and there were two headquarters tanks [belonging respectively to the company commander and executive officer]. So there were 22 tanks in a company. There were three companies in a battalion, and that made for a big battalion. We had 69 tanks in our battalion."

Taking command of his first platoon, Starry wondered if his new charges would take him seriously. "I was bothered by the problem of acceptance by some very grizzled veterans of World War II." Aside from a few replacements, nearly all of his soldiers were combat veterans, many of whom were highly decorated. "It was a strange collection of misfits," he recalled—men who had left the Army after World War II but came back because they couldn't find a job, or those who had left the Army and discovered that they no longer "fitted in" amongst their fellow civilians.

But, as he admitted, the 63d Tank Battalion had a wealth of experienced personnel:

> In the first platoon I commanded, every tank commander had been either a tank commander or platoon sergeant in a tank outfit in World War II—every one of them. The drivers and the gunners were the same way—they had been tank commanders and then they had come back as corporals or sergeants after a year or so out of the service. We had an enormous amount of combat experience.

Despite the experience gap between Starry and his men, he nevertheless carried himself with grace, approachability, and always sought opportunities to learn from his battle-hardened soldiers. "The first platoon sergeant I ever owned, or to whom I belonged," he said, "was an old gent named Willard Lucas." A grizzled Sergeant First Class, Lucas had served in the 5th Armored Division during World War II and had fought in some of the bloodiest battles of the European theater.

On meeting Sergeant Lucas, Donn learned just how important the relationship between platoon leader and platoon sergeant should be. The platoon leader was responsible for the tactical deployment of the platoon while the platoon sergeant oversaw its discipline and technical maintenance. These responsibilities, however, were not strictly demarcated and often overlapped. A platoon sergeant was in reality a partner, subordinate, and a mentor—sharing his expertise, yet contributing to the lieutenant's success. It was often said: "If you have a good platoon sergeant; you'll have an excellent platoon."

On meeting young Lieutenant Starry, however, Lucas simply eyed him and said, "Well, I see I have another lieutenant to train." He promptly issued Starry a toolbox, had him identify and inventory each tool, and sign for the entire contents. These socket wrenches, screwdrivers, etc. were the tools needed to maintain the mighty M26 Pershing tank, the workhorse of the 63d Tank Battalion. It was the Army's first operational "heavy" tank and fired the biggest caliber gun of any Allied tank in Europe. However, as Starry would find out, maintaining the five tanks in his platoon was an arduous task. And, ironically, the tanks seemed to break down more frequently within the motor pool than when out on maneuvers. After Starry signed for the last tool, Lucas told him, "Okay, Lieutenant, I know you've been to West Point. I know you've been to Fort Knox … and all that was very useful, but now what we are going to do is make things practical. I'm going to do that, and the maintenance instruction begins in the motor park tonight at 1930. Please be on time. Bring your toolbox."

Starry acknowledged his sergeant's request but was somewhat taken aback by it. "Well, who is in charge of this mess?" he wondered. Still, Donn concluded it was better to keep his mouth shut and listen to the old sergeant's advice. "I went to the motor park, *and it was an unfortunate thing*," he recalled facetiously. For Lucas made Donn Starry such a proficient mechanic that the lieutenant was later tapped to become the Battalion Motor Officer—a highly stressful and mercurial job that no junior officer ever wanted.

Still, Lucas was an outstanding mentor to the green lieutenant:

> The first time we went to the field and pulled into a bivouac area, Sergeant Lucas came up to my tank and said, "Now if the Lieutenant would be so kind as to go over and sit down under that tree, I will put the platoon in position. I will report back to the Lieutenant when we are ready for inspection." I thought, "Well now, I really should, as the platoon leader, be doing something besides sitting under that bloody tree." But I did as he said. So there I was, sitting under a tree reading my Soldier's Manual … trying to decide what I ought to be learning out of that. I also watched him as he went around. He made them go into position; he made them put up camouflage; he made them make out range cards. He had a kind of checklist of crew duties. He had a little inspection and he checked to see if they had been doing their maintenance. Then he came over to me and reported,

"Sir, the platoon is ready for inspection. If the Lieutenant would please accompany me, we will inspect the platoon. Here's what I want you to look for in tank 31, 32, and 33."

Then he told me some things, because he knew the sergeants and the crew better than I did and he knew where they were weak. When we all got through, he said,

"That's fine, sir. Thank you very much. You did what I asked you do to do, but you weren't tough enough. Now that may be for one of two reasons: one is that you are inclined to be too easy on the soldiers, and we can correct that. The second reason is that you don't know enough about the skills, the things we're checking on, the little tasks that I want them to do. You don't know enough about that yourself in order to ask questions, and you may be a little nervous about that, so we'll fix that. We're going to improve that, because we're going to have classes for you and I'm the instructor."

Starry continued:

Now, he [Lucas] was always very respectful, but it was clear to me that his job as he saw it was to train the platoon leader, and he was not alone. We had a battalion of those sergeants. This was 1949. Every platoon sergeant in that battalion had the attitude that it was his job to make sure that his lieutenant was the best platoon leader in the battalion. Now, as to individual training of the soldiers in the platoon, Sergeant Lucas was very clever about that. For instance, we would go to the field and clean weapons. The first time I went down there to watch this, he had all the soldiers gathered around in a circle. They had a couple of bins of solvent and cleaning materials. But they weren't just cleaning the weapons. He was conducting a class in the assembly, disassembly, nomenclature, functioning, care, and cleaning as they cleaned the weapons.

He was always checking on people. He had a little notebook in which he kept notes on me, the men in the platoon, and probably the battalion commander for all I know. But he had more knowledge in that notebook than all the manuals in the Army. Now today we call that a Job Book. One of the first things he made me do was to get one of those things myself. I had everything in there from shoes sizes and hat sizes for the men … to how many times they had been married and how many kids they had. It was all in my platoon leader's Job Book.

Starry was equally impressed by many of the officers in his battalion. His company commander was a young First Lieutenant George S. Patton IV, son of the legendary World War II general. The younger Patton had been one year ahead of Starry at the Academy, graduating with the accelerated Class of 1946. Patton would later serve in the Korean War and complete two tours of duty in Vietnam. Like his father, the younger Patton would also achieve general rank. But whereas the elder Patton was gruff and bombastic, his son was more measured, with a personality more akin to Omar Bradley. Another comrade in his battalion was First Lieutenant Sidney "Hap" Haszard. Hap had enlisted in the Army during World War II and earned a battlefield commission while serving in the Recon Company of the 1st Infantry Division. According to Starry, Haszard "probably had more experience with combat patrols than any officer in the battalion." Years later, as a Lieutenant Colonel, Hap Haszard would earn the Distinguished Service Cross for his actions at the Second Battle of Bau Bang in Vietnam.

No one, however, left a more lasting impression on Starry than his first battalion commander, Lieutenant Colonel Creighton "Abe" Abrams. By 1949, Abrams had already become somewhat of a legend within the Army. A 1936 West Point graduate, he had commanded the 37th Tank Battalion during World War II. Throughout much of his command, the 37th had been the spearhead of Patton's Third Army. Later in the war, Abrams commanded a brigade of the 4th Armored Division during the Battle of the Bulge and was awarded the Distinguished Service Cross for extraordinary heroism in Normandy. During the war, General Patton had said of Abrams: "I'm supposed to be the best tank commander in the Army, but I have one peer—Abe Abrams. He's the world champion."

"My perceptions of him as a leader," said Donn, "at that period have to be set against the background of what he had been and what he had done." Starry described him as the "most colorful, if not the best tank battalion commander" in the 4th Armored Division in World War II. After the war, however, Abrams had to accept an involuntary reduction in rank—part of an Army-wide reversion program that attempted to normalize the ranks of the postwar force. Hence, Abrams had been demoted from colonel to lieutenant colonel, and was none too happy about it. Coming home from the war, Abrams was sent to Fort Knox where he headed the Command and Staff Department, responsible for rewriting the field manuals and documenting the "lessons learned" from World War II.

"Then," Starry said, "all of a sudden, he is a lieutenant colonel with all of that background and he's assigned to command a tank battalion in an infantry division in Europe. It must have been a very, very discouraging experience for him. He must have come to that job not really anticipating it at all and a little bit ticked off at where he found himself." Abrams's gruff personality and bombastic methods of leadership certainly reinforced that notion in the young lieutenant.

In fact, as Starry remembered, working for Abrams was a discouraging experience. Many nights, Donn would come home and confess to Letty, "I got to get out of this Army, there's no way I can meet this guy's standards." In fact, Donn was convinced that "I had one hell of a learning problem. I just couldn't do anything right. Sergeants always did things right according to him … and I kept saying to my platoon sergeant [Lucas], 'Sergeant, we've got to do this right.' He said, 'We're doing it right.' In the end, we'd do it right, and the Colonel [Abrams] would give him a cigar or a bottle of whiskey, and he'd kick my ass all over the kaserne[4] because of something else he had found wrong."

Starry believed that Abrams's subordinate officers fell into distinct categories. "We had a lot of captains and senior lieutenants who had commanded tank companies in World War II." In fact, many of the battalion staff officers had also commanded companies during the war. "And then there was a distinct gap between that group and the younger lieutenants, none of whom had any experience at all. We had some combat-experienced first lieutenants … but the second lieutenants—there were nine of us in the group I was in when I reported for duty—had no experience at all. Some of us were West Point graduates, some graduates of the ROTC system. And it must have been discouraging for him [Abrams] to look at that gaggle, particularly the second lieutenants, and realize that he was, in fact, starting all over again. He had a job at which he had been very successful several years before and probably felt that he had left behind forever more."

"Colonel Abrams had some absolute standards," Donn said:

> They went something like this: captains *sometimes* turned in an acceptable performance; first lieutenants never; second lieutenants were the dregs of the earth; the noncommissioned officers could do no wrong. I distinctly remember one Sunday morning. My company commander, Lieutenant Patton, had decided that we should rise early on Sunday and go out to our little sub-caliber range … to shoot sub-caliber. We started at 3:30 in the morning because we didn't want the battalion commander to find us out there. I remember the company commander

saying, "God help us if he comes out here. Because they [the soldiers on the firing line] are really terrible." They were, in fact, terrible! [Indeed, many of these soldiers were poor marksmen who had come to the range for remedial training.] But there we were banging away [and] daylight came over the horizon. As luck would have it, a staff car drove up and out came the colonel. My distinguished company commander had absented himself from the scene with the onset of the staff car and so there I was. I went up all soldierly, reported, and said exactly what we were doing: "We've got the non-qualifiers here and we are going to qualify them." He grunted, stuck his cigar in his mouth, walked around and munched on all of us. The errant company commander peeked his head around the corner and got snagged by the battalion commander. I remember his parting words: "There's not a Goddamn soul on this range who knows what he's doing, and that starts with you two."

So, we reassessed what we were doing. After a lot of soul searching, we finally decided that we *were* doing the right thing—we just weren't doing it fast enough, and we had gotten caught at a bad time. One of us suggested wishfully that after the colonel had been to church, things might be better. He was indeed back after church. We stood on the line quaking. He got out of the car, walked up and down, talked to the sergeants—didn't talk to us—watched what they were doing, lay on the ground with a couple of soldiers, and fired a few rounds. By this time, it was 11:00 in the morning; things were much improved from the wee hours. Finally, he turned to the two of us and said, "That's okay—keep on doing what you're doing." He got in his car and drove off.

Dumbfounded, Patton and Starry just looked at each other and shrugged. "Now, I don't know what his motive was," Starry admitted, "but what was certain was that there was no grading on a curve. His standard was so high that it was very tough to meet."

When Starry's Officer Efficiency Reports came in, however, he was shocked to find that Creighton Abrams had rated him the "best officer I know." Starry had never heard Abrams compliment him on *anything*. "Reading the efficiency reports later on, according to the reports I did everything right, and better than everybody else, but you sure wouldn't have known that at the time."

Still, Donn conceded that Abrams was a gifted and forward-thinking commander. While commanding the 63d Tank Battalion, Abrams's goal was "to make a well-trained, professional, tough outfit out of what was then the only tank battalion in Europe." To accomplish that end, however, Abrams tried many techniques that were unorthodox even by World War II standards. "He decided one time that we ought to have a little better experience with live fire and maneuver. So he had us take some machine gun ammunition, and in each company we dipped the [ammunition] belts in paint so that the tips of the cartridges were colored, and we went out and fired them at each other." Indeed, the tank crews were firing *live* ammunition at each other's vehicles.

Luckily, the armor of the M26 was such that the bullets caused no damage to the vehicles' functionality. But the painted tips of the bullets left a telltale sign of how the tanks had maneuvered through the fray. After the exercise, Abrams went around and "counted the paint marks on the side [of a tank] and that told you whether or not you had been hit." The collateral damage to the tanks' exterior gear, however, was hard to ignore. "We shot off some antennas, shot up some phone boxes on the back of tanks, and blew out some optics." And although Division Headquarters was none too happy about the maneuver damage, Starry admitted that "we had great fun and it was superb training."

And Abrams certainly kept his men training. "For the first 24 months I was in that battalion," Starry said, "I was in the field … places like Grafenwoehr, Hohenfels, Vilseck, Baumholder. We would come home just long enough to get our wives pregnant and then take off again. His [Abrams's] story was, unless you're out there maintaining the tanks and shooting them, they're not going to work, and you're not going to work, and all this garrison living is for the birds. You learn a lot that way, particularly from a guy who fought a war as successfully as he did."

During these maneuvers along the West German countryside, "we never sat around and chewed the fat," Starry remembered:

> Abrams, in effect, conducted tutorials, but he did it by asking questions: "Here we are, and here's the enemy's disposition and situation as we know it. What are we going to do if the enemy does this or that?" And everybody would kick in a little bit and he'd come to a place in the conversation and say, "All right, let me give you a set of orders here: A Company's going to do this, B Company's going to do that, and C Company's going to do this. The battalion's got an objective up here, and here's where we're going to do that. Now, I want you to go out, reconnoiter the area, come back with a tentative plan about how you would do what I just told you to do, and be back here by 1400" or whatever. And, we'd go away and do it. Then he'd say, "Okay," and we worked out a plan. If time permitted, Abrams would say, "What if the enemy comes over here? What if they do this? What are you going to do? Here's what I want you to do. Now

go reconnoiter it." We drilled all the time, mentally, and he left time for us to go back and talk it out with the sergeants. It almost became second nature with us. We were always thinking about the What-if's.

Still, Creighton Abrams could be surprisingly jovial towards military families. In many ways, this attitude stemmed from his concern for their welfare. After all, the wives and children of the 63d Tank Battalion stood barely a few hundred miles from the Soviet Army. "Colonel Abrams got into a big argument with the administration one time about the evacuation of noncombatants," Donn recalled. "We had plans for that and, in those days, we had to have ten gallons of water and two cases of C-rations and a bunch of blankets ... stored in a closet inside the front door"—in case the Russians invaded and the families needed to make a quick getaway. However, given the Army's postwar logistical capabilities, Abrams and the other senior commanders knew that the dependents might not make it out in time. Thus, since NATO's forces were already outnumbered, Abrams decided that if some of the dependents couldn't get out, "then some of them might want to fight and they should be taught to use the weapons. So, we took the wives out, and the older kids, those who wanted to, and taught them to be tank drivers, tank gunners, and fire the machine guns. As a matter of fact, for a long time on some models of tanks, my wife was one of the better tank gunners I've ever met. We had plenty of ammunition left over from the war, so we would go out on Sundays and put the wives and those who wanted to–those who didn't we could give them something else to do–through a training program."

Starry also remembered that Abrams paved the way for developing US training centers in Germany. "We opened up Baumholder," he recalled. "The French were using it a staging area for Indochina, and we went over there in 1950–51 for the first time. American units had not been there since the war. We were the first tank unit to go up to what's now Bergen Hohne, the British training area up in the North German Plain ... and we sort of opened that up for American units. He was always looking for some new training experience for us."

While adjusting to Abrams's caustic and curious methods of leadership, Starry had to adjust to the realities of postwar Germany. Understandably, the Germans were still shocked and bitter over their defeat at the hands of the Allies. To make matters worse, their country had been partitioned along ideological lines. East Germany was now a Communist state and West Germany was a fragile democracy. The economies of both nations were in shambles, millions were starving, millions more were homeless, and several had taken to a life of crime.

The younger Patton recalled that the Germans were, as a nation, depressed by their devastating defeat. "They didn't realize what had happened to them," he said. "They were bewildered by the fact that we were there and they had lost. They were trying to survive with substitute items, such as wood-burning cars. There was a thriving black market. As an army of occupation, it was demilitarization, deindustrialization, and denazification. This was known as the '3 D's.' The rules were strict and we were not permitted to fraternize with Germans."[5] Starry added: "The Germans had been bombed out of most of their homes in the larger cities. They were poor. There were still people dying of hunger, even in the early 1950s."

Reflecting on the chaos of the postwar period, Patton recalled an incident when he passed through the Nuremberg airfield. "On the tarmac," he said, "were literally hundreds of B-17s wing-to-wing and nose-to-tail. Over in a corner of the airfield, some Germans were starting a large fire, so I drove over to check them out. I learned that they were going to burn Air Corps field jackets with fleece-lined collars. I said, 'Wait a minute, I'll take two-hundred for my men.' The man in charge said I could have them for two cartons of Chesterfields. I immediately arranged for a truck and cigarettes. With literally thousands of Germans needing warm clothing for a hard winter, it seemed criminal to destroy those valuable and unique Air Force bomber jackets. In all candor, that was government waste of the first degree."[6]

Meanwhile, Starry remembered that there was a "substantial Communist influence, particularly in the industrial cities. For a while, our battalion was stationed in Mannheim. There was some Communist influence in Frankfurt, and throughout the industrial Ruhr. There were some riots and demonstrations in that area." Thus, Starry and his fellow tankers received crash courses in police tactics, including riot control and anti-terrorism. "People raided our ammo dump," he continued, "which was out behind the kaserne in a wooded area. It was fenced in, but they'd dig under the fence and tunnel into the bunkers." Starry was both impressed and frustrated by the Germans' ingenuity. Throughout his tour of duty, there were a few attempts by local Germans (Communists and former Nazis) to blow the ammunition dumps, "but more often than not," he said, "you'd discover that what they were doing was *stealing* ammunition." At first, this caused alarm because Allied leaders had long been wary of a Nazi guerrilla movement coming on the heels of an Allied victory. However, as Starry found out, these ammo raids were little more than a bizarre survival tactic. "They'd take [the ammunition] out, take it apart, then sell the brass shell cases."

But while the communist influence was strong within Germany's industrial heartland, Starry noticed it was almost nonexistent in the countryside, particularly in Bavaria. "That region," he noted, "was dominated by a strong Catholic, right-wing conservative influence. The Communist movement never got into Bavaria at all, to speak of. Anyway, in the countryside especially, they [the Germans] were glad to have us there. They had no military force of their own until the late 1950s, and most of them saw us as the only thing standing between them and the Russians. It may have been that they were more afraid of the Russians than they were of us."

Still, the Allied occupation brought strict rules that tightly regulated how US troops could interact with German civilians. "When we first got over there," he said, "we were not allowed to buy food on the German market because it would have meant taking food away from the Germans." Indeed, the food shortage and mass hunger problems would continue well into the 1950s. Additionally, in many units, it was a court-martial offense to fraternize with German women, although this rule was frequently overlooked as many GIs returned home with German wives after the war.

As the summer of 1950 approached, Donn was nearing the end of his two-year tour as an armor officer. Thus, he would revert to his original status as a Transportation officer and report to the 122d Truck Battalion in Nuremberg. "I didn't know whether to desert, go AWOL, or both, but I was *not* going to the 122d Truck Battalion in any way, shape, or form." In the months prior to his pending reversion, he had sent a series of letters to Washington pleading to stay in his current billet as an armor officer. By this time, Starry had even earned an endorsement letter from Creighton Abrams requesting that the young lieutenant remain a tanker.

Still, no luck.

But fortune cast a warm smile on Donn Starry when he and Letty met Beatrice Patton—General Patton's widow and mother to Donn's current company commander, George Patton IV. Mrs. Patton visited her son frequently and, one fateful night, joined Donn, Letty, and George for a lengthy dinner. Hearing of Donn's difficulties in staving off his pending reassignment, she promptly replied, "Well, I think we can do something about that." Within a few days, Mrs. Patton had contacted Senator Henry Cabot Lodge to work the "fix" for the young Donn Starry.

The senator wasted no time.

Contacting the Chief of Cavalry (to which Armor still belonged), Lodge made it perfectly clear that Starry was to stay where he was—so said the widow of the great General Patton. The Chief of Cavalry, in an official communique, wrote with considerable understatement, "it was possible for certain reasons to obtain an exception and he [Starry] will be transferred to Cavalry by Department of the Army orders in the near future." Merely ten days before his branch reversion was to be official, Donn Starry received orders from Washington permanently assigning him to the US Cavalry. He had narrowly escaped the life of a truck commander. But while Starry grappled with the Army bureaucracy and the realities of postwar Germany, a new war was brewing on the Korean peninsula.

Korea had been a Japanese colony from its annexation in 1910 until the end of World War II. Following the Allied victory, the United States and the Soviet Union divided the peninsula into two political zones along the 38th Parallel. The north became a Communist state while the south remained capitalist. With the goal of reuniting the peninsula under Communist rule, however, the North Korean People's Army (NKPA) stormed across the 38th Parallel on June 25, 1950.

The conflict was unique for the US military because it wasn't a "war" in the traditional sense—there had been no formal declaration of hostilities and it was the first conflict carried out under the banner of the United Nations (UN). President Harry Truman therefore dubbed it a "police action." At first glance it appeared that the conflict was a minor adjunct of World War II. The military used much of the same weaponry and tactics as it had during the previous war, and in the higher echelons of command, Korea featured much the same cast as in World War II. General Douglas MacArthur, who had made headlines as commander of the Southwest Pacific Area, returned as commander-in-chief of the UN forces in Korea. General Omar Bradley was now Chairman of the Joint Chiefs, and General J. Lawton Collins, who had headed the VII Corps in Europe, was now the Army Chief of Staff. Lieutenant General Matthew Ridgway, an airborne pioneer and former commander of the 82nd Airborne Division, returned as commander of the US Eighth Army.

Although the invasion had caught the US by surprise, many predicted that Korea would be an easy victory. MacArthur cheerfully announced that his troops would be home by Christmas 1950. Others thought that the North Koreans would simply quit the field as soon as they realized they were fighting Americans. After all, the US had just defeated Germany and Japan—who were the North Koreans to tussle with the American war machine? However, the Army of 1950 was a far cry from the 8-million-man force that had defeated the Nazis five years earlier. Training and readiness had sunk to an all-time low as the US demobilized its army and discharged its wartime conscripts. By 1949, a soldier's typical day consisted of little more than constabulary duty, organized athletics, and USO dances. Thus, in the opening stages of the war, the US paid a terrible price for its unpreparedness.

After a disastrous encounter at the Battle of Osan, the atrophied American forces retreated south to the port of Pusan, where they rallied to make their final stand against the NKPA. For six weeks, spanning August–September 1950, the UN troops (consisting mostly of American, British, and South Korean forces) beat back the North Korean assault in what became known as the Pusan Perimeter—a 140-mile defensive line around the city. After a miraculous break-out from Pusan, and the simultaneous Allied landing at Inchon, the Americans rallied a counteroffensive which pushed the North Koreans back across the 38th Parallel and as far north as the Yalu River.

As the war in Korea raged on, Starry and his comrades in the 63d Tank Battalion wondered if they would be diverted from their occupation duty to stem the tide of Communist aggression in the Far East.

Sadly, it was not to be.

Because the 63d was the only heavy-tank battalion in Europe, the Army refused to divert any of the unit's personnel away from the Iron Curtain. The war in Korea may have stalemated, but NATO's front-line forces in Germany were presumably the only thing that stood between a free Europe and World War III.

"Several of us tried to go straight from Europe to Korea," said Starry. Many of his classmates were approaching the end of their initial three-year tours in Germany and were anxious for follow-on assignments to a combat zone. However, according to Starry, "the personnel manager's wisdom was: 'No, go to the Advanced Course. We don't know when the war is going to be over, but it'll probably still be going on when you get there.' So we decided to wait it out." All told, the North Koreans were the least of his worries—there were certainly enough issues in Germany to keep him occupied.

One such issue concerned the racial integration of the armed forces. "We had more trouble, in those days, with the Puerto Ricans who came out of the slums of New York and Chicago because of the draft starting up again, due to the Korean War. As a result, [the Army] dragged them up out of the ghettos down there, and we had a horrible time. Our division got, all at once, an infusion of [several] Puerto Ricans, many of whom couldn't speak English. In our battalion, we were issued about a company-sized cohort of those guys, a couple hundred of them."

As it turned out, many of these recruits had gone through Basic Training without understanding half of what the drill sergeants had said to them. These soldiers had to rely on their more fluent comrades to translate the points of instruction. As a result, the Puerto Rican recruits were not proficient on *any* of the military skills needed to be tank crewman.

> There was a total language disconnect [Starry remembered]. I was the assistant battalion S-3 [operations staff] at the time, and I was given the task of forming a training cadre ... to make up for their lack of basic training. I got all the Spanish-speaking sergeants in the battalion together, and we went at it—small

unit training, tank crew training, because they hadn't had much of that. They came out of that exercise as well-trained soldiers, but every once in a while, you had to wonder: "Well, if the tank commander doesn't speak Spanish, how is he going to get along with that guy if he's a gunner?" So, we had to work on the language problem.

Thus, impromptu ESL classes were devised as part of the battalion's training regimen. "They [the Puerto Ricans] made good soldiers," Starry said. "The poor guys simply hadn't understood what was being said to them during their initial training."

Linguistics aside, Starry also had to contend with a postwar maintenance and supply system that had devolved into chaos. "We had a horrible maintenance situation," he recalled. "When I joined the 63d in August 1949, the battalion was stationed in Grafenwoehr, where it had been organized. As I recall, in November or December 1949, we moved the battalion to Mannheim from Grafenwoehr. The division ordnance company moved into the same barracks with us—Sullivan Barracks in Mannheim. Shortly after we got down there, we discovered that we couldn't even field one company of tanks." As it turned out, "the ordnance company, even though it was collocated on the kaserne with us, just couldn't supply the spare parts." Undaunted, Creighton Abrams hopped into his command car and drove to Heidelberg, straight to the office of General Thomas Handy, the chief of US European Command. Abrams wasted no time. "Sir, the only tank battalion in Europe is virtually deadlined." Upon hearing this, General Handy erupted.

"All hell broke loose," Starry recalled.

"They [Abrams and Handy] had an investigation of the ordnance company and court-martialed a few people." As it turned out, the company had lost several thousand dollars' worth of spare parts. During the course of the investigation, Starry said, Handy and his deputy commander "opened up the Mannheim supply depot to us; we were allowed to go in there, and if we could find it, we could have it. So he [Abrams] got us all together—the company commanders and the company executive officers—and he said, 'Now I want to make sure that we don't leave any stone unturned to get everything we need out of that depot.' Well, what he didn't realize was that he was turning the job over to the most overzealous, nonprofessional thieves in the world," said Starry facetiously.

We robbed that depot blind. For about seven days, we ran a fleet of trucks out of that thing, twenty-four hours a day. There were sergeants down there with packing lists ... and we had so many spare parts that we went down to the basements of our quarters and built bins down there to hold them. Well, several months later, [Abrams] discovered what we had done and, once again, all hell broke loose. Then we had a big "turn in all your excess" program. He realized, I guess too late, that he had turned it over to a real bunch of thieves. But, here again, he had the courage to get in his car, go down there and say, "Boss, this thing isn't going very well." And at least he got their attention to the point that we were back on the road very shortly. The changes they made in the ordnance support system were such that we were able to survive after that.

Later, when Donn Starry became the supply officer for B Company, he had a more intense encounter with the postwar supply system. But it was one that taught him a valuable lesson in leadership. "At the end of the war, we'd given the surplus equipment we had to the German government," he said. West Germany, in turn, formed a corporation and sold this equipment to the highest bidder—"I'm talking sleeping bags, clothing, even trucks, to prime the economic pump." However, when the Korean War started, "we bought that stuff back from the Germans ... and re-issued it. But, up to that time, we really were struggling for parts, clothing, almost anything. The supply system was a *bloody disaster.*" Even after receiving their windfall from the Mannheim depot, individual field gear was in short supply for the 63d Tank Battalion. On one occasion, Starry mustered up the nerve to tell Abrams just how shoddy the supply system had become, "which resulted in the roundest ass-chewing I have ever had from anybody." As Starry described it, Abrams "took me apart up one side and down the other. When it was all over, he said: 'Let me tell you something. I'm not pissed off at you because you complained about the supply situation. I know it's fucked up. I'd be the first one to tell you that. The trouble with you is that you don't have a solution.' Well, I went home and I thought about that, and I wrote that down for myself." Thereafter, Donn made it a point never to criticize a situation unless he had an idea for a solution. It underscored an important lesson for any leader: *Don't be all problem and no solution.* Instead of complaining about a situation, suggest ideas for how to fix it.

Although Starry and several of his comrades in the 63d had been left out of the war in Korea, he later remarked that the stabilization was good for maintaining crew proficiency:

> When I left that battalion after more than three years, we still had most of the same tank commanders, platoon sergeants, and first sergeants. Now some of the sergeants had been promoted over the years, so you may have had a first sergeant who had been a tank commander when I first came aboard as a second lieutenant. But the fact of the matter was that the NCOs, from the squad leader/tank commander on up, and most of the officers had been together for more than three years ... the secret to our success was that we could do a lot of things and do them very well.
>
> Creighton Abrams commented on this one time. Someone asked him the difference between the 63d Tank Battalion and the 37th Tank Battalion which he had commanded during World War II, and he said, "The difference ... is that this one [63d Tank Battalion] can do a whole lot of things and do them well. That one [37th Tank Battalion] could only do a couple of things well because we simply hadn't been together long enough and didn't have time to train. When we went to war and landed in Normandy, it was a top-notch battalion but the minute replacements began to come as individuals, as opposed to crews or platoons, the quality of our performance—outside the initial problems of moving, shooting, and communicating—fell off dramatically."

Later in his career, Starry used this as an example to protest the Army's methods for replacing individual soldiers in Vietnam. Despite overwhelming evidence, the Pentagon continued its counterproductive practice of replacing individual soldiers on the front lines instead of whole units.

After the breakout from Pusan Perimeter, UN forces had the North Koreans on their heels and, for a while, it appeared that the war was in its last throes—until the Chinese entered the fight. Beginning in the fall of 1950, the Chinese counteroffensive regained much of the land that had been lost to UN forces following the Inchon landings. Indeed, by January 1951, the Communists had re-occupied Seoul and pushed the UN as far south as Wongju, where the front lines had stabilized. However, during their blitzkrieg to Seoul, the Chinese had outrun their supply lines, allowing the UN to regain the initiative and rollback the Communist tide through a series of counterattacks including Operation

Roundup, Operation *Killer*, and Operation *Ripper*—the latter of which expelled the Communists from Seoul.

That spring, the Chinese attempted one more counteroffensive before being halted by the US X Corps in May 1951. By month's end, the Eighth US Army counterattacked and re-established the front lines just north of the 38th Parallel. For the remaining two years of the war, the UN Command and the Red Chinese continued fighting but exchanged little ground.

By the time Starry returned to the United States in 1952, the major offenses in Korea had ended and the war had devolved into a stalemate. "Peace talks," for what they were worth, had been under way for about a year, and both American and Communist forces had dug themselves into World War I-style trenches, each making minor advances against the other in bloody skirmishes.

Returning stateside, Donn Starry followed the path prescribed by the Army career managers. Instead of deploying to the battlefields of North Korea, he first had to complete the Armor Officer Advanced Course (AOAC). A continuation of the Basic Course, AOAC was a year-long residency course that prepared junior captains for company command and battalion staff. However, it would be another year until Starry would see the inside of a classroom: the Korean War had caused a backfill in attendees.

Thus, while waiting to attend AOAC, he was assigned to the 3d Armored Division, colloquially known as the "Spearhead Division." Although the unit had had a distinguished combat record during World War II, the division had since been re-assigned to Fort Knox as a training unit. "All of the training centers had numbered divisions in them," said Starry. "The 3d Armored Division was at Fort Knox, and deployed in the late 1950s to Germany. They said, 'We want you to take command of a tank company,' and I thought, 'Well, that's fine. I know something about that.'" After all, he had been a platoon leader and a company commander under Creighton Abrams—perhaps the two toughest jobs for a postwar armor lieutenant.

"So I went to this company and met the company commander, who was so anxious to leave that he was just about to hand me the key to the orderly room and say, 'So long.'" But Donn Starry, taken aback by the hasty departure, interjected:

"Wait a minute. I've got to know something about this company."

"Well, it's big," said the outgoing commander. "It has 60-some-odd tanks in it."

"No," Starry countered, "I mean the *company*, not the battalion."

"I'm talking about the company," the outgoing captain replied. "We're in the rent-a-tank business. We rent tanks to the trainees."

"Well," Starry said nonchalantly, "take me around will you?"

But as the former commander showed him the equipment and the training areas, Starry was dumbfounded by how poorly their assets had been maintained.

> Well, in truth, they had 100-and-some-odd tanks in that company; about half of them were static on a range someplace. The other half moved somewhere and, because they couldn't keep track of the equipment—let me remind you that the Korean War was still going on—they took it all off of the tanks. So the tanks were stripped in the motor pool.
>
> Now, if you wanted to teach a gunnery class, you would go to this enormous warehouse and draw the sights and the fire control equipment out of the bins in the warehouse. You would take it out, put it in the tank, and go off and shoot. It may or may not have been the stuff that was on the tank yesterday or the day before; it was just stuff that would plug in the holes. Most of it didn't work very well because the maintenance was sporadic. In fact, it was a disaster. I went around and looked at the tanks, and out of the 60-some-odd that they had in the motor pool, they did well getting 15 or 20 of them running on any given day in order to meet a training commitment.

"I never had an experience like that before," Starry continued. Indeed, a situation like that would have been a mortal sin in the 63d Tank Battalion. "In Abrams' battalion, if your tanks didn't run, you were standing nose-to-nose with his cigar trying to explain why they were down."

Luckily, while wrestling with the realities of his new "rent-a-tank" business, Donn Starry was saved by the bureaucratic bell. "A friend called from the Division Headquarters and said, 'Come up here. We'd like to interview you to be the aide-de-camp to the Assistant Division Commander.'" Starry had no idea what an "aide-de-camp" was, or how it related to the Division's deputy commander, but it *had* to be better than running a piecemeal tank rental service.

Well, I met a superb brigadier general named John Tupper Cole, who was one of the Army's great cavalrymen, twice captain of the Olympic equestrian team, and a super guy. I decided that, whatever the general did, it was better than worrying about those 100-some-odd tanks scattered all over the landscape. So I spent a very enjoyable year working for him.

Part of my impression of the cavalry, with the excellence of the individual and the officers' ability to do things well, came from my association with him. His method of inspecting the training was to go out on the rifle range and walk up and down the line until he found the soldier who was doing the worst. Every time the guy fired, the red flag would be waving across the target, so the general would lie down in the mud, or the sand, or whatever, next to this soldier and spend whatever time it took coaching him to the point where he was not a bad shot. He was a marvelous shot himself, and he had an uncanny ability to take some quivering 17-year-old and, in a matter of a few minutes' time, get the guy shooting through the middle of the target when before he couldn't hit it with both hands. He was very good at that. You'd go to the machine gun range with him, and he'd do the same thing. You'd go to the tank gun range with him, and again he'd do the same thing.

Not only was he good himself, but he knew all sorts of little techniques that you could use to teach the soldiers. I watched him in rifle marksmanship and machine gun marksmanship … and he had a little pattern of things that he looked at. Most of it had to do with holding your breath and squeezing the trigger … and timing your shots. He was quite good at that, probably the best I've ever seen. I was very impressed by that. I asked him about it one time, and he said, "Well, that's what we did in the cavalry." Now, I've met several people before and after him who were products of that same system, and they were all the same—excellent in performance of soldier skills. But, more than that, his ability to train the soldiers and correct their faults in a short period of time was just outstanding.

As the Assistant Division Commander, Cole frequently traveled the continental US for training demonstrations and the normal variety of stateside "dog-and-pony shows." For every occasion, his trusted aide-de-camp went with him. Starry enjoyed the travel; it gave him a chance to see the newest experimental weapons and meet dignitaries of every stripe. On one occasion, however, a simple training demo turned into a near life-or-death struggle. Starry had accompanied Cole to the Nevada Test Site for a troop test of nuclear weapons. However, an airburst from the nuclear bomb collapsed the trench from which Cole was observing the shot. Springing into action, Starry dug his commander out of the collapsed trench. Dusting off the slightly-rattled general, Starry asked for (and received) permission to mount and drive an M4A3E8 tank, which had been placed on the site, to demonstrate the vehicle could still operate unaffected by the blast. "This feat was noted with considerable approval by other tankers present since, at the time, nuclear weapons were viewed in some quarters as constituting the end of the line for armored vehicles."

But after a year of serving under the inspirational John Tupper Cole, Donn Starry was finally sent to AOAC. Admittedly, he found the course to be a bit pedestrian. "I had been a tank platoon leader and a tank company commander, plus a battalion staff officer in Lieutenant Colonel Abrams' battalion, so they were happy to have me come to Fort Knox." Although AOAC taught many of the same concepts Starry had learned on the job in West Germany, he was nonetheless happy to have some downtime with Letty and their young sons, Michael "Mike," aged four, and Paul, aged three.

Meanwhile, the Korean War finally ground to a halt. Less than three weeks after the infamous Battle of Pork Chop Hill, the negotiating parties at Panmunjom reached an accord. The resulting armistice—signed on July 27, 1953—restored the international boundary at the 38th Parallel and established the Korean Demilitarized Zone (DMZ). After the demarcation agreement, the US kept a permanent military presence along the DMZ to deter any further aggression.

Although the US had declared victory, they had essentially fought the Communists to a draw. The enemy dictated the tempo for most of the conflict and the Army's rules of engagement tended to discourage initiative rather than promote it. Still, Starry and his comrades were confident that the next war, wherever it may be, would be fought on better terms. All told, the Class of 1948 lost 15 of its members in Korea.

After completing the AOAC, Starry received orders to Korea in August 1954. The fighting had been over for nearly a year and a half, but tensions remained high and the resulting peace was tenuous at best. Since the conflict had ended in a cease-fire, the two Koreas were technically still at war. The more pressing matter for Donn Starry, however, was the fact that he had missed combat in Korea. Most of his classmates had completed combat tours, and the question lingered:

Would his lack of combat experience harm his chances of promotion among his peers?

Little did Starry realize, however, that he was about to get an "experience" most armor officers never dream of—*clandestine operations*:

> I went to Korea hoping to be a tank company commander again. I was a captain but not very senior. Promotions dragged in those days, and here I'd been a platoon leader, a company commander, a battalion staff officer, and had been to the Advanced Course. I thought I knew enough about commanding a company that it would be a breeze. However, my assignment was to the Eighth Army staff, the G-2 section, which didn't please me very much. However, it turned out to be a good assignment. It was an interesting 16 months because after a short period of being the "commissioned telephone orderly," as we have in many such headquarters, *I became the coordinator of the covert and clandestine collection program targeted against China, Manchuria and North Korea.*

The new assignment was beyond the purview of anything Starry had trained for as an officer. As the Army re-organized its footprint in postwar Korea, "they took the Eighth Army back to Japan," he said, "leaving an Eighth Army Forward in Korea." But according to Starry, this "Eighth Army Forward" had been pared down to a skeleton crew headquarters. Indeed, as a young captain, he was replacing five lieutenant colonels, and assuming their collective workload. "Then one day," he recalled, "as the remaining master sergeant and I were sizing up our work, I decided to see the Deputy G-2." With unrestricted candor, Starry asked him how much of the previous staff's workload could be eliminated. After all, he said, "there's only one of me and there were five of them, and they were all lieutenant colonels with combat experience, and I'm a dumb captain with no combat experience. I've never been a G-2 before, don't want to be one, but need to know what I'm supposed to do."

The Deputy G-2's response was swift.

"Well," he said, "as far as I can tell, we're not going to stop doing anything we were doing before, so you're just going to have to work harder."

"So, for the next year or so," Starry recounted, "that's what we did."

At the time, covert operations in Korea relied on a network of indigenous agents, mostly North Korean defectors. A few, however, were displaced northerners who wanted to reunite with their families in the

Hermit Kingdom. Thus, in exchange for their repatriation, they agreed to spy on the North Korean government and send information back to the Eighth Army. These spies would come to regret their decision, however, as North Korea transformed itself into a totalitarian police state.

To make matters worse, the North Korean government had become more adept at ferreting out its spies and saboteurs. As Starry explained, "we were paying our agents in gold. Gold had a very high exchange rate." The Kim dynasty, however, responded by creating a national monopoly on gold. This effectively outlawed private ownership of the metal. "If they caught you with gold," Starry said, "you were thrown into prison. So gold became a non-exchange item and we started paying our debts with outdated wonder drugs"—namely dope. "There was a big trade in dope, even back then," he recalled wryly. But soon, even the drug payoffs proved ineffective: "we couldn't get enough of it to pay the bills."

Monetary shortcomings aside, the biggest obstacle to maintaining a spy network was the North Korean security apparatus. To effect the Eighth Army's espionage efforts, "we used people who had lived in the north, but had been pushed south by the Chinese invasion and were left behind when we drove the North Koreans back across the 38th Parallel. We'd equip them with radios and other means of communication. We were trying to build an agent network up there to assist downed aviators and parachutists ... and for moving agent traffic inside North Korea. As the North Korean government gained more and more control over the population, it became impossible to do that." It was particularly frightful in the cities, where "block wardens" appointed by the Communist regime would run local neighborhoods with an iron fist. For example, every North Korean home had to display a placard on the front door. "On it," Starry said, "were the names of the people who were authorized to be in that house." Thus, if someone wanted to visit his neighbor, he would first have to pay the block warden for an additional placard, stating he was authorized to be in the home. "If the police came to your house and walked in, which they could do, and found someone unauthorized there, then everyone in the house went to jail. Then they would tear the house down. It doesn't take much of that to intimidate a population. So, as time wore on, over the period of a year or so, it became more and more difficult to send people home. That put us in a totally different construct as far as agent training, agent infiltration, exfiltration, and agent communications were concerned."

It was, in many ways, demoralizing: the Eighth Army G-2 had pinned their hopes on building an active network of repatriated spies, people simply sent back to live where they had lived before the war. "They, along with their families, were going to do whatever it was they wanted to do, and we were going to pay them for simply observing certain things. However, it never happened. As the government closed on the population and got absolute control over it, that whole idea fell apart."

Still, these freshman spies did a remarkable job infiltrating enemy territory:

> We did send a lot of people back and forth across the DMZ. There were only a few safe routes through the minefields, and both sides were using those. In 1954, we had to stop the parachute work. So we were mostly dependent on boats, and to eliminate or to solve a part of the problem of identification … we used fishing boats. We used some of the native fishing boats with those old "hot-head" engines in them, while others were fishing boats with Gray-Marine diesels aboard. With the diesel-powered boats you could get into Manchuria and back in one night. In other words, you could start up in the afternoon off the east coast, put agents ashore in Manchuria, and get back by daylight, or at least get far enough south by daylight that you were out of the North Korean Navy's grasp.

Ironically, however, Starry's best source of information was an apostolic bishop named John Quinlan. He was the apostolic delegate to the Republic of Korea and had become a legend on both sides of the DMZ:

> He'd been a prisoner of the North Koreans during the war, and was credited with keeping most of the people in the camp alive. The North Koreans hated his guts. About once a week, or once every two weeks, there would be a propaganda blast from Pyongyang against the "gangster" Quinlan. He was a marvelous man, and somehow he had communications into North Korea. On two or three occasions that I can remember, we really had a crisis, and it was alleged in [South Korea] that they [the North Koreans] were getting ready to attack. Now, of course, during these times we would crank up the whole intelligence network. The Army commander would send for the Intel people; I would always be standing in the rear rank someplace and, sooner or later, attention would be focused on me to see what I could find out.
>
> Well, I'd get in the jeep and go see the bishop. In response to my request for help, he'd go down into the cellar, crank up whatever commo gear he had down

there, then come back up and say, "There's nothing to worry about. Here's the situation." Apparently, what he had access to was the south end of a piece of the old Mukden cable which, before the war, ran from Pusan to Seoul to Pyongyang and into China/Manchuria. I don't know where it crossed the borders, but it wound up in Mukden. Part of the cable was cut during the war, but apparently not all of it, and he was still communicating on a piece of that. But he actually had telephone traffic with people in Pyongyang. He also had radio communications.

Of course, the North Koreans were sending their own agents across the DMZ as well. However, as the DMZ became more difficult to traverse by foot, the Communists began digging tunnels underneath. "That's what you've got over there now," Starry added. "They did not have the resources that we had, either in boats, people, communications equipment, or anything else." Though audacious in their attempts to infiltrate South Korea, these northern agents were rarely successful. In fact, as Starry recalled, "most of the agents we captured—that had been sent south through the DMZ, or the ones we picked up landing from fishing boats—weren't very well trained. As time wore on, they were not well-informed about what to expect in South Korea or how to act, and frequently they would give themselves away simply by the way they acted."

Meanwhile, to supplement its fragile network of spies and saboteurs, the Eighth Army G-2 resorted to economic warfare. "So, we started a program to counterfeit money," Starry said. "It would be printed in the US, and we'd pay our bills with counterfeit North Korean *won*. That fell afoul of some American official in Japan. He complained ... that we were not in economic warfare with North Koreans. So we had to knock that off."

"I even tried to start a little business, in fact, several businesses, in North Korea. One of them was to be a house of ill repute—a high-class house of ill repute [a brothel in Pyongyang]. I figured that if we could get that going, we could have a continuous source of information from government officials." However, Starry's "house of ill repute" never came to fruition. "The ladies were all lined up," he said, including the principal madam. "I found a lady who had been married to one of the last members of the ruling house in Korea. She was a very influential lady ... she owned the garbage contract in Inchon for the American installations. Now, the person who owned the garbage contract was always wealthy. In addition, she still owned property in Pyongyang and part of her family lived there. Anyway, she said she owned the property and could get a staff together for us. All she wanted from us was transportation. I was to run the transportation and communications arrangements, and she was to get what I thought was a reasonable stipend for her efforts."

However, Starry's creativity was about to earn him a swift reprimand:

> In the intelligence business, not knowing much about it, I felt obliged to report what I'd been doing and account for the money that I'd been spending. So I prepared a report and sent it in through the proper channels. It wound up in the Joint UW [Unconventional Warfare] Task Force Headquarters in Japan. Now, it turned out that everybody thought it was so funny that it became the topic of cocktail party conversation in Tokyo. The next thing I know, I'm standing in front of the Army commander—the ambassador was also there—and I'm told that this operation is immoral, illegal, and a whole bunch of other things, and to close it down immediately. So, I shut the whole thing down.

Around this time, Starry also began to take note of the events happening in Indochina. The entire region had been a French colony from 1887 until the rise of the Viet Minh Independence Movement led by Ho Chi Minh in the 1940s. During World War II, Ho Chi Minh had rescued several downed American pilots in Indochina and supplied the US with intelligence on Japanese and Vichy French troop movements. All this, he had hoped, would curry favor with the US government and generate sympathy for the anti-French rebellion. However, Ho Chi Minh had miscalculated America's support for the French and their growing mistrust of all things Communist.

Casting their lot with the French, America responded by sending the Military Assistance Advisory Group (MAAG) to Vietnam in 1950. MAAG was the command group responsible for all US military advisors in foreign countries. Their mission in Vietnam was to supervise the millions of dollars in US equipment being used by the French. By 1953, however, it was clear that the French were losing ground to the Viet Minh.

Following his unconventional, hair-raising tour in Korea, Starry and his family returned stateside in 1956. Shortly after touching down in the USA, Donn and Letty welcomed the birth of their third child, Melissa (whom the family called "Lisa"), born in October 1956. Young Lisa was soon joined by another sister, Melanie, born in January 1958.

Receiving orders to Fort Holabird, Maryland, Donn became a Combat Arms Instructor at the US Army Intelligence School. "There was a little combined arms instructor there," Starry recalled, "a couple of artillerymen, a couple of infantrymen, two armor folks, a medical service officer, and an engineer. We taught organization, tactics, weapons—we taught all of the field training they have. I guess someone decided that they [the Intelligence School] needed someone who knew something about G-2s," he said, "and would know how to talk to intelligence officers in the classroom. I tried to get the assignment changed, but the answer from the personnel manager was, of course, 'Look, we know best … as always.' So I went."

Professionally, however, the assignment was rewarding. It gave Starry a more intimate look at the burgeoning field of tactical nuclear weapons. Part of his duties as a Combat Arms Instructor entailed teaching classes about the employment of nuclear weaponry.

> There was a nuclear weapons employment course at Leavenworth which I had to attend while I was teaching at Holabird. At that time, target analysis was a tedious business. There were knee curves and other primitive methods for determining blast effects. The nomograph and tabular data forms we use now were not available at that time. As a matter of fact, another officer, Vernon Quarstein, and I developed a system of target analysis that eventually, along with some other work, led to the use of tables as opposed to the graphs and charts we were using and lent themselves to computerization of the whole process of target analysis.

In fact, Starry's performance at Holabird was so good that his superiors recommended him for an early promotion to major in June 1958.

Although fascinated by the advent of smaller-scale nuclear weapons, Starry noticed a dangerous trend in military thinking—too much emphasis on nuclear capabilities and less attention to conventional warfare. This lopsided emphasis on strategic and tactical nukes, Starry feared, would lead the Army into an erosion of its core capabilities. In fact, he felt so strongly on the matter of nuclear weapons that he later wrote an article titled "Fifty Years at the Business End of the Bomb" (Appendix B).

Still, Donn Starry recalled his time at Fort Holabird with fondness. "They were very good to us," he said, even if it wasn't a prime posting for a mid-career armor officer. According to Starry, Holabird had been "the home of the Counterintelligence Corps, but in the mid-1950s the combat intelligence schools were moved from Fort Riley to Holabird. In addition, they organized a new [discipline] called 'field operations intelligence' which, of course, is a clandestine collection—a HUMINT program. All of that was centered at Holabird. They had put Colonel [later General] Henry Newton there to organize the school; he did a super job. It was well-run and had a good set of facilities, which General Newton was noted for providing in all the schools he ran:

> They looked on us in the combat arms group as a source of expertise. Most of us had been to some service school, whereas they [the Intelligence School Staff] had *no* experience in school management. As a result, we were asked to do all sorts of things for them, some as simple as figuring out how to get to the students the issue material on time before the class, which is kind of sophomoric; still, we were asked to set that up for them. Because we had expertise in subjects they knew nothing about—nuclear weapons employment, operations and tactics—they were really very happy to have us and very good to us.

But, "it was a miserable place to live," he admitted:

> There were no quarters on post. Fort Holabird was right in the middle of downtown Baltimore, almost on the waterfront, behind nearby Dundalk, Maryland. There were few, if any, what would now be called condominiums—in Baltimore they call them row houses—in that area. It was largely populated by people who worked at Bethlehem's Sparrow's Point steel mill. A lot of military people lived on our block which made it easier, but it was still not a desirable place to live. So, from a family standpoint, in an attempt to escape from that, we spent a lot of time touring battlefields at Gettysburg, Antietam, the Valley … and others. From that standpoint, it turned out to be educational. My kids still go to places like Gettysburg: "Yeah, that's the cannon we stuffed our little sister into on such and such a visit." So apparently, it made some impression on them.

Fort Holabird closed in 1973 and the area has since been redeveloped into an industrial park. Sadly, in 2001, a fire destroyed what remained of the Counterintelligence School.

As a newly minted major, Donn Starry then reported to the Command and General Staff College (CGSC) at Fort Leavenworth, Kansas. A year-long residency course, CGSC prepared majors for staff work at the higher echelons. It also had a reputation as one of the most demanding schools in the Army:

> I'd been teaching and writing operations orders for the Intelligence School students. They [the students at the Intelligence School] weren't really interested in tactics at the platoon and company and battalion level, although we taught a little bit of that; rather, the question was, "Where does the intelligence staff officer fit into the staff organization at all levels of command?" So we were teaching everything from the field army on down. As a result, I got a *much* broader exposure to that kind of instruction. That was particularly useful … because I found out at Leavenworth that I knew a lot more about the various subjects than did my classmates. We had used Leavenworth-issued material to teach our students at Holabird, simply because no other school in the system put out material at the level we were concerned with teaching. So it turned out to be a fortuitous thing for me, at least.

Reflecting on his time at CGSC, he said: "You've always got a little problem of relevance between the school and the real world. Mind you, by the time I went Leavenworth in 1959, I'd been away from troops since 1953–54 when I was at Knox. So, there was a little gap there." Nevertheless, Donn found ways to make his time at Leavenworth enjoyable. For instance, he and a few classmates organized a mission church, known as Mission of the Centurion, which later became the Episcopal congregation of Fort Leavenworth.

Starry also played a hand in the selection of the Army's new field cap: the OG-106. "One day in 1959," he recalled, "the QMG [Quartermaster General] of the Army came to Leavenworth to speak to the class. To make himself popular, he brought along guidons which he issued to each section. Some irreverent soul stood up; after congratulating the QMG on the splendid guidons, he asked why the Army couldn't make a fatigue hat as nice as those guidons." To this point, the Army's field cap had been the M-1951 fatigue hat, which largely resembles the patrol cap of today's Army. However, since its introduction, the headgear had been derided as appearing "too slovenly" even for field wear. After a moment of awkward silence, the perturbed QMG answered: "That's your problem—you guys are the users—put in your requirements." Before long, "we got a lot of people to sign a document describing the hat we wanted," Donn said. "I even furnished a real New York Yankees baseball hat given to me by Ralph Houck to use as a sample." Collectively, the officers wanted a crisper headgear that resembled a baseball cap. Three years later, they got their wish—the Army fielded the new OG-106 fatigue hat. Although the first iteration of this headgear did, in fact, resemble a baseball hat, Starry described it as one that "required the wearer to have a pointed head and forehead-protruding horns to prevent the brim from flopping in his eyes." The OG-106 went through a few more alterations over the next 20 years, and Starry remembered that he was satisfied with the final iteration of it. However, much to his chagrin, the hat was phased out when the Army converted to the Battle Dress Uniform in 1981. With it, the Army re-adopted the old M-1951 cap with the new camouflage pattern. In a mildly facetious note to Army Chief of Staff General Edward "Shy" Meyer in 1982, Starry questioned: "So now, twenty years, later, we finally have an about right baseball hat, just as we abandon it for battle dress?"

Graduating from CGSC in June 1960, Donn Starry received orders back to Germany. His return to the "frontier of democracy," however, would once again put him under the tutelage of the legendary Creighton Abrams.

CHAPTER 3

Fields of Armor

Starry reported for duty in the 3d Armored Division in August of 1960 as a major, newly graduated from Leavenworth. Coincidentally, Creighton Abrams (now a general) had been the Assistant Division Commander the previous year. After completing a brief tour as the Deputy Chief of Staff (Operations) for US Army Europe, the formidable Abe Abrams returned as the 3d Armored Division commander. At the time, Starry was Operations Officer (S-3) for the Division's Combat Command C.

As Starry explained, "the armored divisions were always organized into Combat Commands—A, B, and C. The infantry divisions from about 1956 onward were organized into battle groups. They went from regiments to battle groups in the infantry, but armored divisions never gave up their combat commands. Then, with the 1963 reorganization of armor and infantry divisions, everybody went to brigades. Combat Command A became 1st Brigade, B became 2d Brigade, and C became 3d Brigade."

However, from what Starry could see, the European contingent was in bad shape. "They had gone through a very bad series of years in the mid-1950s when strategic retaliation was the order of the day," he said. Indeed, the Eisenhower administration had placed too much emphasis on nuclear weapons. As Starry recalled, "there was some question as to whether or not we needed land forces at all." As a result, US Army Europe had suffered under eight years of neglect. "It showed the ravages of those years of neglect and underfunding. The billets were in bad shape; the kaserne was in bad shape. The equipment was not in too bad shape, although we had the M48 tank, the modern counterpart of the M26—and a gas hog."

To make matters worse, there had been virtually no emphasis on training. When Donn reported to the Combat Command C headquarters in Friedberg, he recalled that it was a Wednesday afternoon. The following morning, Thursday, the Assistant S-3 told him: "We have to get ready for the Friday parade. We have a parade every Friday. We've got the practice parade group lined up on the parade ground if you want to come and look at them."

A parade every Friday? Starry didn't quite like it.

Why would a forward-deployed unit be conducting weekly parades when their mission was to defend West Germany from the Communists? "There were people lined up all the way around the parade ground," Starry continued. "No battalions, just folks in little groups." The Assistant S-3 then began identifying the "little groups" as the Combat Command C sports teams: "Now over here we have the combat command football team," he told Starry, "this is the combat command soccer team; this is the combat command drum and bugle corps. Over here is the combat command squash team, and these people are the cross-country team."

By this time, Starry had heard enough.

"What we had at that time was an enormous sports program," he recalled, "fostered by a corps commander who shall remain nameless. But that's all they did—sports. There was no soldiering going on. They were all out there playing games. In fact, the corps commander had a rule that every soldier had to play a different sport every quarter, different from the one he had played the previous quarter. There were large groups in orderly rooms just keeping track of that."

Luckily, when the sports-obsessed corps commander rotated back to the US, his replacement abolished the athletic programs. General Abrams then issued a four-word order to every officer in the 3d Armored Division: "Get back to work."

"That's what we did," said Starry. "We started with the individuals and worked our way up to the units. When we were done, nearly four years later, we had a good outfit."

Starry later credited Abrams as the only commander he had met who really understood how an armored division was supposed to operate:

By that, I mean the disciplinary, administrative, personnel, and logistics management things went straight from him to the battalion commander ... the concept of the operation is that the brigade is a control headquarters—it's a tactical headquarters, and even in garrison as a training exercise, he hewed that line very closely. If you had an administrative problem ... he never called the brigade commander—he called the battalion commander direct. The brigade commander didn't always understand this, and so we had a little difficulty keeping the brigade commander informed from time to time, but [Abrams] was very insistent on it. That was a good training vehicle ... because what it does is it forces the subordinate commander not to lean on the next guy up the line ... but to pick up his share of the marbles and start playing the game.

Starry also noticed that Abrams was tough on his battalion commanders. Granted, his demeanor towards the field-grade officers was not quite as gruff as it had been towards the lieutenants of the 63d Tank Battalion, but it was still the type of relationship where exacting standards had to be met. He frequently visited the battalion commanders to discuss their annual training plans. "He always walked in unannounced," Starry recalled. "He'd say: 'I'd like to know what you think you're going to do, what your goals are, how long you think it's going to take to get it done, and what it's going to cost.'" From that point, the battalion commander would talk about his training goals for however long it took to convince Abrams that there was a solid plan in place, "or at least to the point that [Abrams] was convinced that you either did or did not know what you were talking about."

Meanwhile, General Abrams, recycled and retooled many of the same readiness programs he had instituted in the 63d Tank Battalion. Maintenance became a top priority, as did small-unit training. Reflecting on Abrams's command tenure, several things stood out for Starry: "One is that he inherited a set of war plans for the defense of the V Corps sector [of which the 3d Armored Division was a subordinate unit] that, as an S-3 ... I just found ridiculous. They [the defense plans] were based on the notion that, in one area of the corps sector, we were going to create an 'impenetrable barrier' through which the enemy could not come, and we were going to do that with minefields and barbed wire." Starry found the concept laughable because there was *no such thing* as an impenetrable barrier. In the context of modern warfare—with aerial bombardment, long-range artillery, combat engineers, and tactical nukes—the very idea of an "impenetrable barrier" had been rendered obsolete. To boot, the terrain slated to host this "barrier" was a 60-kilometer front covered by only *three* battalions. Starry realized that there was no way the 3d Armored Division could mount an effective defense under these conditions. Thus, from his narrow view of the battlefield along the 3d Division's front, Starry noted the conditions that would pave the way for his AirLand Battle doctrine more than a decade later.

Budgetary constraints and implausible defense schemes notwithstanding, the biggest problem for US Army Europe was the political climate. Shortly after Starry's arrival in Germany, the Berlin Wall made its debut on the international stage. A formidable structure separating East from West, the Wall was referred to as the "Anti-Fascist Protection Rampart" by its Communist constructors. The distinction was dubious, however, as it was simply a means to keep East Berliners away from the lures of capitalism. Meanwhile, Soviet Premier Nikita Khrushchev, never one for mild manners, had become openly more hostile towards the West. His provocative rhetoric at the United Nations, and his hardline stance at the 1961 Vienna Summit, hadn't won him many friends in the free world.

Meanwhile, the situation in Vietnam had steadily gone from bad to worse. After the French were defeated at Dien Bien Phu in 1954, peace negotiations at Geneva separated Vietnam into two political entities: a northern zone, governed by the Communist Viet Minh, and a southern zone, which became the Republic of Vietnam.

Per the Geneva Accords, the Republic of Vietnam was to hold a reunification election in 1956. However, Ngo Dinh Diem, the South Vietnamese president, cancelled the elections and vowed to stamp out and lingering Communists in the Republic of Vietnam. The Viet Minh who remained in the south (the first incarnation of the Viet Cong) reciprocated by launching a low-level insurgency in 1957.

After the French withdrew from Vietnam, MAAG stepped in to assist Diem in his anti-communist efforts. The US advisory mission continued into the early 1960s until the insurgency grew to a level which Washington could no longer ignore. In 1964, MAAG was dissolved and replaced by the Military Assistance Command, Vietnam (MACV),[7] thereby giving the US a wider scope to send conventional forces into Southeast Asia. Almost simultaneously, President Kennedy lost his confidence in Diem's ability to rule South Vietnam. On November 2, 1963, just weeks before Kennedy's own assassination, Ngo Dinh Diem was deposed and murdered in a coup d'état that was sanctioned, if not partially orchestrated, by Washington.

With Diem now out of the way, the Hanoi government felt it was time to escalate the war and "liberate" South Vietnam. They felt that it wasn't enough to provide guns and ammunition to the Viet Cong. The time had come to intervene militarily with units of the People's Army of North Vietnam. They argued that these better-trained and highly motivated soldiers could infiltrate the south and make short work of the unmotivated South Vietnamese Army.

"I was the S-3 [of Combat Command 'C'] from about August of 1960 to April of 1962," said Starry. "Combat Command 'C' was traditionally the reserve brigade, the reserve combat command of the 3rd Armored Division, so we always had to go where one of the other brigades was and do counterattack planning." As it turned out, his previous duties at Fort Holabird (and his year-long schooling at Leavenworth) had over-prepared him for the rigors of brigade staff work:

> So, when I went to be the S-3 of that brigade, I'd been an instructor for almost four years in tactics [at the Intelligence School]. I'd also been a student at Leavenworth for a year, and at least from the standpoint of the operational concepts of the Army … I was probably as up to date as I could have been. The most interesting thing I found at Leavenworth as a student was that I was the only person in my section who knew how to write an operations order. I taught that [at Fort Holabird] for four years. As a result, I could sit down with a clean piece of paper and fairly quickly write an operations order that was fairly correct, to include the punctuation, which was very important in those days. So, that was good background for being a Brigade S-3.

In fact, Starry's tenure as the S-3 was so impressive that Abrams tapped him to be the Plan Officer for the V Corps in Europe. Abrams had relinquished his command of the 3d Armored Division in 1962 and returned stateside for a year-long tour as Deputy Chief of Staff for Operations in the Pentagon. When he returned to Europe in 1963, Abrams was awarded command of V Corps. By the time he assumed this new command, he was writing the order to bring Starry onto the V Corps staff.

"But I wanted to stay in the brigade," Starry admitted.

Indeed, Starry was due to be on the promotion list for lieutenant colonel—and he desperately wanted battalion command. Specifically, Donn had his eye on 1st Battalion, 32d Armor Regiment (1-32 Armor). The unit had one of the best reputations in the 3d Armored Division and commanding such a unit would undoubtedly pay dividends for Starry's mid-level career. He said to General Abrams: "I want to stay in that brigade so I can go to that battalion, be the [executive officer] for a while, and if the promotion thing works out right, I can move right into command."

Abrams grumbled, "Well, let me think about it."

Four days later, Abrams called the 3d Brigade commander and said "All right, tell Donn he can go to the 32d."

"Well," Starry recalled, "that was a great favor," for this new assignment gave him a chance to overhaul the unit's warrior ethos. When Starry arrived at 1-32 Armor as its executive officer, he was thrust into a command climate that allowed him to thrive. "The battalion commander was [Lieutenant Colonel] Bill Mangum. Bill liked to let his executive officer run the battalion." Some commanders, if straddled with a competent and motivated executive officer, are happy to let their second-in-command oversee the unit's daily operations. "Then, when Bill left, I took command of the 32nd."

"It was a good battalion," Starry remembered, "and had been for a long time:

> My predecessor was a good battalion commander who had continuity in command, and good people. We had a lot of cohesion. But ... we had a shortage of majors and senior captains. So, we had a situation in which we had plenty of lieutenants. But, what I found out was that I couldn't have a mixed bag of [company] commanders out there. In other words, I couldn't have a couple of companies commanded by lieutenants and a couple of companies commanded by senior captains unless I was willing to issue *two* different sets of instructions.

After all, given that these captains had three to four years of experience over the lieutenants, a battalion commander could not issue the same kind of instructions to a lieutenant:

> So ... I kept the captains on the staff in the principal staff positions and let the lieutenants command the companies. I would also argue that the younger people

with more imagination and a little bit more "get-up-and-go," are perhaps the kind of commanders you want to go to war with, at least in the initial stages. I would rather coach and develop teamwork with a group of people like that than to work with older officers who had had those jobs before and had a lot of preconceived notions. I think coaches have the same problem with teams; I remember some conversations with my football coach about that.

But placing young lieutenants into command positions was only part of Starry's plan. Early in his command tenure, Donn realized that some of the training philosophies were flawed. For instance, when Starry arrived in Germany in 1960, "there was a big debate going on about whether officers should fire [their tanks during gunnery]." Starry was shocked to learn that this was even a topic for debate. As far as he was concerned, *every* armor officer should fire his tank (and qualify) during gunnery. "The platoon leader was the first guy down range in his tank; the company commander with his; the battalion commander with his." Indeed, this was the way he had been brought up under Abrams's leadership in the 63d Tank Battalion. This trend of exempting officers from gunnery, as Starry saw it, "was a cop-out on the part of those who were not technically qualified to get in the tank and go do what they were supposed to do, particularly battalion commanders."

Thus, when he took command of 1-32 Armor, Starry gathered all the tank commanders in the battalion into one room:

> No one else was allowed, motor sergeants were not allowed and the sergeant major was not allowed. We were getting ready to go to the ROAD [Reorganization of Army Divisions] organization, and so I had my own four tank companies plus a fifth tank company. So I got all the tank commanders in the room and I said, "Now there are 89 tank commanders in this battalion. The whole operation of this battalion depends on what we do if the war starts. Some of us are better than others. There are officers, there are sergeants, there are platoon sergeants and so on in this group, and I expect every tank commander to be just as proficient as the next guy."

He finished the discussion, however, with a challenge: "I'm going to beat all of you," he said, "and I expect every commander to beat everyone in his company and the platoon leader to beat everyone in his platoon and so on." It may have seemed like a tall order, but Starry believed that every officer should lead from the front. Nevertheless, he spiced up the challenge by adding: "Any crew who beats my crew, I'll owe them all a steak dinner and a case of beer." Nearly every tank commander in the room responded: "All right, you're on."

It was a great motivator for the tank crews, but as Starry recalled, "it cost me untold hours of personal agony, nights, and weekends." Not the least of his worries was the condition of his own tank crew: "I had a crew composed of a drunk, a perpetual AWOL, and another guy that had a family problem of some kind." Despite being saddled with a tank crew of misfits, Donn was determined to mold them into "top guns." Huddling his crewmen, Starry wasted no time: "Now, I'll tell you what, fellas," he said, "we're going to have to practice on Saturdays and Sundays, and we're going to have to practice at night. That means you're all going to have to be here *and be sober* in order to do that, and you're going to have to meet my schedule. Now we'll work out the rest of your work so that it gets done, too."

Thus began the grueling task of building his crew into a well-oiled machine. As he had predicted, it was task that spanned several nights and weekends. But Starry's efforts had the tertiary effect of boosting the battalion's morale and motivation. For instance, amid his nightly training regimen,

> we'd been out all night doing some night tracking exercises and some sub-caliber firing. I was walking down through the motor pool, chatting with the platoon sergeants during a maintenance period one afternoon, when one of the platoon sergeants came up and said:
> "Sir, you're serious about this, aren't you?"
> I said, "About what?"
> He said, "About beating our asses."
> I said, "Why do you ask?"
> He said, "Well, I drove by here last night and the only thing I could see was your crew and yourself out there, working the targets and whatnot. We're not doing that." I said, "Sarge, if you intend to compete in the big competition, you better get your ass out here and do the same thing." So, after that, you began to see them *all* doing it. Well, we fired and were the high battalion in the division that year. Now, with that little crew I had, we were second high in the battalion. We were beat out by a crew that set a new USAREUR [US Army Europe] record.

True to his word, Starry rewarded the winning crew with a case of beer and a steak dinner. He later remarked, half-jokingly, how grateful he was that he only had to purchase the smorgasbord for *one* crew.

During his command, Starry also developed the concepts for what became the Battalion Training Management System (BTMS). During one of their training exercises, 1-32 Armor received a visit from the Research Analysis Corporation (RAC). General Abrams had sent the RAC team to "collect data on target acquisition times. They brought some Air Force gun camera systems with them to record tank versus tank engagements. We spent about a year doing that. It was a great experiment and a lot of fun. We learned a lot from it. We found that we had to lay out these scenarios meticulously, in great detail, in order to do the instrumentation."

Suddenly, it dawned on Starry and his Battalion S-3 that they ought to be preparing *every* training exercise with that level of detail. For too long, battalions across the Army had simply done training exercises without asking themselves: "What do they know when they go into the training experience? What do we want them to know when they get out of it? And what goes on in the middle to make that happen?" According to Starry, that was the beginning of BTMS. "If you go back in the literature," he said, "we created the genesis of it in that battalion. We had a thing called the Readiness Training Program which consisted of tasks, conditions and standards. In the end, I think we were getting a lot more out of training time than we had ever been getting before." The concepts born from 1-32 Armor's training program are still in use today: every Army training event is prefaced with "Task, Conditions, and Standards."

This prototype of BTMS was also a safeguard against the highly turbulent personnel replacement system. Typically, there was a 30 percent annual turnover rate for soldiers serving in 1-32 Armor. This was a result of the individual replacement system and the three-year tour limits for Army personnel in West Germany. Under this early version on BTMS, "skills necessary to achieve and sustain combat capability were grouped. Newly assigned soldiers were tested on those skills and then, based on cumulative test data, the battalion training program was designed around an evaluation of how frequently those skills needed to be practiced in order to maintain individual and unit proficiency."

Another improvement to the battalion's training culture was a revision of the administrative standards. Starry consolidated every policy into what he called the Battalion Training Manual. "We'd had a couple of changes in division commanders," he said, "which resulted in a flurry of directives from division. Everybody was confused about what they were supposed to be doing." Adding to the confusion was that the previous commanders of 1–32 Armor had issued conflicting guidance to their tank crews. "Well, I got a bunch of the platoon sergeants together and we had a big talk about that. And they were carrying around little directives like that, from one battalion commander to the next. None of them were the same; there was no standardization."

Thus, Starry eliminated every contradicting order from the previous battalion commanders, and annotated the most current standing orders from Division. The result was the Battalion Training Manual. "So, when you went to do whatever it was ... all the way from investigations to motor pool operations, you just turned that tab, looked down, and there was your guidance on what to do. We finished that thing and threw away about two filing cabinets full of standing orders and instructions. It dramatically simplified the administration."

Almost simultaneously, he developed the concept of "Who Fights With Me Tonight?" Combat readiness was the top priority for American ground forces in West Germany. By necessity, it had to be. The NATO contingent along the Inner German Border was presumably the only deterrent against a ground invasion from the Eastern Bloc forces. Thus, every soldier along the "Frontier of Democracy," whether an infantryman or a cook, had an equal stake in the readiness of his unit. Starry thus developed "Who Fights With Me Tonight?" as a means to ensure that every seat in every vehicle (whether a combat vehicle or support vehicle) would be occupied by a soldier in the event of a Communist invasion. Thus, every evening, 1–32 Armor would construct a battle roster of crews ready to man their vehicles should the unit be alerted at night. "Any roster shortages in regularly assigned crews were filled as necessary by clerks, mechanics, and others normally assigned noncombat duties."

In August 1964, the Starrys returned stateside. With a successful battalion command under his belt, Starry received orders to the Armed Forces Staff College in Norfolk, Virginia. Donn remarked that, during the 1960s, "the Army and the Marine Corps had a rule that you had to have gone to your service command and staff course, either at Quantico [for the Marines] or at Leavenworth [for the Army], before you could go to Norfolk. So, all of the Army officers who went to Norfolk were graduates of Leavenworth, and all of the Marine Corps officers were graduates either of Leavenworth or the Quantico school. The Navy has never put the kind of emphasis on progressive schooling that the other services have, so the Naval officers at Norfolk were people who were essentially between assignments. So, for them it was a brand new world. That was also the case for the Air Force officers. Now, of course, that has all changed."

Reflecting on this inter-service synergy, Donn recalled that the Army and Marine Corps students often tutored their Navy and Air Force counterparts on the dynamics of higher-level staff work, "which is not all bad," he added. As Starry saw it, "it made us coalesce our thoughts on what the Army is, what the Marine Corps is, how they do business, and so on. It provided a better base line for us. It taught all of us a lot about the other services that we never would have known otherwise." Starry later remarked: "Norfolk is an opportunity to learn something about the other services that you could never get anywhere else. That place should be given some doctrinal development responsibilities, which is part of the key, I think, to developing what I called joint tactics, techniques and procedures."

Years later, when Starry was the commander of US Readiness Command (REDCOM) at MacDill Air Force Base, he realized that, "nobody wanted to let us tell them about joint doctrine. There wasn't any real honest-to-goodness doctrine for tactical and operational level employment of joint forces, but there needed to be some, and that's the place to develop it." Completing the five-month course at Norfolk, Starry stayed on for an additional six months as an Army faculty advisor, wherein he had the opportunity to co-author the latest revision to the *Joint Officer's Staff Guide*.

Meanwhile, the powder keg in Vietnam finally exploded. In the wake of Diem's assassination, Saigon went through a series of violent coups d'état staged by South Vietnamese generals who took turns being "strongman of the month." At the same time, the Viet Cong continued to grow in Mekong Delta and began exerting their influence in the Central

Highlands and the Coastal Plains. In the middle of it all, the ARVN remained poorly led and largely unmotivated.

In August 1964, Congress passed the infamous Gulf of Tonkin Resolution. The new law was drafted in response to a naval skirmish involving North Vietnamese boats and the US destroyers *Maddox* and *C. Turner Joy*. Essentially, it gave President Lyndon Johnson the unprecedented authority to use conventional military force in Vietnam without a formal declaration of war. Still, Johnson was confident that he could find a diplomatic solution to the Vietnamese problem.

All that changed, however, on the night of February 15, 1965, when Viet Cong sappers attacked the US airbase at Pleiku. That night, a fed-up Johnson went to his National Security Council and said, "I've had enough of this." The following month, he authorized a systematic bombing campaign and on March 8, 1965, the first US Marines waded ashore at Danang. Meanwhile, the new MACV commander, General William C. Westmoreland, continued pressing Johnson for more troops. By Westmoreland's estimate, he would need nearly 180,000 troops by the end of 1965.

This was a bit unsettling for Johnson, who had wanted to pursue the war in Vietnam without detracting from his Great Society programs. Thus, in another bad decision for America's war effort, Johnson ignored the advice of his military chiefs and decided that the war could be fought "on the cheap." There would be no mobilization of the Reserve or National Guard, and no declared state of emergency, which would have allowed the Army to extend the enlistments of its best-trained troops. Instead, the war would be manned by cannibalizing the Army's divisions in Europe while 20,000 new (and reluctant) draftees were shuttled into Vietnam every month.

Back in the US, the newly promoted Colonel Starry moved from one staff school to another. He enrolled at the Army War College in Carlisle Barracks, Pennsylvania, with the Class of 1966. As the operational picture in Vietnam became clearer, the US Army began instructing more of its personnel in the art of *counterinsurgency*. By the fall of 1965, it was clear that Vietnam was a war unlike any other.

Unlike World War II and Korea, where the enemy had been clearly defined and somewhat predictable, the US found itself battling a faceless enemy that lurked amongst the population. The North Vietnamese Army (NVA) abided by *some* of the established rules of war, but the Viet Cong abided by none. It was a war with no front lines and no rear echelon. Plus, the conventional concepts of holding key terrain and pursuing the enemy across international boundaries had gone by the wayside.

During his course of study, Donn researched and wrote several treatises about the tenets of counterinsurgency. Typically, US doctrine had shied away from it, although Field Manual 31-20 *Operations Against Guerrilla Forces* and Field Manual 31-21 *Organization and Conduct of Guerrilla Warfare* had given the US military a primer on how to defeat unconventional forces. Drawing lessons from these and other publications (along with a critical study of the French defeat in Indochina), Starry concluded that victory in Vietnam would require more than just a military solution—"that successful counterinsurgency operations would require a wider spectrum of skills and training—economic, political, and social as well as military—and would require new doctrine … and new and different weapons, organization, and other relevant skills." These were great concepts, but putting them into practice—especially on the fly—would be no easy task.

Starry went to Vietnam from Carlisle in August 1966 for his first tour:

> Because I was a recent War College graduate and had commanded a battalion already, I was assigned to USARV [US Army Vietnam] Headquarters, a fate worse than death. I spent three or four months as part of the G-3 Plans shop in USARV … which at that point was located in Saigon. It had not yet moved out to Long Binh and was essentially a logistics headquarters. It was a terrible place. I had one miserable assignment in 40 years in the Army, and that was it. I wanted to command a battalion [in Vietnam], but in December I came out on the promotion list to colonel and obviously wasn't going to command a battalion. I was very frustrated.

Starry bitterly recalled:

> USARV had too many people. They really didn't know what they were supposed to be doing. It was all make-work. You had to be in the office by 6:30 or 6:45 in the morning, and you couldn't leave until 6:30 or 6:45 at night. When you got there at 6:30 or 7:00 in the morning you had to look around and say, "What the hell am I supposed to be doing today?" You looked at all the guys up and down the hall, hundreds of them, doing the same thing and you just had to

wonder: "Here I've uprooted myself from my wife and my family and they're all back there suffering from this whole thing. The press is against the war, and here's old Dad out here doing this. So, what in the world am I doing here?"

There really was no logical answer. The old logisticians were over there, fumbling around trying to figure out how to get organized. Some of the logistical units in the field were doing super work building ports, establishing airfields ... but still that whole headquarters was a common zoo.

At the time, the USARV deputy commander was Lieutenant General Jean Engler, an ordnance officer and a 1933 West Point graduate. "Nice man," Starry said, "but clearly in over his head." Starry was impressed by the big-screen system Engler kept in his command briefing room—but he wondered why Engler never went out to inspect the logistical units he nominally commanded. Rather, his staff officers would go out and snap photographs of the port and airfield construction, convert the film into 35mm slides, then bring in the slides to brief the general. "You had to wonder" Starry said, "if he was afraid to go out there. He was succeeded by General Bruce Palmer, so we had a soldier instead of a logistician in charge, and things began to get a little better. But it was a disaster in the beginning."

However, in fairness to General Engler, Starry conceded that this was before MACV created a separate logistics command for its supply and construction needs. "They organized the Logistics Command separately, got another ordnance general to command that, and then [re-] organized USARV." Thereafter, operations at the higher echelons ran more smoothly.

Luckily, Donn would serve only four months at the USARV Headquarters. "Subsequently," he recalled, "General Art West came over with his MACOV (Mechanized and Armor Combat Operations, Vietnam) Study Group, and I got hooked up with that in the fall of 1966. I spent about five months of my tour with that study group." MACOV, however, would be no trivial, academic exercise. To the contrary, it would be an intense front-line observation, often conducted in the heat of battle. Indeed, throughout the course of the study, five MACOV team members were wounded in action, including General West himself. "As part of the MACOV Study," Donn recalled, "we went around and visited every tank, mech, and cavalry squadron, troop or company in the theater."

To this point, there had been considerable debate as to whether tanks and mechanized vehicles could operate effectively in Vietnam. Popular images of rice paddies and near-impenetrable jungles had dissuaded Army leaders from bringing mechanized forces into the fight. But the problem, according to Starry, stemmed from commonly held misbeliefs and an ignorance of history. The Army realized too late that "they had deployed a lot of the wrong kinds of forces," he said. "They brought the infantry divisions over without their tank battalions. They thought there was no place for tanks. The data that we gathered in the MACOV Study [however] shows that Vietnam was a place where you *could* use armor.

"The mythology," he said, "started with Bernard Fall's book, *Street Without Joy*, which described the death of Groupe Mobile 100. Groupe Mobile 100, even if you read Bernard Fall carefully, was not a mechanized unit. It was a column of trucks … truckborne infantry. The image that we drew out of that battle was that Vietnam was no place for tanks or armored vehicles of any kind, simply because they destroyed this armored group on the road up there in the Central Highlands. It wasn't an armored group at all, but just a bunch of trucks under a stupid commander who made some dumb tactical mistakes that cost him his entire command."

Thus, MACOV's first order of business was to prove the naysayers wrong. Terrain and weather were challenges, certainly, but they were *not* inhibitors. After all, the South Vietnamese had grown quite adept to using armor in the jungle. The biggest challenge, as Starry saw it, was knowing *when* and *where* to use tanks effectively. Operational tempo in Vietnam depended largely on the season—wet or dry. Using this data point, Starry and his team took a critical look at the four Corps Tactical Zones into which South Vietnam had been divided. For each of the four zones, Starry analyzed the trafficability for tanks and armored personnel carriers [APCs].

The results were astounding.

For example, in the IV Corps area, which included the Mekong Delta, APCs had an 87 percent "go-trafficability" in wet or dry seasons. "In fact, APCs were found to be more mobile than foot soldiers during the wet season." For tanks, however, the dry season gave a 61 percent "go-trafficability" in the IV Corps region. During the wet season, tank mobility plummeted to *zero*.

Tanks (including the M48A3 Patton and M41 Walker Bulldog) fared better in the other Corps Tactical Zones. In III Corps, encompassing Saigon and the surrounding provinces, trafficability ranged from 92 percent in the dry season to 73 percent in the wet season. In I Corps, covering the northernmost provinces, tanks could achieve 44 percent in the dry season and only 36 percent during the monsoon season. In the Central Highlands of II Corps, tanks did nearly as well in the wet season as they did during the dry season—54 and 55 percent, respectively.

Having thoroughly analyzed the terrain and trafficability, MACOV then turned its attention to doctrine, operations, and equipment. As early as 1965, the Army had deployed *some* of its armored assets to Vietnam. But, as Starry noted, this had been done in a rather piecemeal fashion, and most armor/mechanized units had left their vehicles at home prior to deploying. Aside from the M48A3 tank, one of the earliest armored vehicles to appear in Vietnam was the M113 Armored Personnel Carrier.

Starry took note of the M113's adaptability and pervasiveness in Vietnam. By design, the vehicle was little more than a "battlefield taxi" intended to deliver infantrymen to the front line. However, since its debut in 1960, the Army had gradually adapted it to other roles: ambulance, fire-support vehicle, mortar carrier, and an air-defense platform. Since its arrival in Vietnam, it had become a veritable workhorse. "With the emergence of the M113 as a fighting vehicle," Starry's group noted, "armor, scout, and mechanized units are engaging the enemy in mounted combat, while current doctrine prescribes this form of combat only for tank units." Reliance on the M113 prompted several innovations, including two additional side-mounted M60 machine guns, stronger belly armor, relocation and strengthening of fuel lines, and stand-off side shielding designed to cause the premature detonation of the enemy's lethal rocket-propelled grenades (RPGs). These reconfigured M113s were called "armored cavalry assault vehicles" (ACAVs).

Starry was less impressed, however, with the M551 Sheridan. The M551 was a light tank, officially designated an Armored Reconnaissance Airborne Assault Vehicle, capable of being landed into theater by parachute. However, its aluminum hull and troublesome 152mm main gun made the Sheridan one of the most despised armored vehicles of its day. The main gun fired an MGM-51 Shillelagh antitank missile. Once fired, the Shillelagh missile was guided to its target by a wireless control system aboard the vehicle. However, if anything obstructed the signal from the wireless transmitter, the missile would boomerang and often hit the Sheridan or other nearby vehicles.

Despite the Sheridan's obvious design flaws, the Army nevertheless wanted to send it to Vietnam in 1967. Starry, however, led the effort to prevent its fielding. He noted that the Sheridan lacked adequate armor, did not possess any night-fighting capabilities, and could not fire conventional munitions. Indeed, at the time, the 152mm gun could only fire the Shillelagh missile. This may have been all right for the battlefields of Western Europe, but there were *no* targets in Vietnam that called for an antitank missile. Thus, the lack of armor, and the unbefitting missile launcher made the Sheridan a liability in the jungles of South Vietnam. Under these conditions, Starry argued that the "Sheridan was no more than a very expensive, and quite vulnerable, machine gun platform." What the vehicle truly needed, he said, was a main gun capable of firing high-explosive and anti-personnel rounds. Starry's efforts delayed the Sheridan's introduction, but, sadly, he couldn't stop the vehicle from being fielded.

During the next two years (1967–69), the Army took Starry's recommendation for an improved armament and delivered the Sheridan with a new 152mm gun that could fire conventional high-explosive and anti-personnel rounds. Both rounds, however, featured caseless ammunition that were highly hazardous to the crew:

> That stuff would blow up if it was hit by an incandescent fragment of some kind. So, if a vehicle was hit by a rocket-propelled grenade … you had a catastrophic detonation within a few seconds. The vehicle would burn for a while—and then the fuel cells and ammunition would begin to cook off. In 15 minutes or so, the whole vehicle would begin to blow. But the fact is, most of your casualties were suffered in that first flash. And you only have to see one crew burn up before you realize that you don't want that machine in your inventory. The ordnance guys claim that what I'm saying is not true, but I'm sorry, I've seen it happen more times than I care to remember.

To make matters worse, the vehicle's hull and armor received no upgrades. The aluminum hull could not protect the crew from mine explosions. The thin-skinned armor proved no better; indeed, anything larger than a 12.7mm machine gun could result in a catastrophic kill to the vehicle. As Starry succinctly noted: "The whole system was in no way crew safe." Ironically, though, the Sheridan would come back to haunt him during his command of the 11th Armored Cavalry.

Starry and his MACOV teammates also noted that several commanders had failed to continue combat operations at night. "The bulk of the US operations and all of ARVN regular unit operations are conducted during the hours of daylight," General West noted. "At night, our units go into a tight perimeter defense. At first light they move out and, if it's a mechanized or armor unit ... the first thing that happens is that the lead tank and/or APC hits mines." These mines had been placed during the night by Viet Cong sappers, the likes of which could have been interdicted by a nighttime patrol.

Starry was also highly critical of commanders who watched the battle unfold from the safety of their helicopters. "As a matter of fact," he recalled, "we wrote in the MACOV Study in 1967 that 'the helicopter in the air costs the commander his feel for the war on the ground.' It's a question of the relevancy of your resources and putting them all together to do the job at hand. If you're flying around in the air over a firefight at altitudes of 1,000, 2,000, 3,000, or 4,000 feet (if the flak envelope will allow it), from that height the whole place looks like a pool table. It all looks so simple. I've observed generals and colonels flying around up there giving instructions that were totally out of line with what was happening on the ground simply because they had no visualization of the ground." Later, when commanding the 11th Armored Cavalry, he was careful not to acquire the same bad habits. "While I did some commanding from the helicopter," he noted, "I made it a practice to deliberately spend at least three or four days a week on the ground with units in operations. I had a couple of command tracks equipped for me with crews in them; they were just like a standby airplane. All I did was land and get into the command track and off I went."

Reflecting on his time with MACOV, Starry recalled:

> The thing that bothered us the most was that there was an enormous amount of information available from the people who had been in Saigon since the French left. Our people, Americans, who'd been in the [MAAG advisory] mission over there had an enormous amount of information. Unfortunately, it was all classified

and kept in the State Department files and not distributed. Army schools never got hold of that information, and no one ever studied it. There was no attempt to extract lessons learned from it. There was no attempt to look at it and evaluate tactics, force structure, strategies, and so on, at the operational level. So, there it sat, an enormous body of information, because it had some State Department classification on it and couldn't be released to anybody.

So, the mythology came into being that Vietnam was just a swampland and had a monsoon climate and was not suitable for much of anything except dismounted infantry and the animals that lived in the jungle. That was not the case at all. We had very imperfect knowledge of the landscape … and I suppose it's easy to be 20/20 in hindsight, but some of that should have been apparent up front. The information was available in this country [the United States] to give us a better handle on that.

Although not necessarily a "game changer," the MACOV study did have some qualitative effects. For one, it staved off deployment of the M551 Sheridan for at next two years. Starry also recalled that it was the first time that "the potential of armored forces was fully described to the Army's top leadership." Moreover, it prompted General Westmoreland (an artilleryman and perennial skeptic of using armor in the jungle) to request more armor and mechanized assets deployed to Vietnam.

Concluding his work with MACOV, Starry spent the next three months in Malaysia at the British Jungle Warfare School on a program to train military tracker dogs. "The British had had great success with tracker teams using Labrador Retrievers," he said, "in the confrontation in Borneo and the emergency in Malaysia." Hoping to duplicate that success in Vietnam, the US Army sent a team of dog handlers to train with the British Tracker Wing. "We bought 30 or 40 Labradors from the British," Starry continued. "The dogs had been deployed in operations in Malaysia and Borneo. We bought them, and the British trained our soldiers to use them. A tracker dog will track a human from wherever the scent is picked up. If the person goes into a hole in the ground, the dog will track him right into that hole."

The risk, however, was that the tracker dog could lead his handlers right into an ambush. According to Starry, this was how a tracker dog differed from a scout dog. Scout dogs (like German Shepherds) would typically stop within 100 yards of their scented target and alert their handlers of the target's location. The tracker breeds, however, didn't do that; they would lead their handlers straight to the target. But Starry discovered that a tracker dogs' mannerisms would change as it got closer to a target. "The Labrador will get a little nervous," he said. "So, if you know the dog, and you've been doing it awhile, you can sense that you're getting very close. When the dog starts getting nervous, you know that there's somebody within 30 to 40 yards of where you are."

The military tracker dog program proved to be a success, but it came too late to have an appreciable effect on the war. Indeed, by the time the program was ready to launch in 1968, the Viet Cong had already been decimated as a fighting force. Because most of the post-1968 battles were fought against North Vietnamese regulars, there was less need for tracker dogs. Still, the dogs performed remarkably well in sniffing out the occasional Viet Cong saboteur. "It was an interesting experiment," Starry said, "and I happen to believe that it has a lot of promise for counterinsurgency-type operations."

Starry came back from Vietnam in the summer of 1967 and went to work on the Army Staff in the Assistant Vice Chief's office as an operations analyst. "I stayed there until February 1968, when I went to work in OSD [Office of the Secretary of Defense] as a special assistant to Dr. Solis Horowitz, who was the ASD [Assistant Secretary of Defense] in those days. These were the days when the OSD Systems Analysis groups were running rampant over the services. It was a very interesting time. We worked some very difficult papers, all of which turned out our way because Dr. Horowitz had Mr. McNamara's ear. That was the de facto end of Systems Analysis power in the OSD." But this bureaucratic victory, significant as it was, could not turn the tides of the war.

Indeed, from what Starry could deduce, the American public was growing more restless over the war in Vietnam. Still, throughout 1967, it seemed that Allied forces were making strides against the Communists. That year, "some two-thirds of the hamlets were judged secure and under the control of the central government" and US forces had killed nearly 81,000 Viet Cong and NVA. If these trends continued, General Westmoreland predicted that an orderly withdrawal could begin as early as 1970. However, in January 1968, the Tet Offensive drastically changed the course of American intervention in Vietnam.

By this time, Hanoi realized that the NVA stood no chance of defeating US forces in open combat. The Communists, therefore, settled on a different approach: if they couldn't defeat the Americans on the battlefield, then they would try to disrupt the cheerful narrative of "rural pacification" and bring the US to the negotiating table. Under the cover of a cease-fire during Tet (Vietnamese New Year), Hanoi directed the Viet Cong to launch a massive, simultaneous attack on several key US and ARVN installations. It was bold move and, in truth, Hanoi wasn't entirely certain that it would succeed. But, if it stood any chance of undermining South Vietnam's credibility and shake the confidence of the American war effort, it was worth the risk.

Although the US and South Vietnamese forces effectively crushed the Viet Cong uprising, the American media painted a *very* different picture of the Tet Offensive. Television broadcasts showed frightening images of the Viet Cong storming the American Embassy in Saigon and the bloody fighting in Hue and Khe Sanh. Taken together, these images led Walter Cronkite, America's most trusted news anchor, to declare that the war was now unwinnable. All at once, President Johnson and Secretary McNamara lost their credibility as public opinion turned savagely against the war. Scrambling to save the administration's dignity, Johnson announced on March 31, 1968 that he would not seek re-election and would instead devote his attention to ending the war in Vietnam. Although Tet proved to be a resounding failure for the North Vietnamese, it gave the Hanoi bureaucrats exactly what they wanted—a crisis of confidence in the American war effort.

Amidst the public backlash, Starry also noticed that the American people were growing increasingly hostile towards the military. To make matters worse, many Americans were blaming the military simply for its involvement in the war. Indeed, US servicemen who had once been heralded as "heroes" were now being protested, spat upon, and called "baby killers."

From his post in Washington, Donn noticed that Secretary McNamara was taking the failure particularly hard. As the former CEO of the Ford Motor Company, McNamara had tried to apply the same "bean counter" metrics-based business ideals to the Department of Defense. He had failed. "He left office early in that period [February 1968] and Clark Clifford replaced him. When Nixon was elected in the fall of 1968, Mel Laird came into office. So, during most of the period that I was there, Clark Clifford was the Secretary of Defense. It was during the period that McNamara changed his mind about the Vietnam War and for that reason resigned. Clifford, of course, was part of the antiwar movement, so he spent most of his time away from the Pentagon making speeches about getting out of Vietnam. The department was really run by the Deputy Secretary of Defense, Paul Nitze, for most of that period. McNamara left about the time I got there."

By now, Johnson's turnabout on Vietnam had morphed into President Nixon's policy of "Vietnamization"—a redeployment of American combat forces while training the South Vietnamese to take the lead in combat operations. Vietnamization was essentially a three-step process: increase the ARVN's combat and logistical capabilities, systematically return the Corps Tactical Zones to Vietnamese control, and withdraw American ground forces. Little did Starry realize, however, that he would find himself on the front lines of this redeployment effort. For in February 1969, he was pulled from the bureaucratic confines of the Pentagon and sent back to Vietnam.

Arriving once again in Saigon, Starry found himself in the MACV Plans Office (J-3):

> After a very brief period as the head of Operations Analysis for J-3, I became the head of the task force to Vietnamize the war. This was in March 1969. By then the new administration had taken office. It's quite clear that they had begun work the previous November and December [of 1968] trying to figure out how to "get out of" Vietnam. In Vietnam … we would soon be told to plan redeployment of US units [and] General Abrams set to work in December considering one division, then in January and February, he added an additional requirement to examine taking out *two* divisions. In April 1969, redeployment had become *National Security Study Memorandum 36*. It set forth the requirement to develop a plan to first redeploy 25,000 people, then another increment of 100,000, or perhaps more later on that year.
>
> General Abrams and Major General Carter Townsend, who was his chief of staff, plus myself and four majors (two Army, one Air Force, and one Marine Corps), were the only people in the headquarters who knew what was going on. The majors did the "spadework," and I would draw up a plan. The whole exercise was run through backchannels between the Chairman, the President, and the SecDef, mostly the Chairman and the SecDef, and General Abrams

and General Townsend. As the MACV Chief of Staff, General Townsend had knowledge of it and sort of steered us along with what we were doing.

Essentially, we had to decide who to redeploy, how many, when, and so on. Then we had to bring in the J-2 [Intelligence] to make an assessment to find areas where the threat would allow redeployment of US forces. For many reasons, we decided to redeploy the 9th Division out of Dong Tam [in the Mekong Delta]. In April, General Abrams summoned me one morning and handed me a message from General Westmoreland, the Chief of Staff.

It said we can't redeploy a division as a division.

Our proposal had been to lift the whole division out, lock, stock and barrel, and send it home. We wanted to march it down the streets of Seattle, Washington, or some other large city, flags, flying, bands playing, bugles blaring, and soldiers marching with their heads up and proud in the sunshine. Well, the personnel managers got hold of that. The equality folks got hold of that. They said:

"You can't do that, because in that outfit you have some people who have been there 2 or 3 months and some who have been there 8 or 10 months. The 8-or 10-month folks deserve to go home, but these other people haven't paid their dues. They have got to stay. What we should do is take the short-term people from this outfit, replace them with some long-term people from other outfits. Then, we'll put all the new folks over in the other outfit. We'll just send the long-term folks home as individuals, not as a unit."

Well, you follow what was going on. General Abrams argued back and forth with General Westmoreland ... for about two weeks; finally, he was overruled. With tears in his eyes, he said to me, "*We'll suffer for this. The Army will suffer for this in the end, and I don't know how badly.*" Little did either of us know that it would turn out to be the process that ruined the Army in Vietnam.

When we had over 540,000 people in Vietnam, there was no problem. But, as we wound down to the last few thousand, we had the spectacle of officers standing up in the morning in front of squads, platoons, and soldiers whom they didn't know and who didn't know them or know one another. The officers didn't know the soldiers, the soldiers didn't know the officers, and they were supposed to go out and fight a battle that morning. They were indeed—not very successfully! What happened [in Vietnam] had nothing to do with the ethic of the officer corps. The institution did that to itself. We did it to accommodate the personnel managers.

Reluctantly, and against their better judgement, Abrams, Starry and the others on the J-3 Task Force redeployed the 9th Division as a mishmash of total strangers. "Before we finished that redeployment, we were at work on the second increment, which was to occur in August. However, it was delayed because the North Vietnamese staged a period of high activity. We delayed the redeployment until September just to see what they were going to do. We also drew up plans for yet another increment, which was to be the third redeployment. This one was to take place in the spring of 1970."

However, in December 1969, Starry was posted to command the 11th Armored Cavalry Regiment. It was to be the most exhilarating command of his career.

CHAPTER 4

Blackhorse

The Armored Cavalry Regiment (ACR) was an organization unique to the United States Army. Independent, heavily-armored, and rapidly deployable, the ACR's purpose was to provide armored reconnaissance, surveillance, and mobile security to heavy forces in the field. Unlike conventional armor and infantry units—which are descendingly organized into brigades, battalions, and companies—cavalry units are respectively organized into *regiments*, *squadrons*, and *troops*. Each ACR contained three armored cavalry squadrons and a regimental air cavalry troop. An armored cavalry squadron normally consisted of a headquarters troop, three armored cavalry troops, a pure tank company, and a self-propelled howitzer battery.

The armored cavalry troop was the centerpiece of the ACR's ground network:

> The three cavalry troops were equipped with what we called armored cavalry assault vehicles (ACAVs). The ACAV was actually an M-113 … on which we had mounted a gun shield forward that housed a .50 caliber, and two shields side-mounted that housed 7.62mm side-firing machine guns. The ACAV had a drop-down hatch in the back and a top hatch that opened up and out. The guys normally rode with the top hatch open because of the mine problem. If we hit a mine, they preferred to be blown out than blown up inside the vehicle. And we beefed up the floors—the decks forward in the driver's compartment—usually with sandbags, so that, to some extent at least, it would mitigate the effects of the mine damage. But it's a fragile vehicle. And if you hit a big mine—standard, 23-pound, Chinese-manufactured, Soviet-developed antitank mine—it could make a big mess out of those vehicles.

Meanwhile, the squadrons' tank companies were equipped with the M48A3 Patton tank. One company, however, was equipped with the dreaded M551 Sheridan, which had somehow wormed its way into Vietnam despite Starry's efforts to kill it. The howitzer batteries operated the mighty M-109, firing its 155mm high-explosive shells. "And the helicopters," Starry added, "those little light observation helicopters, the OH-6s. And we had the Huey Cobra and the Huey UH-1. Originally that's all we had."

During the Vietnam War, the US Army had five active ACRs: the 2d, 3d, 6th, 11th, and 14th. The 2d, 3d, and 14th ACRs were forward-stationed in West Germany, while the other two were stationed in the continental US. Of these five regiments, only the 11th ACR deployed to Vietnam.

The 11th Armored Cavalry Regiment came to Vietnam with a storied history. Activated in 1901 as a horse cavalry regiment, the 11th had participated in the Philippine–American War and the Punitive Expedition against Pancho Villa. After converting to tanks, various elements of 11th deployed to the European theater during World War II, where they saw extensive action in the Normandy and Central European campaigns. In the years following World War II, the regiment had adopted the unit insignia of a silhouetted prancing horse, hence its nickname: *Blackhorse*.

Since its arrival in Vietnam, the 11th ACR had gained one of the most respected reputations in theater. Deploying from its home base in Fort Meade, Maryland, the Blackhorse Regiment arrived in Vietnam in September 1966. Over the next three years, the 11th would participate in several high-profile missions against the NVA and Viet Cong—including Operation *Cedar Falls* and Operation *Manhattan*. By the time Starry took command on December 7, 1969, the regiment had been conducting combat operations in the Long Binh province.

The night before Starry took command, he had dinner with General Abrams in Saigon. "He was very concerned by the fact that many US commanders were still in the frame of mind that 'you little guys [the South Vietnamese] get out of our way.' He said to me after the change of command: 'Don't push yourself on the Vietnamese. They're going to have to learn to pick up the combat load, and you're going to have to help them learn that.'"

Taking the reins from Colonel Jimmie Leach, the previous commander, Starry noticed that the regiment's maintenance program was in shambles:

> As I recall, the operational ready rate of vehicles was less than 50 percent and hadn't been above 50 percent for some five or six months … and the fact that there was no balance between the operational schemes and the availability of vehicles and weapons systems. We were at the beginning of the dry season, which helped a bit. But, in any event, we had a maintenance situation that I thought was intolerable. The first part of it had to do with the spare parts situation. The second part had to do with what the officers and the supervisors themselves knew about maintenance and how much maintenance was being done. I tackled both of those problems while running operations. The first thing I found was each squadron had somewhere between 2,500 and 3,000 lines in the prescribed load list [PLL].

Starry was incredulous.

That quantity was nearly *ten times* the number of items typically found on a cavalry squadron's PLL. Where did all the extra gear come from?, he wondered. It didn't take him long, however, to discover that the Sheridan was the culprit. Indeed, the vehicle that Starry had tried desperately to keep out of Vietnam had returned to plague his property book.

As it turned out, the Army "had pushed large packages of spare parts when they issued the Sheridan. Many of those parts had to do with the missile system. We were not using the missile system, but the parts were still on the PLL." Naturally, this cluttered the supply depots and had contributed to the inefficient maintenance system. Trying to get a handle on the situation, Starry went back to the regimental supply depots to see what items he could purge.

"I made them purge the squadron PLLs," he said. "Not long after we started the purge, the biggest squadron had about 325 lines in its PLL. So, we had reduced the line item count … by a factor of almost 10." At the same time, Starry began studying the regiment's "usage cards"—a consolidated report of the spare parts that were frequently expended during combat operations. These "high mortality parts," as Starry called them, had to be replaced constantly in order for the vehicles to maintain their combat functionality. It was the chronic shortage of these parts that had led to the regiment's deplorable readiness rate.

To correct the situation, Starry gained an audience with the Logistics Command commander (a 3-star general). Accompanied by a few of his maintenance and supply sergeants, Starry convinced Logistics Command to adjust the regiment's supply rations based on the reported usage factors. After a long-winded conference, the general finally said: "All right, you send me a list and I'll authorize it."

"Within about four months or so," Starry said, "we had increased the stock of high mortality parts, and the OR [operational readiness] rate started to go up and continued to go up. We went into Cambodia in May 1970 at about 98 percent OR and, although we lost a lot of vehicles in Cambodia, we cannibalized and came out with about a 98 percent OR. So, over the period of just a few months, we straightened out the maintenance situation."

Starry also had to contend with the fact that his regiment had been fragmented and parceled out to other units. "One of the findings of the MACOV Study," he recalled, "was that in Vietnam, infantry commanders tended to piecemeal their armor out, as infantry commanders always do. Armor units were never employed as units, and so it was with the 11th Cavalry." Coincidentally, one of the preceding regimental commanders was Colonel George Patton IV, whom Starry had served with in the 63d Tank Battalion nearly 20 years earlier. According to Starry, the regiment "wasn't as badly fragmented in 1969 as it had been when George Patton was in command of it in 1968. For some four or five months during his command … all he had under his control was the headquarters troop and part of the air cavalry troop. Everything else had been allocated out."

When Starry took command, however, he insisted on having his regiment remain intact. To him, it made no sense to have an ACR in Vietnam if it wasn't going to be employed as a singular unit. For according to Starry, a cavalry regiment, even in a jungle environment, could cover as much ground and deliver more firepower than two airmobile divisions. Once Starry had the squadrons back under his control, he gave each of them an operational sector within the regiment's combat zone. "We carved out an AO [Area of Operations] for each squadron," he said. "Everything that went on in that AO was the squadron commander's responsibility, to include artillery and air."

Despite the initial setbacks with maintenance and operationally fragmented units, Starry was blessed to have a first-rate command sergeant major—Don Horn. The pair had worked together in 1-32 Armor when Starry had been the battalion commander. "Don Horn had been first sergeant of three companies in the 32d Tank Battalion," Starry recalled. Later, Horn became the Operations Sergeant Major for 3d Brigade, 3d Armored Division in Friedberg. "He was probably the best operations sergeant I ever met," said Starry. By the time Starry assumed command of the 11th Armored Cavalry, Horn was on his *second* tour as the regimental command sergeant major.

As such, Starry wanted to give Horn a more active role in the regiment's daily operations. Like most regimental commanders in Vietnam, Starry had a command liaison helicopter from which he could observe and control his troop movements. Most commanders would bring their air liaison officer or artillery support officer along for the ride. Starry, however, chose to bring his sergeant major:

> The sergeant major and I, the two door gunners, and the two pilots were the only people I would allow in that [helicopter]. The sergeant major was responsible for the fire support—air, helicopters, and artillery—and I was responsible for the maneuver units and what he couldn't handle in terms of fire support. If he got overloaded, I'd pick up one or the other. We had a system worked out so that two people ran the operation. He kept the maps, the records, and worked the radios. I helped occasionally with that. We had a super pilot, Larry Parsons, who'd been a scout pilot.
>
> For most my tour we were in northern War Zone C [part of the III Corps Tactical Zone], and we had on the ground, either just south of the border or just north of the border, sufficient North Vietnamese antiaircraft units to force us to modify our air operations in the area. We really never flew much over the treetop level. At treetop level the reaction time was such that the enemy ground gunners couldn't get at you. Even so, we got hit a couple of times. Fortunately, no one was hurt. My air cavalry troop commander, Don Smart, got shot down so many times I told him that I didn't have enough airplanes to keep him in command and that he was going to have to modify his tactics, which he did. So, it was a risky enterprise, and we learned to fly low and stay there.

On one occasion, Starry had to organize a rescue mission to recover the crew of a downed scout helicopter. "This was in early April," he recalled. "He [the pilot] was flying along the border. The border was ill-defined in that area [and] he took a burst of AK fire from the ground. When he crashed, he ended up across the border. We thought at the time that he was across the border, but there was no border marking to confirm it. We saw him go in and knew about where it was." At the time of the incident, Starry was in his command vehicle alongside Lieutenant Colonel Grail Brookshire, the 2d Squadron commander. Without hesitation, the pair went off in search of the downed crew.

> It took us about a half hour to get the guys and the wreckage out and pulled back on our side of the border. The helicopter did not burn, fortunately. The guys were wounded and covered with fuel. The scout/observer had a couple of rounds through his leg, and the pilot had a hole in his hand or an arm. Anyway, we got them out and washed them off. If you wear a flight suit impregnated with fuel, it'll just burn your skin something terrible. We stripped them and washed them off, then wrapped them up and hauled them away. We did all that in about a half hour. You could hear the North Vietnamese rustling around out there in the jungle, so we put a couple of platoons out as security while we worked the problem with the helicopter. We hoisted the helicopter up on the back of a retriever and hauled the whole thing out. We would have been attacked, but we popped a few shots at them as we left just to convince them that we were still there. This forced them to pause a little bit before they started closing in on us. Anyway, we hightailed it back to the other side of the border.

For his heroic actions that day, Starry was awarded the Silver Star.

Starry made the big decision before he went into Cambodia to go into combat *on the ground*, at least until he and his men got through the flak belt. "I went in on the ground simply because I was afraid I would lose control of the regiment if I started out in the air … and got shot down or forced down someplace in the middle of nowhere." But from an operational point of view, he found the same situation that one finds almost everywhere:

> The hardest thing to teach people at the small-unit level, battalion and below, is how to integrate all of their resources. It's particularly difficult in a battle situation. You get into a firefight and, unless you've drilled yourself to methodically go down a checklist—air, artillery, Cobras [attack helicopters], maneuver units, resupply, all of those things—you'll forget some of them. In other words, it's just hard to teach people to remember to use everything. However, there is a drill. For a long time, I carried a bunch of 3×5 cards. I did it as a company commander and even later as a battalion commander. I did the same thing as a

regimental commander, because I didn't trust myself in the heat of battle and the excitement to remember all those things. I was always grabbing those cards and looking at them to make sure that I hadn't forgotten something. I think we all tend to believe that, by the time we get to be lieutenant colonels or colonels, we have all of that in hand. That's not the case!

When selecting subordinate officers for command positions, Starry preferred to have seasoned veterans in command of the squadrons. "I don't think we ever put in someone who hadn't been there [in Vietnam] before. I preferred to have somebody who'd been in the regiment and knew how we operated ... A couple of them had been the regimental S-3 ... and one had been the regimental executive officer for a while."

"One of the things I did with new squadron commanders," he continued, "if I didn't already know them well enough ... was put them in a helicopter and take them up." He then watched them to see how well they could control their formations and integrate their tactical assets. Recalling his experience with the MACOV Study Group, Starry said:

If I had to make a single observation out of that whole study, which consumed seven volumes and made a lot of other conclusions, it was that we had a whole lot of people out in command from the troop/battery/company level on up who really weren't as good as they should have been at putting all that stuff together and fighting the battle. I remember hearing then-Colonel Abrams talk about that as a big shortcoming of his battalion in World War II. He commented that it was a matter of training and discipline. You had to train the officers and the key NCOs, but particularly the officers; they had to learn to discipline themselves ... to make sure that there weren't some resources available that they could bring into the fight that they had ignored. In some cases, that resource might win the battle for them.

Starry remembered that "the squadron commanders that I had to relieve ... or get out of command a little early were people who simply couldn't figure out how to do that very well."

When selecting troop commanders, however, Starry had to take whatever the Army gave him. Troop commanders were typically young captains. "It was really not possible," he said, "to insist that they be people who had been in the theater. Most of the captains came to me new and had not been there [in Vietnam] before. Most of them had only a couple of years of service. We tried to use our own people who had been promoted; that is, the platoon leaders who were promoted to captain. Inevitably, they made better troop commanders than those who came from the outside who had not been there before." However, Starry never placed a new captain from outside the unit directly into command. "We would put him on the squadron staff to give him a chance to get familiar with the ground, the operating conditions, the enemy, and so on. After watching him for a while and giving him a chance to get acclimated, then we'd sometimes put him in as a troop commander."

But regardless of skill or experience level, every incoming trooper had to attend the regimental orientation before joining his comrades in the field:

> The regiment had a training detachment in the base camp that we put everybody through. The sergeants and the officers received a reorientation on weapons, enemy tactics, and so on. The soldiers received a little indoctrination on the enemy, living conditions, hygiene in the field, and the kinds of things that bother soldiers in the field. The longest courses were a couple of weeks. The majors and the senior captains who had been to Vietnam before were frequently there for no more than three or four days, just long enough to reacquaint them with what had changed since they'd been there the last time. If a man had not been there before at all, we left him in there for the full two weeks, I didn't care what his rank.

Throughout, Starry carefully vetted his subordinate officers before placing them into positions of leadership. During these initial interviews with potential squadron, troop, and platoon commanders, he always asked them the same question:

> "Are you afraid?"
> I asked that question because I had come to believe that, if you weren't afraid or were unwilling to admit it, then you didn't belong out there. And, if you hadn't figured out what to do about it, you *really* didn't belong out there. I got some interesting answers to that question—really interesting answers. Most of them were not willing to admit that they were afraid. Finally, as they talked through the problem, they would say, "Well, yes, I guess I am."

In that vein, Starry remembered two of his most memorable lieutenants:

> A lieutenant came in one night and, in the course of the conversation, he said he wanted to be in the Civic Action Program working in the villages ... He had a degree in social work from a good university, and he was interested in that. I said:

"That's fine, but we require every lieutenant to spend six months on the line in a platoon so that, when you're working the other part of that problem, you understand why you're doing it. You will understand the battle context in which we're trying to work this whole problem. Also, if they get into a problem down in your village, or wherever you're working, you will be qualified to call in artillery fire, direct close air support, call for gunships, and fight."

Several times during the course of the conversation, it came up that he really wanted to get into that program. I said, "Okay, six months in a platoon and then you can do that." To the question, "Are you scared?" he sort of hedged and never really answered it directly. So, I sent him off to be a platoon leader in the 2d Squadron.

The following afternoon, as Starry was preparing to mount his helicopter, he received a frantic call from the 2d Squadron commander.

"What have you sent me?" the bewildered commander asked.

"What's the matter?" Starry replied.

"This kid is out here in the middle of my firebase and has now refused to take command of his platoon." Starry quickly turned his aircraft around and landed at the 2d Squadron base camp.

What he saw next would shock him:

Our Rome plows [tactical bulldozers] were crashing the trees down, and we'd been burning a bunch of trash. It was a scene right out of Dante's *Inferno*. Here's this kid, standing with his duffel bag on his shoulders, frozen in the middle of the road. He'd gotten off the helicopter, but that's as far as he got. He walked out from under the blade arc, looked up at the trees, watched the trees come down as the plows went by, heard the artillery going out, the small arms zinging around, and he froze right in the middle of this place. Somebody went and got him and finally took him over to the squadron commander.

He said, "I can't do it."

So, I put him on the helicopter and sent him back to the regimental command post. We gave him a nice, warm, safe, overhead covered bunker to work in. I gave him a letter from me that said: "Having been posted to the command of so-and-so, it was reported to me that you had refused to accept command. I would like for you to take a few hours to think this over and please reply by endorsement, by hand, on the bottom of this page what your intentions are."

Part of the letter pointed out some of the possibilities that could come as a result of refusing to assume command. I didn't think it was a threatening letter, although some people complained that it was. But it was all there—his rights and his obligations. I made him think the whole thing through and gave him 24 hours to sign the letter as to his intentions.

However, when the young lieutenant returned to Starry's office, he *still* refused to take command of his platoon.

Starry was not impressed.

The young man had been an ROTC scholarship graduate from a good university. "What in the world were you doing in four years of ROTC in that university?" Starry demanded. "What in the world did you think you were getting ready for?"

"I don't know, sir. I never thought it through."

"You went to the Armor School. What in the hell did you think they were getting you ready for?"

"I don't know. I never stopped to think about it," he said.

"Now that you've made me think about it," the lieutenant continued, "I guess I always was scared to death the whole time, but unwilling to admit it, so I just put it aside." Starry unceremoniously put him on a helicopter and sent him back to Long Binh where he served out his tour of Vietnam as the assistant club officer.

A few weeks later, another lieutenant arrived at the regiment and when asked "Are you scared?" he answered in the affirmative. "Yes, sir, I'm scared. Colonel, I've thought about that a lot, and here's what I've decided—I've decided that I'm about as well trained as the Army can afford to make me. I need more training, but that little school we went to in the rear with the weapons, the enemy training, and all that stuff was super. I enjoyed it, and I got a lot out of that. I don't know what kind of a platoon leader I'm going to be, but I think I've got it all sorted out in my mind. I'm ready to give it a try. As far as fear of being killed is concerned, I've thought about it a lot and have looked at what is going on in our country in that regard, and I've decided that there are a lot of things a lot worse than dying for your country, and some of those things have to do with going away and hiding in some village in the mountains, or going to Canada, or not being willing to serve."

Sadly, that eager and conscientious lieutenant was killed three months later while leading a patrol near Loc Ninh. "He was a good platoon leader," Starry recalled:

> He was probably one of the best ones we had. I asked his sergeant afterwards what happened. They ran into an ambush. The lieutenant was out in front and

was smart enough to understand what had happened to them. He gave a little signal of some kind that they'd worked out to deploy and attack just before he was hit. The platoon sergeant told me afterwards,

"We had practiced that a hundred times. We practiced it in the base camp. We practiced it in the motor pool. We practiced it wherever we were doing our maintenance. We practiced it out in the jungle when nothing else was going on. We had about a half a dozen drills, and the guys all knew them. I didn't have to give a command. After the lieutenant was hit I didn't give a command, I just went with the fire team that I was supposed to go with, and the thing worked just like it was supposed to."

They wound up blowing away the better part of a North Vietnamese infantry company. They won the fight, cleaned up the battlefield, and marched out of the jungle carrying their lieutenant on their shoulders. It was all because he'd gone in there and organized the thing and drilled them so that, when the fight came, they did what they'd been trained to do and it worked like gangbusters.

Some psychiatrist would have a field day with that story. Philosophically, ecclesiastically, or whatever, how do you justify the fact that one kid lived out his tour as an assistant club officer in Long Binh and came home because he was a coward and another guy who had the courage to face up to it went out and got killed? I'm not able to solve that problem. It's beyond my skill level.

Yet all around, the 11th Armored Cavalry Regiment were a fine group of soldiers. Unlike other units composed of draftees serving one-year tours of duty, the 11th ACR was primarily a regiment of volunteers. Starry believed this was because armor/cavalry soldiers tended to stay within the same cluster of units. Still, the regiment suffered under the same replacement system that plagued much of the Army. The high turnover rate of personnel meant that vehicle crews were often scrambling to rebuild their synchronicity. "I think there were a lot of [tactical tasks] we could not do simply because we had not had time to learn how to do them and hadn't been together long enough as a unit to do them. As for the fundamental skills, which battle sharpens up very quickly, I think they did about as well as I could expect them to do under the circumstances. They were good troops. We tried to take care of them by rotating them in and out for a maintenance stand-down period ... we took time out for maintenance and that improved the ready rate. At the same time, it gave them a chance for a little break."

By virtue of being an armored cavalry regiment, the troopers conducted both mounted *and* dismounted operations—a throwback to the latter-day dragoons of the 19th century. "The ambush operations were all dismounted," he said, "because if you took the [tanks], it was a dead giveaway. The troops learned to … use all the tricks of woodcraft that people use to cover trails. You usually leave a soldier or two on the vehicle to man the guns and provide communications, security, and over-watch." If the ambush patrol were about to be overrun by an enemy force, the tanks and APCs would bound forward to provide direct fire support.

"We worked those trail networks out there," Starry said:

> You could go in there and see all the soldiers working at reading the signs on the ground. I learned some of this from going through the Jungle Warfare School when we were doing the tracker training in 1966–67. The soldiers who were teaching at the Tracking Wing were New Zealanders, native Maori. They were very well educated people, but retained their traditional skills. As I watched them work and looked at what they were doing, it became apparent to me what they were doing was well described in my "ancient" *Boy Scout Handbook*. The more we watched our own soldiers in the 11th Cavalry, the more we tried to train them well in those skills. We concentrated on the simple tracking and scouting procedures. Because of that they could read the trails. The lead scouts could tell you how many people went down the trail, how long ago, and about what they were carrying. And they were hardly ever wrong. That's mechanized soldiers, not infantry. You can't put airmobile infantry in there and have the lead scouts be that proficient instantly, since they won't know what it looked like before. So, I'd like to think we had a steadier, more stable, better balanced, more proficient, and, at the same time, safer kind of an operation. We had fewer casualties because we stayed there longer and became more familiar with the terrain and situation than did the units that just popped in, stayed a few hours or a couple of days, and then pulled out.

But whether fighting mounted or dismounted, Starry noted how much the regiment's operations differed from their counterparts in the airmobile infantry. These comparisons were astounding because it seemed that the armored cavalry troopers produced better results. As Starry described it, airmobile infantry was a means of getting soldiers from one place to another very quickly:

> It beats the hell out of walking through the jungle. My impression of them was that, while they got from "Point A" to "Point B" rather quickly, once they got there they didn't know where they were, they didn't know what the enemy situation was … and they didn't know the terrain. In short, they didn't know

anything. It was inexperienced lieutenants leading inexperienced sergeants, and together the whole outfit was scared to death out in an environment with which they were not familiar.

As opposed to that, we put the cavalry troops out and left them there. They knew the ground, they knew the trails, they knew the enemy, they knew the situation, and they knew the animals that lived in the jungle. I've seen infantry companies waste a whole basic load firing at a couple of monkeys because they were something that stirred in the jungle. The cavalry soldiers could almost smell monkeys and had superb fire discipline. In Cambodia one of the troops ran into a large group of refugees in a rubber plantation. Had it not been for the fire discipline we had established, with the troop commanders controlling the fire, they would have blown away several hundred people before they realized what was happening. Once you start a cavalry troop firing, if you can't stop it immediately, you've got a disaster on your hands. You can wipe out a village in a matter of two or three minutes. In this particular case the troop commander was in front, where we required them to be, and he maintained control long enough to determine, in his mind at least, that they were not something we should fire on. We avoided a near disaster with that situation. All of the troops were very good at that. It's risky, because you have a tendency to withhold fire, particularly in populated areas, until the leader is sure that he's facing an enemy and not friendlies. But you have to do that or you're going to have a My Lai or something like that on your hands. We knew about My Lai and were fearful of killing a lot of people who didn't deserve to be killed.

As I said, we made the troop commanders and the platoon leaders ride up front where they were supposed to be, instead of in the rear, where you found a lot of the leaders in other units, and they were in charge of the fire discipline. I think that's the only way to do it.

Simultaneously, Starry noted that the cavalry troopers tended to stay in the field longer, which in turn sharpened their skills against the NVA. According to Starry, there were never any "safe areas" in the regimental sector:

You were always surrounded by somebody. So, it wasn't like the airmobile infantry, when they went back to their base camps, got drunk, and went to the massage parlors. I always felt that that was a mistake, because the soldier spends a week doing that, then you take him back out to the jungle and you have to reacclimatize him all over again. He's gotten all full of booze and women and the safety of that base camp, and then you take him back to war again. Psychologically it's a bad thing. I always felt that we had a better balance. We weren't just thrashing around in the jungle for a few days and then going back … sopping it up in the base camp. We were out day after day … grinding away at the same old problems, and we learned to take care of ourselves much better than the infantry, the airmobile infantry units in particular, did.

The true test of the regiment's mettle, however, came in the borderlands of Cambodia. For the past several years, the NVA and Viet Cong had been operating within the Kingdom of Cambodia, in direct violation of that country's neutrality. The violation, however, was no secret. By this time, nearly everyone in South Vietnam knew that the Communists funneled supplies through Laos and Cambodia. Since the late 1960s, however, enemy activity in Cambodia had been on the rise. Thus, President Nixon had a tough decision to make: How would he reconcile the planned American withdrawal and the practice of Vietnamization against the clear and present danger ruminating in the Cambodian borderlands? His answer came in the form of a televised address to the nation on April 30, 1970. Supplementing his decision to withdraw 150,000 American troops, Nixon announced:

> In cooperation with the armed forces of South Vietnam, attacks are being launched this week to clean out major enemy sanctuaries on the Cambodian–Vietnam border. Tonight, American and South Vietnamese units will attack the headquarters for the entire Communist military operation in South Vietnam. This key control center has been occupied by the North for five years in blatant violation of Cambodia's neutrality. This is not an invasion of Cambodia. The areas in which these attacks will be launched are completely occupied and controlled by North Vietnamese forces. Our purpose is not to occupy the areas. Once enemy forces are driven out of these sanctuaries and once their military supplies are destroyed, we will withdraw.

As the president spoke, a task force of 25,000 US and ARVN troops began their assault into Cambodia. The area of operations was a 40-mile stretch of the border known as the "Fishhook." South Vietnamese forces would call this Operation *Toan Thang 43* (Vietnamese for "Total Victory"); the Americans would call it Operation *Rockcrusher*. "These were the first operational cross-border attacks by conventional ground forces of the war."[8] For the operation, the 11th ACR teamed up with the 1st Cavalry Division and 25th Infantry Division. "The Cambodian Task Force was commanded by General Bob Shoemaker," Starry remembered, "who was an ADC [Assistant Division Commander] in the 1st Cavalry Division."

Alongside Starry's regiment was the 1st Brigade of the 1st Cavalry Division, which was stationed in Tay Ninh, the 2nd Brigade of the 25th Infantry Division, and a brigade of the ARVN Airborne Division.

From the outset, however, Nixon imposed heavy restrictions on the assaulting force. For instance, the operation would occur on a very short timetable: American forces would have only until June 30, 1970 to clear the enemy from the borderlands. The truncated timeframe, however, was largely a function of the weather. "May is a transition month," Starry recalled, "between winter dry and summer wet seasons. Each day, beginning in April, sees a little more rain. The water table begins to rise in mid-April, and by June the ground in War Zone C and along the Fishhook part of the border is virtually impassable to tracks." Furthermore, US troops were put on a 30-kilometer tether. There would be no engagement of enemy forces beyond the prescribed distance.

In the field, however, these objectives were less clear. In fact, several ground commanders, including Starry himself, were unsure of what this mission was intended to accomplish. "We really weren't given any clear-cut objectives," he said. "Bob Shoemaker himself admitted that he really didn't know what we were going in there for." Sadly, the *Stars and Stripes* newspaper became a more reliable and timely source of information than any communiques from DC. Indeed, from the pages of *Stars and Stripes*, "we knew that the purpose of the exercise was to disrupt the logistics operations over there by getting into the cache sites and digging them out. That forced the North Vietnamese regular forces back from the border and gave the South Vietnamese time to get themselves a little better organized to take over as part of the Vietnamization process."

But as Starry admitted, the objectives from on high and the timing of the operation were ill-defined. "So we sat down and laid out some objectives for ourselves. Based on what we knew of the enemy situation and the lack of any instruction from higher headquarters, we made our own objectives." Namely: "Find the bastards, and pile on!"

Meanwhile, Allied intelligence estimated that there were several NVA training and supply bases within the Fishhook region. The focal point of the operation, as it turned out, was the district of Snuol—known for the Terre et Rouge rubber plantation. According to the 11th ACR's interpreters, Snuol was a hotbed of NVA activity, housing a major enemy cache. "The units involved," said Starry, referring to his squadrons, "had been engaged in 'Search and Destroy' or, more correctly, recon-in-force operations daily. Now they were to attack into territory held by a well-organized, strong enemy who had deliberately avoided [us] unless it suited his purposes to fight us. So, it was to be a new experience, and while we were confident of our own strength and ability, we were apprehensive about the unknown content of this battle, about to begin."

Of particular note to the operation was the Central Office for South Vietnam (COSVN). It was described as the "Supreme Communist Field Headquarters", or, according to most news outlets, the "NVA Pentagon." COSVN was reportedly located somewhere within the Cambodian borderlands. If the invading task force could find COSVN, it was to be captured, exploited, and destroyed.

But according to Starry, the preoccupation with finding COSVN was symptomatic of the poor intelligence gathering that plagued America's involvement in Vietnam:

> The press became enamored with the idea that we were going to find COSVN ... a thing that looked like the Pentagon to most correspondents. I tried to explain to a couple of them that, if there was a "COSVN Pentagon," it was four or five guys with a radio in a hole in the jungle. We had all sorts of ridiculous reports about what was over there. The intelligence situation was, at best, confusing. It was alleged that all of the stuff in Cambodia had come down the [Ho Chi Minh] trail network. But we had been reporting for months that that was *not* the case. It was coming in by truck convoy out of the port of Kompong Som (Sihanoukville) ... being delivered by Cambodian Army truck units working for the North Vietnamese. But the initial intelligence information said that it was all coming down from the north. We got into the caches [after capturing Snuol] and I made them [the troopers] pull out the bills of lading which, incidentally, were all there. Sure enough, they'd all been unloaded from third country freighters in Kompong Som. There was a dividing line somewhere farther north of us ... where we found the [materiel] had indeed been coming down the trail network from the north. But it was some distance away and completely out of our area of operations. Everything that we [11th ACR] found in Cambodia, as far as I know, was stuff that had been brought in through the Cambodian port.

The second problem with the intelligence picture was that there was a great deal of misinformation generated by the special operations people who were working across the border. Starry had always been suspicious of them:

They were there when I was in Vietnam the first time. I had limited contact with some of them and had the impression that they really weren't doing what they said they were doing. That is, they weren't going deep enough to find out what was going on. They weren't getting across the border far enough to find anything. They'd go out and sit around in the jungle for a little while, get scared to death, and then come back and write themselves up for a bunch of awards. Most of what they reported was probably not true; at least we found that to be the case.

For instance, on the eve of Operation *Rockcrusher*, Starry met with a senior Special Forces operator at Bu Dop, "and he told me about all of this stuff over there [in Cambodia], the buildings, the concrete gun emplacements, the antitank guns, the antiaircraft guns with sliding concrete overhead covers … none of which we had seen. Now, mind you, we flew that border every day. We even had photography runs to try to find these things. We found absolutely nothing that those people said we were going to find, which of course confirmed my suspicions about them."

On April 28, 1970, the units of the Cambodian Task Force moved into position near the border, ready to attack within 48 hours. "The enemy across the border consisted of the 1st NVA Division and 9th VC Division," Starry said, supplemented by one independent regiment. Three regiments of antiaircraft artillery, largely 12.7mm and 14.5mm heavy machine guns, were deployed along the border. The night before the attack, Starry met with his squadron commanders to review the battle plan and discuss where the commanders would be throughout the engagement.

Because the enemy's air defenses were so tight, he would not allow any squadron commander to stay aloft in their helicopters. All commanders would be on the ground inside their command tracks. The regiment's 2d Squadron, commanded by Lieutenant Colonel Grail Brookshire, would lead the assault. "The two of us [Starry and Brookshire] would go in behind H Company [the squadron's tank company] which would lead the 2d Squadron." Meanwhile, 3d Squadron would follow close behind, soon moving up to the right flank of 2d Squadron. The regiment would then attack in sector, with the two squadrons abreast while 1st Squadron followed as a rearguard and mobile reserve force. "The 11th Cavalry was to go directly through the southernmost border of the Fishhook. The 2nd Brigade of the 25th was to go in on our immediate left. The 1st

Brigade of the 1st Cavalry Division was to go in almost due north of Tay Ninh City, to the west of 2nd Brigade, 25th Division. We all took objectives commensurate with our respective fronts."

For the 11th Armored Cavalry, Snuol was the prize. Indeed, if these training and supply bases were as big as the informants said they were, then capturing Snuol could be decisive victory. Getting to Snoul, however, would be no easy task. The NVA and Viet Cong were guaranteed to mount an aggressive defense. And the terrain would be no ally. Starry recalled that it "consisted of mixed double and single canopy jungle, some lighter and less dense jungle along the border. Farther north was some high grassland, almost a savannah, and the great long laterite ridge of the Terre et Rouge rubber plantation … with its orderly alignment of producing rubber trees." Taking the onset of the wet season into consideration, "we felt we would be all right so long as we did not allow tracking—following along the tracts of the vehicle in front."

At daybreak on May 1, American artillery opened fire on suspected enemy targets and launched preparatory fires on landing zones selected by the ARVN airborne unit. Starry's regiment, meanwhile, began their assault into the jungle borderlands.

H Company, under the command of Captain Miles Sisson, moved into its attack positions amongst the scattered trees of the jungle savannah. Immediately behind H Company's last vehicle was Donn Starry himself, mounted atop his M113 ACAV. Rumbling alongside the regimental commander were Lieutenant Colonel Brookshire and young Major Fred Franks, the 2d Squadron Operations Officer (S-3), both in their respective command vehicles. As planned, 3d Squadron followed closely behind in a textbook column formation while 1st Squadron secured the supporting artillery, including a battalion of 155mm M109s as well as the regimental supply lines that stretched for miles back into South Vietnam. Meanwhile, the supporting helicopters from 1-9 Air Cavalry (part of the 1st Cavalry Division) remained on "ready alert," waiting until Starry's regiment could destroy the antiaircraft guns "and make flying over the area something less than a suicide mission."

For the first few minutes of the operation, the regimental maneuvers seemed to be going well. However, because the border was so poorly defined, the Americans didn't know how close they were to the enemy.

As a result, the regiment began trading fire with the North Vietnamese sooner than they had expected.

> One of the things the manuals tell you is that your line of departure should be in *friendly* hands and be identifiable. The line of departure we drew was in *enemy* hands [an honest error due to the unclear border markings], and we damn near got blown away before we got to it. We attacked with about eight or ten sticks of fighters [F-4 Phantom jets] and about six or eight battalion volleys of artillery on that position before we even got to the line of departure ... the little bastards figured out something was going on ... and opened up on that lead tank company with volleys of RPGs and rockets. Fortunately, nobody was hurt and no equipment was seriously damaged. Most rounds were short because they fired too soon, and during the reload process we attacked. The minute the stuff landed, we attacked, because we knew they had to reload or rearm somehow. We figured that, if we could catch them in the middle of that rearming process, they'd break and run for cover, which they did. They broke and ran, and we shot them up with canister and machine guns as they boomed off through the jungle.
>
> Farther west, 2-47 Infantry (Mechanized) and 2-34 Armor proceeded north, unopposed, to secure landing zones to be used later in the day by units of the 1st Brigade, 1st Cavalry Division. 2d and 3d Squadrons, after their early fight at the border, moved north against light opposition until about 1600, when lead elements from Miles Sisson's tank company entered a 200-meter long, burned out area about six kilometers inside Cambodia. When 2d Squadron moved into the clearing, a lone scout helicopter from the regimental air cavalry troop uncovered a large enemy force in a long trench on the edge of the area.
>
> The jungle erupted with enemy fire.
>
> As the firing intensified, it became evident that the enemy was in a position on three sides of 2d Squadron.

Realizing that his 2d Squadron was about to be surrounded, Starry jumped on the radio and ordered 3d Squadron to punch right and break through the enemy's defenses. As 3d Squadron's M48 tanks and M113s roared into the melee, Cobra gunships hit the enemy's rear, turning the NVA's escape routes into a blazing inferno. At 4:45 that afternoon, the enemy force (estimated to be a battalion plus) broke contact and fled from the field, leaving 52 of their dead in the woodline. "Two 11th ACR troopers were killed in this action," Starry recalled, "the only two soldiers to die in Cambodia on 1 May."

Though saddened by the loss of his two soldiers, Starry was proud of how the regiment had conducted itself on the first day of battle. True, many of them were battle-hardened from the "search-and-destroy" missions in Long Binh, but today was the first fight where armored cavalry operated as it would in a conventional war—leading the charge, crashing through enemy defenses, with enough firepower to sustain itself in a prolonged battle. And throughout the day's operations, Starry remained at the forefront of battle. According to him, the first battle validated his notion that a leader ought to lead from the front:

> The commander of the 1st Brigade of the 1st Cavalry Division elected to try to command the operation from his bunker in Tay Ninh. I tried to suggest to him that he risked losing control of the situation. By the time his brigade got across the border, there would be at least 50 kilometers between where he was and where his troops were. The FM [communication] links were pretty fragile at that distance, and they didn't have a good relay system. I just felt that he was going to lose control. He did, and by the second or third day out, he'd been relieved of command … it's an interesting lesson in command and control. Here's one commander who's going to do it from a secure bunker and he loses complete control of the thing because of the distances involved and he really can't visualize the battle. Other commanders commanded from a helicopter, in spite of the fact that they know that there were regiments of flak in front that must be suppressed before they could fly safely at altitudes where they could see what's going on and control the battle.

Starry humorously recalled that General Bob Shoemaker, the task force commander, chided him for going into battle on the ground and positioning himself behind the lead tank company. "That was considered to be too dangerous a place for the regimental commander," Starry said. However, Starry quickly diffused the situation with a bit quick-witted humor: "The reason I'm going to be out there" he said, "is that, if you want to fire me, you'll have to come find me, and I don't think you're going to want to come out there that far." Shoemaker, knowing his argument had just been bested, decided to let the matter drop. However, Starry continued:

> I don't know whether he wanted to fire me or not, but what happened to other commanders was just *exactly* what we had predicted. That brings up the question of where the boss ought to be in a fight. Although it's of some risk to yourself, I think you have to be close to the front. I don't necessarily say that the regimental commander ought to have his saber drawn and be out in front of the lead cavalry troop, like a George Armstrong Custer, but nonetheless you have to be there. The other reason I wanted to be out there is that it was unknown

territory and an unknown enemy. Even in a helicopter, had it been safe to fly, I did not have enough confidence in my own ability to visualize the situation down there so that I could make intelligent decisions. I think you just have to be there and see it. You have to be right there because the decisions have got to be made instantly. It was a good decision.

By the afternoon of May 2, Starry's regiment had crossed in Cambodia, linking up with the ARVN airborne brigade north of the border. "Now began the search to find the enemy caches," he said. But the NVA, regrouping from their rout the previous afternoon, counterattacked along the 11th ACR's front. Starry described it as more of a nuisance than an actual threat, but it showed that the enemy was prepared to guard the Snuol cache at all costs. In fact, during the ensuing counterattack, 3d Squadron's command post was hit by a barrage of B-20 rockets which, according to the troopers, "sounded like a freight train and exploded like a small ammunition dump."

By nightfall, the front-line troops had laagered to resupply and dug into their night defensive positions. Despite a few contacts during the day, namely the B-20 rockets and other small arms, there had been no heavy fighting. As if to remind the troopers of the change in season, the early evening clouds had brought a brief thunderstorm. Although the deluge was short and did not impede the regiment's mobility, it nevertheless made the troopers miserable. But with the passing of the storm and the re-emergence of the moon, the landscape settled into an eerie luminescent glow of shadows and stillness. The gunners aboard the M48s, ACAVs, and Sheridans meanwhile scanned the perimeter, searching for any signs of life beyond the edge of their battle area. As the dull hum of tanks' winding turrets pierced the stillness, the dismounted troopers set up Claymore mines as they hunkered down for the night.

Suddenly, in E Troop's sector, a flash of light erupted from beyond the tree line, followed by the distinctive hiss of an incoming RPG round—the NVA was trying to mount a nighttime counterattack. "Then there's a sudden whoosh of incoming rockets," Starry recounted, "a *whump whump* of incoming mortar rounds ... and salvo after salvo of RPG rounds land in and among the Sheridans and ACAVs." E Troop opened fire on shadows moving in the darkness some 800 meters away. As it turned out, the NVA had placed their RPG teams out of a nearby tree line, occupying bomb craters and using fallen timber for cover. As the cavalrymen began returning fire against their phantom enemy, the troop commander began calling artillery and mortar fire into the tree line. Waiting for the right moment, the commander blasted the Claymore mines against the maneuvering RPG teams. With the enemy in full panic, and buckling under the weight of the Blackhorse onslaught, the NVA began fleeing into the night.

Meanwhile, the troop first sergeant, seeing a nearby ACAV hit by an RPG, leapt out the back of his command track, grabbed the nearby medics and fire-fighting equipment, and made a beeline towards the disabled vehicle. By this time, the enemy RPG and mortar fire had died down and, minus the occasional burst from an AK-47, it seemed that this nighttime skirmish had ended.

But fate was about to cast a grim shadow on the front-line troop.

As the enemy shadows faded into the night, a Sheridan gunner saw the silhouettes of a straggling RPG team in his sights. As he steadied his hand on the trigger, ready to let loose a cannister round, one of the RPG gunners turned and blindly fired his last round, hoping it would hit something or someone inside the perimeter. Tragically, that random, un-aimed round screamed into the perimeter and found its mark on the first sergeant just as he was moving to help the wounded. He was killed instantly. Starry recalled:

> Just the day before, I had landed where the first sergeant was directing a recovery operation to ask if he needed help. I said, "You're pretty exposed out here." He said, "Colonel, I know they are watching us from that tree line over there. So, I've got to get this track unstuck before they can get set up and bring the RPGs around. The troops are a little spooky, so the old first sergeant is here to keep them working instead of worrying." When they wakened me in the night to tell me he'd been killed, I cried. I was and am a better soldier because of him and dozens like him. Out of heroism grows faith in the worth of heroism. Out of shared danger grows faith in the little bit of heroism that's in each of us, and in our ability to summon it up when it's needed.

On May 3, Starry received orders to attack 40 kilometers north and, within 48 hours, capture the town of Snuol and its critical road junction. Route 7 was the main thoroughfare into Snuol, running north–south along the laterite ridges of the Terre et Rouge plantation. Starry chose the prominent ridgeline as the regiment's axis of advance. "Three streams crossed the axis," he said, "and where Route 7 crossed these streams, there were three bridges—all blown by the enemy in their retreat to the north. At 0730 on 4 May, 2d and 3d Squadrons attacked north towards Snuol. By 1300, the lead tanks had broken out of the jungle and were on the ridge astride Route 7. Once on the road, 2d Squadron raced north ... reaching the first destroyed bridge by mid-afternoon."

So, the question was how to get across the river. The S-3 of the 3d Squadron took the commander of the 1st Engineer Battalion, 1st Cavalry Division, and went up and reconnoitered the riverbank. They were crazy, because they were well behind enemy lines and nobody knew what was out there. They went in using a scout helicopter, came back out, and never had a shot fired at them. The cavalry division decided that it would bring in its bulldozers and put in a bridge. So, by the time we got there and had the site covered by fire, the division was bringing in the bulldozers. You had to assemble the little bulldozers on the ground, which was going to take a great amount of time. While we were squirreling around with that, in frustration I took a sergeant and an AVLB [Armored Vehicle Launching Bridge] and started out down that river line, trying to find a place where we could put the AVLB down. Every once in a while, some guy from the other side would take a pot shot at us, which would zing off the bridge. The sergeant would lay the thing down, discover that it wouldn't work there, and then we'd move on to someplace else. We were about to give up when the sergeant said:

"Sir, you fire a little bit over there to make sure that the bank is clear and I'm going to put this thing down to the riverbank and see if I just can't sink it in the bank. That way we can go down this side, go over the bridge and up the other side. There's enough dirt down there to hold it if we can get it mashed in. If I take the thing down the forward slope of this stream, those guys are going to shoot at me again."

So, I took my M-16 and fired a couple of magazines into the other side of the river. He drove that AVLB down there, laid the bridge out, sort of patted it down a couple of times, and then backed out. I went back and got a cavalry troop and brought it up. We laid down a little suppressive fire on the other side and put the cavalry troop across. Within 15 minutes we had a whole squadron across and headed north, while these guys were still fumbling with their bridge. They finally got it in the next day. Meanwhile we'd put the whole regiment across that one little AVLB ... and proceeded north.

With the regiment now strung out over 60 kilometers, Starry decided to consolidate Blackhorse south of the second stream crossing. "Throughout the night," he recalled, "1st and 3d Squadrons closed up on lead elements of 2d Squadron, now reconnoitering for crossings over the next two stream obstacles." Meanwhile, 1-9 Air Cavalry, during one of its long-range aerial patrols, discovered an extensive enemy complex further up the border. Starry soon discovered that this complex was indeed a weapons cache. "Later named, 'The City,' this area eventually yielded up more than 1,300 individual weapons, 200 crew-served weapons, millions of rounds of ammunition, and tons of other supplies," Starry said. "It was by far one of the most significant caches of the entire war. Weeks were required to evacuate its contents."

The 11th ACR finally reached the outskirts of Snuol on May 5, 1970. Starry momentarily stopped 2d Squadron, still in the lead, just south of Snuol. During this tactical pause, Starry sent a patrol to reconnoiter the town while he brought forward the regimental artillery and organized the necessary air support.

> Refugees reported many NVA troops in the town and that its civilian inhabitants had fled. Scouts from the regimental air cavalry troop observed heavy-caliber antiaircraft fire from more than a dozen locations around the airstrip near the plantation house in Snuol. On the edge of town were probably two [NVA] regiments. I don't know where the third regiment was. They had a division, the 1st NVA Division, and I think they were looking for us to land on the airstrip … there was the typical plantation chateau with the typical grass-covered airstrip. They had several antiaircraft positions around the airfield. A kilometer or so away, the regiments were dug in around the village. As nearly as we could tell, they were looking for us to airmobile into the airstrip and try to work into the town from there. So they were set up to defend the town, but from the direction of the airstrip.

Consequently, Starry decided to surround the city, with 2d Squadron moving to the east, and 3d Squadron closing from the west. It was mid-afternoon when the encirclement of Snuol began, with tanks from Companies H and M leading the assault:

> As tanks and ACAVs rumbled across the Snuol airstrip, they were hit by RPGs and small-arms fire, which ended abruptly in a barrage of cannister rounds from the lead tanks. Meanwhile, 3d Squadron, moving through the rubber trees to encircle the town, triggered an ambush. Colonel Griffin [the 3d Squadron commander] laid down artillery fire behind the enemy position, set up gunships

to cover the right flank, and attacked with I Troop. As 2d Squadron moved in from the southeast in a coordinated attack, an inexperienced gunship pilot from the 1st Cavalry Division Aerial Rocket Artillery (ARA) battalion fired rockets into lead elements. This unfortunate incident caused the gunships to be called off, opening one side of the trap, allowing some enemy to escape. The two-squadron attack, however, broke the enemy's defenses and, in small groups, enemy soldiers began to flee in all directions.

They [NVA] destroyed the village in the process. They did an enormous amount of damage in there themselves. We were blamed for most of it in the press reports. Storefronts were broken in. There were a couple of small fires, but no great conflagration. It wasn't that big a village—a couple of small fires and the petrol station where the fuel pumps had been knocked down. We didn't, as far as I know, do any damage to that village. There was no looting and pillaging or breaking down buildings and knocking out storefronts. That was all done before we got there.

Still, the fight for the airstrip—particularly the antiaircraft guns—had been no easy affair. Both Starry and Major Fred Franks, the young 2d Squadron S-3, were critically wounded during the melee:

We rolled up onto the southern edge of the airfield at Snuol and could see in front of us, right off the edge of the airfield, a gun pit with one of those great big antiaircraft machine guns. Then off 50 or 60 yards away, on the edge of the rubber plantation, were two other gun positions that we could see. We sent a cavalry troop after the guns in the rubber trees and the Vietnamese got up and ran. They were in hot pursuit over there. I was in my command track in the middle of a cavalry troop and the gun in front of me was pointing at the helicopter overhead. The OH-6 had in it Major Fred Franks, the S-3 of the 2d Squadron, who said on the radio, "This guy is pointing his gun at us." So I looked up and sure enough he was. The gun was swinging around and I thought, "My god, we're going to lose that helicopter and those guys."

I rolled off the back of my track with my rifle, which was all I could get my hands on at the time, and grabbed a couple of guys and headed for the gun pit. I rolled over the edge of the parapet as this gunner was swinging the gun around to get the helicopter in his sights. I knocked the gunner away from it; he went back with his arms up and surrendered. I gave him to somebody. The second guy, who was standing there holding the ammunition belt, dropped the belt, jumped over the parapet, went down the trench, and crawled into a bunker.

So I went after him.

I was looking for the interpreter to try to coax him out of the bunker. Still I had a hand grenade in my hand. The interpreter, the Vietnamese scout we had with us, was coming along hollering at this guy, and I looked over to do something and then looked back. By that time the little bugger had thrown this damn grenade out of the bunker that he was in.

Well, you have read about things happening under those circumstances, and they're quite true. Your whole life passes in front of you. You weigh out all sorts of alternatives—I can throw myself on the thing and get a Medal of Honor and be a hero, but that doesn't make much sense because it'll probably sting a little bit when it goes off. I could pick it up and throw it back into the bunker and get him, but goddamn it, the fuse is awfully short. I could kick it away, but that doesn't make much sense. While I was in the process of going through that systems analysis, I looked over and the helicopter had landed and Major Franks was standing there. I remember thinking:

"If I don't do something, poor old Fred's going to get blown away."

Well, that was more important than all the other alternatives, so I dove for him and that's about the last thing I remember.

Sometime in the process of diving after Fred, the grenade went off and the two of us went rolling around on the ground. I lost my helmet and my rifle. I still had a grenade in my hand. Somebody got that away from me and went and dumped it in the bunker, and eventually we got the little guy. I had about 15 or 20 holes of one size or another in me. The worst wound Fred had was in a leg, which eventually became infected to the point where he had to have it amputated. Several other people were also wounded. I guess he and I were the most severely wounded of the lot.

Indeed, Major Franks was the most critically wounded soldier from that awful melee at the airfield. He was medically evacuated from Vietnam and, following his amputation, was fitted for a prosthetic limb. Normally, the loss of a limb meant the end of one's military career. However, Franks fought an uphill battle to stay in the Army and prove that he could still serve despite his prosthesis. Franks ultimately won that battle with the Army bureaucracy and remained on active duty for the next 25 years. He later rose to prominence as the commander of the US VII Corps during the Gulf War.

Humorously, Starry and Franks commemorated their shared wounds on May 5 every year thereafter. Indeed, every Fifth of May, the pair would call each other. They referred to it as the "Fellowship of Cinco de Mayo."

With fiery shrapnel buried in his leg, Starry was promptly evacuated from the battlefield for treatment. "I'll tell a story about the hospital," he said wryly:

If they did this to me, you have to wonder what was going on in the hospital with the soldiers who got wounded. We went to the aid station, and from the aid station they patched us up, stopped the visible bleeding, and sent us to the hospital in Long Binh. I was operated on late that night. In fact, apparently, they spent most of the night picking stuff out of me. They cut a big hole in my stomach to see where the big piece in the middle had gone. Now, I made all the soldiers wear flak jackets, but it was a very hot afternoon and so the friendly regimental commander, in disobedience of his own orders, had taken off his flak jacket.

By sometime early the following morning, they had probed around in me sufficiently to get most of the metal out. Anyway, I'm lying there in the bed, having slept a little, not feeling very well, and open one eye, and there stood this doctor, a major. He says:

"Don't worry about this. We'll have you out of here in a few days. I think you probably need to go to Japan, where they'll do some more surgery on you, and then, if we can get the thing stabilized, you'll be in the States in short order. There's nothing to worry about. You don't have to go back to war," or words to that effect.

So I tried to grab the bastard, but found that I was not able to do that quite as briskly as I wanted. I finally managed to get myself into a half-assed sitting position, and then I called him several things that were later reported by the nurse as being obscene. I said, "You get the hospital commander and the two of you report right here," and they did. I told the hospital commander the story, and I said:

"Let me tell you something. I'm one case, but if this guy's going around telling the soldiers this sort of thing, you've got an unconscionable situation in your hospital. These guys are soldiers. Some of them want to go back to war. I want to go back to war. I'm not leaving this place until you guys send me back to the damn war. You're not going to send me anyplace else. A lot of other soldiers in here feel the same way, and here's this screwhead trying to tell us, 'Oh, don't worry, we're going to get you home and get you out of here.' He's subversive."

He said, "Calm down. I'll give you a shot, sir." So, I finally got calmed down. I don't know whether or not the major went around making his speech any more. He had obviously made it several times before he got to me. How much of a problem did that cause in the hospital, I don't know, but as far as I was concerned, that guy was subversive.

For the next 12 days, Starry agonized over when he would be well enough to rejoin his regiment. The shrapnel wound had been the most excruciating pain of his life, but he refused to let it derail him. During the first few days of his recovery, Starry endured the painful debridement process, for which the anesthesia was only partially effective. "The first thing they do with the wounds," he said, "is stuff them full of gunpowder

… that absorbent stuff. Then they have these ghouls who come around once a day and jerk that stuff out and pour sulfuric acid on the wound and then stuff more stuff back in. When it stops watering, they sew it up."

By the fourth day, Starry's wounds had been sufficiently disinfected to warrant a permanent suture. However, he still had to convince the hospital staff that he was well enough to rejoin his men—no easy task considering the metrics of the Army's healthcare system. Grabbing hold of the doctor who had operated on him—"not that quack Major"—Starry made an appeal: "Okay, I have got to start doing exercises—sit ups, pushups, whatever you think I can do. What I want to know is, did you cut muscle when you cut into the wound?"

"No," the doctor replied. "I separated the muscles. We didn't cut any."

The doctor then invited Starry to do any exercises he felt he could handle. "So I went over to physical therapy, found a nice nurse/physical therapist, and said, 'Okay, sweetie, we are going to get me back into shape, because I'm going to get out of here as quickly as possible.'"

The nurse took one look at Starry and said, "That's going to be a *long* time."

"No, it isn't," Starry fired back, "it's going to be a very short time. We're going to do sit-ups today."

Painful as it was, Starry found that doing sit-ups two to three times a day dramatically speeded the recovery process. In fact, by the end of his 12th day in the hospital, Starry's strength had rebounded such that the hospital staff deemed him "Fit for Duty." Returning to his regiment in Cambodia, however, Starry admitted that he was "still kind of wired together." In fact, the regimental surgeon had to come by the command post every night "and do a little patching … just to make sure that I was still intact." In the end, however, Starry credited his own tenacity for getting him released from the hospital. "I'm sure it would have been a lot longer had it not been for that."

Meanwhile, the 11th Armored Cavalry celebrated its victory against the NVA. "After the capture of Snuol and a limit of advance had been imposed, operations turned to searching out the caches and fending off increasingly heavy and persistent attacks by NVA units either seeking to escape or to return and recapture their base camps."

Starry was surprised by how much property damage the NVA had done to Snuol during their retreat. From the appearance of the battlefield, it seemed that the North Vietnamese had tried to ignite a hasty "scorched earth" policy, setting the ground ablaze to slow the Americans' advance. Luckily, the fires were localized and fairly easy to contain. Most of the Cambodians had fled Snuol prior to the town's occupation but, strangely enough, the manager of Terre et Rouge had remained. "The French plantation manager and his family were in the basement of the chateau. Within an hour or so of the time we cleared the airfield—I didn't see this, because by that time I had been wounded and carted away—but within an hour or so … a little red airplane came in and landed on that airstrip from somewhere. Shortly afterward the Frenchman and his family came out and got into the little red airplane and flew away."

From a tactical and operational standpoint, the capture of Snuol had been well worth the effort. From the tonnage reports, the amount of equipment captured was unbelievable:

> Brand new, Russian-made, some Chinese, some US, but mostly Russian-made equipment. Machine guns, mortars, small arms, AKs, tank gun ammunition—interestingly enough, no tanks, but tank gun ammunition—and this followed General Abrams' analysis of the enemy, which said that, "They project their logistics nose out into an area, and then they conduct an operation after they get the logistics laid down." For a long time they were doing that in South Vietnam. In other words, they'd go across the border with the carrying parties and a little security and they'd lay down the supplies. When they felt they had enough supplies to support their operation, they'd move the units in on top of their supplies and then conduct their operation. That's exactly what they were doing in this case. We found a really extensive hospital complex in the Fishhook area, to include x-ray machines. I mean, it was a regular base area.

Following the capture of Snuol, President Nixon called the invasion of Cambodia, "the most successful military operation of the entire war." General Abrams seemed to concur. The enemy had lost more than 10,000 troops to American firepower. Moreover, the operation had essentially destroyed the NVA's logistical system in Cambodia. In the end, American forces collected 20,000 individual weapons, 2,500 crew-served weapons, 1,800 tons of ammunition (including mortars, rockets, and small arms rounds), 29 tons of communication equipment, 55 tons of medical supplies, and 431 vehicles."

Tactical and strategic victories aside, Starry noted that the capture of Snuol highlighted several important lessons for any battlefield commander. If nothing else, the commander had to be *in* the battle with his unit. Throughout the operation, Starry saw two of his fellow commanders relieved because they had lost control of their formations. One had tried to command and control his unit from a bunker several miles away; the other had not factored the terrain into his battle plans. "Meantime, the Blackhorse pressed on with its commanders up front, outdistancing and outperforming all others in the battle except the little ARVN colonel and his gutsy paratroopers. The price for being up front was high." Indeed it was: Starry, Franks, and Captain Sisson—the commander of H Company—had all been seriously wounded. Of the senior leaders, only Lieutenant Colonel Grail Brookshire, the 2d Squadron commander, had emerged from the fight unscathed.

After consolidating the enemy tonnage, 11th ACR and her sister units began withdrawing from the area, "which ended with Captain Ralph Miles and L Troop crossing the border headed south on the last day of June." For his audacious leadership and courage under fire during the capture of Snuol, Donn Starry was awarded the Bronze Star Medal with the Combat "V" device for Valor.

CHAPTER 5

From the Ashes of Vietnam

Fresh from the throes of war, Starry went from the jungles of Southeast Asia to the sterile confines of the Pentagon. "I remember getting off the airplane at Dulles Airport, and I'm about four days out of command of a cavalry regiment then in the middle of a bloody firefight in Cambodia. Life was a very intense operation. Then, all of a sudden, I was back, and there were no flags. I didn't expect everybody to call out the honor guard to greet me or anything else, but as I walked through that terminal and watched these Americans going about their normal business, I thought, 'There are Americans over there, too, and they come home to this! They deserve a hell of a lot better than this.'" Starry was fortunate, however, not to have been greeted by any protestors.

But from his perch in the nation's capital, Starry saw the situation in Vietnam and the condition of America's Army go from bad to worse. Despite the political victory of Vietnamization and Nixon's promise of a "Peace with Honor," public opinion was still savagely against the war. Returning troops were still being targeted by angry protestors and, to make matters worse, a new protest group of disillusioned veterans had emerged from the unrest: Vietnam Veterans Against the War (VVAW). Staging rallies, organizing marches, and even testifying on Capitol Hill, VVAW's members included John Kerry (future Democrat senator and 2004 presidential candidate) and Ron Kovic (author of *Born on the Fourth of July*).

On college campuses, student protests had begun targeting the schools' ROTC programs. At the height of Vietnam, Starry's eldest son, Mike, was an Army ROTC cadet at the University of Kansas. Young Mike recalled that the vitriol against the ROTC cadets became so intense that the professor of military science ordered his cadets *not* to wear their uniforms on campus.

Amidst the public backlash, however, Hanoi seemed poised to pursue peace. Although the Tet Offensive had created the "crisis of confidence" for which they had hoped, the tactical performance of their military had been less than stellar. The Viet Cong had been rendered ineffective, the US invasion of Cambodia had disrupted the NVA's regional supply nodes, the increased bombing campaigns against North Vietnam (Operations *Linebacker I* and *II*) wrought havoc on the Communists' morale, and the NVA's Easter Offensive of 1972 had been a disastrous failure. Thus, it came as no surprise when the North Vietnamese came to the negotiating table at the Paris Peace Accords in 1973. The resulting truce called for an immediate cease-fire, a full withdrawal of American forces, and a permanent demarcation of North and South Vietnam. The North Vietnamese, however, had no intention of abiding by the accords. When Hanoi was certain that the US would not intervene, the NVA invaded South Vietnam in the spring of 1975.

In response, ARVN troops mounted an unsuccessful defense before retreating through Hue, Danang, and finally Da Lat. With the North Vietnamese closing in on Saigon, the ARVN made its final stand at the Battle of Xuan Loc. As NVA tanks rolled into Saigon on the morning of April 30, 1975, the South Vietnamese government finally surrendered.

Watching these events unfold from the States, Donn Starry was incredulous. In Vietnam, the US had won every battle, yet somehow managed to lose the war. After nearly a decade of misguided war policies—and over 58,000 combat deaths—America had abandoned an ally that she had promised to defend. Watching the last helicopter evacuate from the rooftop of the American embassy in Saigon, it seemed as though the entire war—the bloodshed, the sacrifice, and the untold cost in human suffering—had been an exercise in futility. Starry admitted:

> We didn't know the country. We didn't know the enemy, and we made no organized attempt to find it out and disseminate it. It wasn't studied at the higher levels at all. We had a flawed operational concept at the theater level of warfare that flowed from some mistaken notions in this country and confusion at the

executive level of government about what we were supposed to be doing there. On the other hand, with a few exceptions, we really did not lose any battles. A North Vietnamese officer pointed out, "That's right, but it's irrelevant." I think the Army acquitted itself very well, given the circumstances. The soldiers did well. The officers did well, under the circumstances and given the conditions—our lack of ability to train them as units, to give them the unit cohesion they needed to do well in battle consistently, the one-year rotation policy, the confusion of goals, and the situation at home. As the war wore on, they came out of an environment in which there were all sorts of adverse commentary about the war and what we were doing and not doing and so on. Given all those things, I think the soldiers did admirably well.

Moreover, Starry was critical of how the US government and the press corps had failed the troops:

I would argue that the country, by and large, the management, the administration, the Congress, certainly the press, let its Army down. I think you see that reflected in the current spate of attitudes toward the Vietnam War and the things that you see going on now. The books being written are almost revisionist history. The press is now saying, "Oh, my goodness, we shouldn't have done that." When Peter Braestrup wrote that super book of his, *Big Story*, about Tet, they damn near drummed him out of the press corps. Now they're saying, "Well, yes, Peter was right and we were wrong." But, damn their souls, they did it at the time and they stuck by it. They knew what they were doing. You can't condone that. I don't care if they're having second thoughts about it now ... and as far as I'm concerned, we lost a lot of good soldiers because it was the perception in North Vietnam that the war was going to be won in the United States, not on the battlefields of Vietnam. I don't know how many times we intercepted message traffic out of the North that contained a statement like, "We don't want to do this operation," or "We don't want to do this thing," or "We don't want to have this happen because of potential adverse impact on our base of support in the United States."

All the while, Starry found himself on the front lines trying to rebuild an Army stuck in Purgatory. Emerging from Vietnam, the Army found itself straddled by a growing culture of "apathy, decay, and intolerance." Throughout the early 1970s, nearly half of the soldiers stationed in Germany and Korea admitted to drug use, including heroin, hash, and marijuana. Desertion and violent crime were on the rise and barracks became war zones in their own right as soldier gangs ruled through fear and intimidation. Racial unrest had also found its way into the Army. On one occasion, a race riot between black and white soldiers at Fort Bragg, North Carolina spread into the streets of nearby Fayetteville. In garrison communities across the country, officers, noncommissioned officers, and even their families, were frequently attacked by renegade soldiers.

Meanwhile, the Army routinely lowered its recruiting standards just to maintain its end-strength. But even with these lower entry standards, and the transition to an all-volunteer force, the Army still fell 20,000 men below its quota. By 1975, nearly 40 percent of new recruits had no high school diploma and many more had criminal records. Faced with the prospect of a thankless job, a hostile American public, and increasingly undisciplined soldiers, young officers and noncommissioned officers began leaving the Army by the thousands.

Back at the Pentagon, Starry received his promotion to brigadier general. Attaining flag rank, however, was no charming experience. "The problem with getting promoted to general officer rank," he said, "goes something like this: For reasons that I have never been able to determine, a lot of people believe that they have 'arrived' when they make general. Nothing could be further from the truth. As a matter of fact, brigadier generals get treated with less respect than second lieutenants do in many places. I got much better treatment as a second lieutenant, in many instances, than I did as a brigadier general."

In fact, Starry's new role as the Director of the Manpower and Forces Directorate seemed to be little more than an "errand boy" for the Deputy Chief of Staff for Operations (DCSOPS) and the Assistant Chief of Staff for Force Development (ACSFOR). In this new job, however, Starry had to determine the manpower requirements for a postwar Army—no easy task considering the transition to an all-volunteer force.

"We didn't know whether or not the Army was going to go back to 16 divisions, which it had before the war, or down to *six* divisions." The idea of so few active divisions, however, was alarming. Six divisions would total less than 300,000 soldiers, barely half the manpower needed to meet the Army's global commitments and provide homeland defense. Eventually, the Army settled on 16 postwar divisions which, by the end of the 1980s, had grown to 18 divisions. But, as Starry realized, there was no existing plan for determining force structure in 1971. In fact, during his opening days as the Director of Manpower, Starry asked the

DCSOPS, General John Vessey, "How many divisions do you guys want in this Army of ours?"

"Well," he said, "isn't there a plan for that?"

"No, there's no plan for that."

Thus, he and Starry spent an entire Saturday afternoon in Vessey's office figuring out how many divisions the post-Vietnam Army needed. To make ready for war in any theater, and continue its defense of Western Europe and South Korea, Starry and Vessey determined that the Army should have 16 divisions (at least 850,000 soldiers). "By that time," Starry recalled, "General Abrams was about to take over as Chief of Staff. We finally convinced [him] that he had do something about it. In those days Jim Schlesinger was the Secretary of Defense, and he and General Abrams used to get together on Saturday mornings and have a little cigar-chewing session. General Abrams came back from one of those meetings, called us up to his office, and said, 'You've got your 16 divisions.'"

The new divisional strength, however, came with a caveat. Starry had requested 850,000 troops. "We could not have less," he said. "The last time we had 16 divisions we had about 986,000 people in the Army." Unfortunately, Abrams could only get Schlesinger to agree to 765,000, "and that we would justify additions to that as time wore on." Yet even during the Reagan years, when the US Army was arguably at its zenith, Starry noted that the organization was still "overstructured and understrength." According to Starry, this practice means "that you increase the turbulence of the people going back and forth trying to fill up the structure. The more you increase the structure ... the more you increase the rotation problem. The result is that you get units that approach the rotation limits of the guys in Vietnam. You can't run good operations that way."

During his tenure as the Director of Manpower, Starry made several trips to Europe to evaluate the needs of the Army's defensive posture. "It was six or seven years since I had seen Europe," he said. "When I left it in 1964, we had a good Army over there. It was solid, we had good equipment, we had good soldiers, and we had been together for a long time. We had some problems, as we always do in a place like that, but essentially it was a first-class fighting force that was ready to fight."

Sadly, the war in Vietnam had stripped the Army in Europe of its best soldiers and equipment. "When I went back in 1970 and 1971," he continued, "it was in shambles ... absolute bloody shambles. If you went and talked to the sergeants, the lieutenants, and the captains, they didn't think they could win that battle over there. And there's nothing more frightening and discouraging ... than American soldiers and American officers who don't believe they have a Chinaman's chance in hell of winning the battle that they've been sent to fight."

To make matters worse, the high turnover in personnel and equipment to feed the war in Vietnam had destroyed unit cohesion in Europe:

> They were almost as bad off as the guys in Vietnam were during the latter stages of the redeployment ... when you stood up in front of your squad or your platoon in the morning, you couldn't recognize anybody out there, and they didn't recognize you. Yet you were supposed to go out and fight a successful battle. There was no unit cohesion. They had apparently been deprived of sufficient funds to maintain the barracks, maintain the family housing, and provide themselves with sufficient fuel and ammunition to do training. Those things were always problems, but I have never been convinced that the funding levels were so low that they had to neglect the things that they had obviously neglected.
>
> But they did neglect them, and I lay that on the doorstep of the senior commanders who let it happen without doing anything about it. I remember I went over there one time and went down to see one of the very senior commanders in the theater who happened to have been a good friend of mine. It was early in the morning, and he had a set of 5×7 cards on his desk. He was going through these cards shaking his head. I politely inquired as to what they were, and he said,
>
> "Well, these are all the telephone calls that came in during the night."
>
> You know, at that time, there was a little unrest among the troops. They had had some riots in some of the prison facilities, and everybody was worried about the soldiers' complaints. So, they'd established this Dial CINC [Call the Commander-in-Chief of US Army Europe] hotline, and what he was reading to me from these 5×7 cards was the Dial CINC input from the night before. I looked at some of those cards and, just looking at them, and knowing soldiers as I did, I began to suspect that there was a little "leg pulling" going on.
>
> Several days later I was back in Friedberg, visiting my old haunts, and one of the sergeants major invited me to come down to the NCO club and have dinner with him and sit around and shoot the bull with some of the guys who'd been in the 11th Cavalry in Vietnam. Some of them were guys out of the battalion that I'd commanded earlier, or at least out of the division, the 3d Armored Division. So we went over and had dinner and sat around drinking beer, talking, and I was just listening to what was going on. Late in the evening everybody took out a coin, and they started matching coins. I watched this for a while. Of course, by the process of elimination, it got down to three or four guys. At that point

Donn Starry as commander of the 11th Armored Cavalry Regiment in Vietnam, 1970. *Starry Family Collection*

Donn Starry in one of his earliest known photographs, mounted atop a cavalry horse at the Fort Riley National Guard Camp. Starry's father was a World War I veteran and Kansas National Guardsman. Thus began the younger Starry's exposure to military life. *Starry Family Collection*

Starry as a young teenager, circa 1941. *Starry Family Collection*

Private Donn Starry shortly after his induction into the United States Army in August 1943. Because he had applied to West Point, he was assigned to Company D, 3319th Service Unit (West Point Prep). *Starry Family Collection*

Starry as a West Point cadet during his "Plebe" (freshman) year, September 1944. He graduated with the Class of 1948, the first West Point class to resume the four-year curriculum following World War II. *Starry Family Collection*

A Starry family photo, 1947. Pictured on the left is Starry's father, Don Albert Starry. Despite the similarity in their names, the younger Starry was not a "Junior" because the latter's first name was spelt "Donn" with the double "n." The elder Starry returned to active duty during World War II and served in Washington DC, where he later retired at the rank of Colonel. *Starry Family Collection*

As a cadet, Starry excelled on the West Point swim team. He dedicated so much time to the sport that his classmates nicknamed him "Fish." As a student coach, he led the Plebe swim team to two consecutive undefeated seasons. *Starry Family Collection*

Donn Starry and his fiancée, Leatrice "Letty" Gibbs enjoy a leisurely stroll at West Point following Donn's graduation. The couple had known each other since childhood and were married on June 15, 1948. *Starry Family Collection*

The young Lieutenant and Mrs. Starry at the Officers Club in West Germany, circa 1950. *Starry Family Collection*

Above: Lieutenant Donn A. Starry, 3d Platoon Leader, C Company, 63d Tank Battalion, poses for a group photo with his sergeants. Starry recalled that many of the sergeants in his battalion were grizzled veterans of World War II. *Starry Family Collection*

Left: Sergeant First Class Willard Lucas, Starry's first platoon sergeant. Starry cited Lucas a great mentor and trained who helped mold the young lieutenant into a seasoned tactical leader. *Starry Family Collection*

Right: Lieutenant Starry checks radio communications during a field exercise near Nuremburg, West Germany, 1951. *Starry Family Collection*

Below: With two local Boy Scouts, Starry inspects their gear for a camping trip, circa 1958. Starry took an active role in sponsoring and supporting local youth activities. *Starry Family Collection*

As the commander of 1st Battalion, 32d Armor Regiment, Starry (right) converses with Lieutenant General Creighton Abrams, the V Corps commander, during a terrain walk in West Germany. Starry and Abrams had a long-standing professional relationship. Over the course of twenty-five years, Starry served under Abrams on five different occasions. *Starry Family Collection*

Donn and Letty enjoy a moment of levity aboard his tank during the Battalion Family Day, 1963. In whatever unit he commanded, Donn and Letty sponsored several morale and recreation activities for the soldiers and their families. *Starry Family Collection*

Donn Starry (far left) poses with the crew of his tank, HQ-60 (Headquarters Six-Zero, the battalion commander's tank). During Starry's command tenure, his battalion achieved the highest gunnery scores in US Army Europe. *Starry Family Collection*

Starry takes a brief respite from training maneuvers in the town of Ockstadt, West Germany. Pictured next to him is a reporter from the *Kansas City Star* who had been dispatched to Germany to write a "hometown hero" piece about Starry and his command of 1-32 Armor. *Starry Family Collection*

Starry proudly salutes from the commander's hatch of HQ-60 during a parade in West Germany, 1963. *Starry Family Collection*

A Starry family portrait taken in 1966 while Donn was in Vietnam. Back row (left to right): Mike, Letty, and Paul Starry. Front row (left to right): Melissa, Melanie. *Starry Family Collection*

Lieutenant Colonels Donn Starry and Alexander Haig near Lai Khe, South Vietnam in 1966. Haig and Starry had been classmates at West Point. Haig later became Secretary of State under President Ronald Reagan. *Starry Family Collection*

A heavily-modified M113 Armored Cavalry Assault Vehicle (ACAV). Adapted from the base model M113 Armored Personnel Carrier, the ACAV was the veritable workhorse of armor and cavalry units in Vietnam. *US Army photo*

The M551 Sheridan Armored Reconnaissance Airborne Assault Vehicle. Essentially, a "light tank" with airborne-drop capabilities, the M551 had several functionality problems. Starry had no confidence in the vehicle and he remembered that its design flaws needlessly cost soldiers' lives. *US Army photo*

During his second tour in Vietnam, Starry served as a redeployment planner in the "Vietnamization" process. *Starry Family Collection*

Starry assumes command of the 11th Armored Cavalry Regiment, December 1969. *Starry Family Collection*

Starry with his regimental Command Sergeant Major, Don Horn, near Quan Loi, February 1970. *Starry Family Collection*

The Regimental Command Group at their base camp in An Loc, Vietnam, 1969. *Starry Family Collection*

Colonel Starry lands in a rice patty while on a reconnaissance patrol. Unlike many field commanders, Starry stayed in the field with the troops and squadrons, sharing the burdens and the occasional humorous moments of combat. *Starry Family Collection*

Left: A team of combat engineers clear mines in Cambodia while supported by an M551 Sheridan from the 11th Armored Cavalry Regiment, 1970. Despite the vehicle's safety hazards and design flaws, Starry had little choice but to utilize the vehicle during the regiment's combat operations. *US Army photo*

Below: Starry checks out an ACAV and its crew, Vietnam 1970. Following his experience in Vietnam, he authored *Mounted Combat in Vietnam* as part of the Army's official *Vietnam Studies* series. *Starry Family Collection*

During the first day of the Cambodian incursion, Starry's command vehicle threw its track, prompting him to hitch a ride on the back of another ACAV. Here, Starry is pictured on the rear of the ACAV, cigar-in-mouth, as the vehicle sallies forth into enemy territory. *Starry Family Collection*

M48 Patton tanks of the 11th Armored Cavalry Regiment enter Snuol, Cambodia on May 5, 1970. The operation was a resounding success; the 11th Armored Cavalry captured the largest enemy cache in the region. *US Army photo*

Colonel Donn Starry during a moment of introspection, Vietnam 1970. *Starry Family Collection*

General Creighton Abrams, the commander of American forces in Vietnam, address the Blackhorse regiment following their combat operations in Cambodia. Starry, the regimental commander, stands behind him, flanked by the regimental staff. *Michael Roche*

Donn Starry enjoys a lighthearted moment with a few of his 1948 West Point classmates in Vietnam. *Starry Family Collection*

Left: Donn Starry as commander of Fort Knox and the Armor School, 1973. Starry wears a black beret which, at the time, had been adopted by armor and armored cavalry units as a "morale-enhancing" uniform item. Cavalry troopers continued wearing the black beret until 1979 when the headgear was restricted to Ranger units. In 2001, however, the black beret became the standard headgear for all US Army soldiers. *Starry Family Collection*

Below: Starry formally opens the Army Community Service Center at Fort Knox, Kentucky, 1973. During his tenure in Fort Knox, Starry and his wife, Letty, worked tirelessly to improve the morale of the soldiers and their families. *Starry Family Collection*

Starry inspects an honor guard from the British Army's 4th Royal Tank Regiment during his visit to the UK in 1974. *Starry Family Collection*

Starry sits with Major General Moshe "Musa" Peled, the commanding general of the Israeli Defense Force Armour Corps. During Starry's command of Fort Knox, he made several trips to the Israeli battlefields from the Yom Kippur War, studying the comparative tactics of the Arab and Israeli forces. These postwar observations were the genesis of Starry's AirLand Battle doctrine. *Starry Family Collection*

Left: Starry stands in front of a prototype Apache attack helicopter, moments before its inaugural test flight at Fort Knox. As the commander of America's premier combined arms center, Starry often had a "front-row seat" to the field trials of the Army's newest weapon systems. *Starry Family Collection*

Below: V Corps Headquarters in West Germany. Shortly after Starry assumed command of V Corps, the *Baader Meinhof* (a left-wing German terrorist group) detonated a bomb in the Headquarters parking lot. Luckily, Starry was away from the building during the attack. The *Baader Meinhof* continued harassing the unified German government well into the 1990s. *Starry Family Collection*

As commander of the US V Corps, Lieutenant General Donn Starry stands on the West German border with Lieutenant General Richard Worsley, Commanding General of the British Army on the Rhine (BAOR). BAOR was the forward-stationed element of UK forces in West Germany. Starry prized his relationship with his NATO allies (British and West Germans). He had a close personal friendship with Worsley and other senior British and German officers. *Starry Family Collection*

Starry during one of his many "terrain walks" in the V Corps. These terrain walks were the hallmark of Starry's corps command. He frequently took his subordinate commanders to their assigned defensive sectors and analyzed how they could best support the wider defense of Western Europe against a possible Soviet invasion. *Starry Family Collection*

Above: Starry reviews the V Corps troops upon his arrival as the new corps commander, 1976. For Donn Starry, there had been no formal "Change of Command" ceremony. Starry simply assumed command by signing the Assumption of Command orders in the TWA lounge at the Frankfurt airport because his predecessor had been hastily relieved of command. *Starry Family Collection*

Left: Starry greets V Corps engineers during a River Crossing exercise along the Fulda River. *Starry Family Collection*

Army Vice Chief of Staff, General Walter Kerwin sits alongside Starry, preparing for a visit to the V Corps' defensive area command posts east of Frankfurt. *Starry Family Collection*

Starry stands in front of a captured vehicle belonging to a Soviet Military Liaison Mission 6 (SMLM 6) operative that had been illegally observing a V Corps command post exercise. The SMLM 6 operative was released to Soviet authorities early the next morning. *Starry Family Collection*

Above: Starry receives his promotion to four-star general in 1977 from Army Chief of Staff General Bernard Rogers. *Starry Family Collection*

Left: Starry as the commander of Training and Doctrine Command (TRADOC). *Starry Family Collection*

During his command of TRADOC, Starry spent very little time at its Fort Monroe Headquarters. He was frequently making visits to various Army posts to speak with soldiers and officers and glean information on how to improve training. Here, Starry inspects an M-16 Assault Rifle with a soldier at Fort McClellan. *Starry Family Collection*

Starry visits the 7th Army Training Center in Grafenwoehr, Germany in 1979 alongside Brigadier General Crosbie Saint. As the commander of TRADOC, Starry frequently made trips to the kasernes and training centers in West Germany. Crosbie Saint later became a four-star general and commander of US Army Europe. *Starry Family Collection*

General Starry, TRADOC commander, during one of his frequent visits with Israeli Defense Force (IDF) leaders. His first visit with the IDF was at General Creighton Abrams direction in 1973. He conferred with the IDF on tactics, operations, and on many technical development matters that were dramatically changing the modern battlefield. *Starry Family Collection*

Starry's "branding iron," a gift from his soldiers during the latter years of his career. Starry would often sign his documents with a styled "Y" enclosed by a hand-drawn star—thus, a pictorial representation of the name "Starry." *Starry Family Collection*

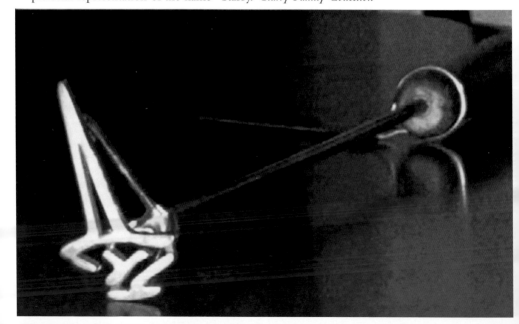

Starry gives an exaggerated grin for the camera during the first-ever video conference at TRADOC. Starry always sought ways to improve training and operations in whatever unit he commanded. *Starry Family Collection*

Starry stands with the newly-inducted members of the Sergeant Morales Club (SMC). SMC was established in 1973 to promote "the highest ideals of integrity, professionalism and leadership for the enlisted force serving in Europe." Throughout his career, Starry strove to maintain good working relationships with non-commissioned officers (NCOs). During his years commanding Fort Knox, V Corps, and TRADOC, Starry worked tirelessly to rebuild the NCO corps that had been savagely devastated by Vietnam. *Starry Family Collection*

Above: Starry (far right) relinquishes command of TRADOC, 1981. Secretary of the Army John O. Marsh stands on the far left, flanked by General Glenn K. Otis, the incoming TRADOC commander. *Starry Family Collection*

Left: Starry as the Commander-in-Chief of US Readiness Command (REDCOM), 1981. *Starry Family Collection*

Three generations of Starry soldiers. The elderly Don Albert Starry (left) and General Donn Starry (right) stand with young Mike Starry (center) following his promotion to major, 1982. Mike Starry would later serve in the 1st Cavalry Division during the Persian Gulf War. He retired as a full colonel in 1998. *Starry Family Collection*

As REDCOM Commander, Donn Starry (center) stands alongside Lieutenant General Robert Kingston (left) and Secretary of Defense Caspar Weinberger (right). Kingston was the commander of the Rapid Deployment Joint Task Force (RDJTF) and eventually commanded CENTCOM when the latter was created following REDCOM's dissolution in 1987. *Starry Family Collection*

Above: Donn and Letty Starry, 1983. The couple were married for nearly 60 years until her untimely death in 2008. *Starry Family Collection*

Left: Starry receives the Distinguished Graduate Award from the United States Military Academy, May 2009. *Starry Family Collection*

they stopped the game. Then these guys, one at a time, would get up, leave and come back, apparently having made phone calls.

So I said to one of them, "What are you guys doing?"

And they said, "Well, we've decided that we ought to put a little input into the Dial CINC program. We sit around here almost every night and decide who's going to call that night. The mission of the caller is to make up the most preposterous story he can. Whether or not it's true doesn't make any difference. We just make up a leg puller. Then we dial it in, because we think the whole thing is so damned ludicrous that that's all it deserves."

Starry was baffled:

Now here sits the senior US Army commander in Europe going through those 5×7 cards, worrying, shaking his head, and becoming all despondent because of what's on the cards. I suspect, if it was going on in Friedberg, it was going on in a lot of other places. It was all a big laugh to them. The program was considered unnecessary and nonrelevant. Now, when you get a situation like that, something really needs to be done.

Short of going over there and taking command of part of it, which I was later to do, the question is, "How do you solve that problem?" You talk to the lieutenants and the sergeants about the tactics and why they think they can't win, and they say, "Well, we're outnumbered." So, the big problem was out. Hell, we were outnumbered when I was a lieutenant over there in the 1949–50 timeframe—much more so, in fact, in terms of sheer numbers than we were in the early 1970s. They had no confidence in their tactics, they had no confidence in their operational schemes, they had no confidence in their logistics system, and they had no confidence in themselves. It was pathetic, particularly when I looked back on my own experiences in Europe in the 1960s. The difference was so dramatic that it was really alarming.

Fortunately, Donn Starry would be at the forefront of reversing these trends during his next two assignments.

The first attempt to revive the shattered Army began in 1973. Both at home and overseas, the Army adopted a "zero tolerance" policy for drugs, and began enforcing new standards of discipline. In Europe alone, the Army discharged more than 1,300 soldiers who were known to be drug addicts, gang members, and other small-time criminals. By removing these criminals from their ranks, the Army could once again focus on training and rebuilding soldier discipline.

During the latter years of Vietnam, unit training and readiness sank to an all-time low. The single-minded focus on counterinsurgency had eroded many of the Army's core competencies and ignored the more immediate threat from the Communist Bloc in Eastern Europe. Furthermore, "training" had been reduced to classroom instruction—where soldiers and officers learned the theory of warfare instead of practicing their craft in the field. According to Brigadier General Robert Scales, "the most realistic peacetime battlefield for infantrymen and tankers was still the firing range."

Determined to reverse these trends, senior Army leaders established the Training and Doctrine Command (TRADOC) in 1973. TRADOC emphasized a return to realistic field-based training which focused on small-unit tactics and basic combat skills. The inaugural commander of TRADOC was General William E. DePuy. An infantry officer, DePuy had received his commission as a second lieutenant in 1941. Assigned to the 90th Infantry Division, he fought on Utah Beach during the D-Day landings and served in the Battle of the Bulge. During the Normandy campaign, he received a field promotion to major and was awarded command of an infantry battalion—all at the age of 24. During Vietnam, he commanded the 1st Infantry Division, where he quickly distinguished himself as one of the toughest field commanders in the Army. By the early 1970s, he had become somewhat a celebrity within the military.

Before assuming his post at TRADOC, DePuy has been the Assistant Vice Chief of Staff when Starry was Director of Manpower. "Because we were trying to restructure the Army, rebuild it … he was in that business up to his elbows," said Starry. "It was General DePuy's bag, but he didn't have a staff to cope with it. So, my directorate and I really worked for [DePuy] directly almost the whole time I was in charge. Over that year or so we developed a rapport." Thus, it came as no surprise when DePuy and Abrams tapped Starry to command the Armor Center at Fort Knox, Kentucky.

When Starry achieved the rank of Major General (two-star) in 1973, he set his sights on division command. An Army division was typically commanded by a two-star general and was considered a prime posting for a general officer on his way to the highest echelons of command. Thus, when General Abrams (now the Army Chief of Staff) called Starry into his office to discuss follow-on assignments, Starry told him: "You know, I really want to command the 3d Armored Division ... because I spent five years in that division, and I know that ground." Abrams chewed on his customary cigar for a few moments and said, bluntly, "I know that, but you're going to Fort Knox. Don't screw up the tank program. Just start with the doctrine, describe the equipment requirements, re-shape organization, and get the Army off its ass!"

"Yes sir," Starry replied.

Although commanding a training center did not have the glamour or panache of division command, the job typically carried more responsibility. "The school operation in the big centers like Knox, Benning, Sill, and Bliss is a much bigger, more comprehensive, and more demanding operation than commanding a division," said Starry, "even if the division assignment includes commanding the installation. You've got a school, a set of schools, for officers and for NCOs. You've got a training center for initial entry training. You've got the whole combat developments spectrum of events going on out there, to include a board, plus you've got the community. So, you've got a thing that's larger than a division as far as troops go. It's engaged in a variety of activities that are much more diverse and demanding on your time, really, than is commanding a division. You've got to worry about the community, the post, and the installation, all at the same time."

For Letty Starry, however, returning to Fort Knox was a culture shock like no other. Now as a post commander's wife, she had more "help staff" than she had ever expected. "We had a cook and a gardener," said Melissa Starry, "and we actually had somebody else who was in charge of making sure the uniforms were clean and pressed." But the most memorable aide was Sergeant First Class Maurice Norman—Starry's enlisted secretary, or "aide-de-camp," as the position was called. Norman was a mess cook and often prepared the family's meals. Whenever Donn or Letty were unavailable to take the children to a scheduled activity, Norman would gladly provide transportation. In fact, he developed such a close rapport with Starry's children that they began calling him "Nanna Norm." And when Starry took command of V Corps in 1976, he demanded that Sergeant Norman be transferred along with him. "And even after Norman retired," said Melanie Starry, "he went to work privately for Mom and

Dad." Indeed, the beloved Nanna Norm remains a close friend of the family to this day.

"I was at Knox when we were trying to reorganize the Army and trying to look at the equipment," Starry recalled. "We hadn't done any equipment development to speak of for 10 years or more." Indeed, by the mid-1970s, many of the Army's combat vehicles had fallen a generation behind their Soviet counterparts. While Americans continued training on their 1950s-era equipment, the Soviets fielded the T-72 Main Battle Tank and the dreaded BMP—the first true "infantry fighting vehicle." To keep pace with the Warsaw Pact (and make up for time lost during Vietnam), Army Chief of Staff General Creighton Abrams put forth a new weapon systems plan known as "The Big Five." Specifically, Abrams sought to develop five new platforms that the Army needed to regain its tactical edge. These included a new main battle tank, an infantry fighting vehicle, two helicopters—an attack aircraft and a troop transport—and a missile defense platform. Respectively, these weapons became the M1 Abrams, the M2 Bradley, the Apache and Black Hawk helicopters, and the vaunted Patriot missile. "And, in addition to that," Starry said, "we had a very active TRADOC commander who was trying to develop tactics and techniques … and get the Army straightened out. It was a busy time, a very busy time."

General DePuy's tenure as the TRADOC commander focused on the central theme of doctrine: "What is the Army going to do now?" Out of necessity, there had to be a revitalization of the Army's tactical doctrine. With Vietnam out of the way (and "counterinsurgency" now regarded as passé) doctrinal focus returned to the defense of Western Europe.

Meanwhile, Donn Starry was driven by a desire to rectify the ills he had seen within the Army in Germany:

> How could we at the Armor Center help get ahold of those tank battalions, cavalry squadrons, and mech battalions over there, even though they didn't belong to me doctrinally, and get the people off of their butts, mentally and psychologically, with some new scheme that would at least help restore their faith in themselves and their ability to do what they were there to do? I've long believed that with soldiers, with anybody for that matter, if you get them involved in something that's a little bit different, or new, you get an immediate positive response to that, psychologically,

which makes things happen. I was not sure how much Fort Knox could do about that, but I was convinced that it was a problem throughout the Army as a whole.

And, after I got to Knox, I went back and forth to Europe. We'd go around to the battalions and the squadrons, trying to talk to people about what was going on and what was coming up. Of course, it takes a long time for that stuff to gestate in the training system, in the school system, and in the development system. And so, as time wore on, it was more and more apparent that that lag, timewise, was preventing us, really, from producing the results that we thought we needed to produce in Europe.

At the same time, Starry took a serious look at the armored warfighting doctrine. Vietnam had relegated armor battalions and cavalry squadrons to route security and direct-fire support. Thus, an entire generation of tank and cavalry crewmen had lost their conventional skills. "We spent the summer of 1973 squirreling around with that," said Starry of his first few months in command. "I organized a cavalry task force because I felt that, functionally, cavalry was something that, in the armored world, we probably needed to look at first. We'd fallen into some bad habits in the cavalry over the years, particularly in Europe." Indeed, by doctrine, the cavalry's mission was to provide armored reconnaissance, surveillance, and mobile security to heavy forces in the field. However, those skills had been eroded by high turnover rates, lack of funding, and a culture of apathy. Moreover, in Europe, cavalry commanders had become content simply to satisfy the metrics of border duty. Because these missions were more constabulary than maneuver-based, the art of traditional cavalry was slowly being lost. "Because of that," he said, "I thought we needed to have a reevaluation of cavalry tactics and perhaps even organization and equipment, although I wasn't certain about that in the beginning. So, we started with the cavalry task force and, at the same time, we tried to depict what we thought war on the modern battlefield was going to look like."

Ironically, the Yom Kippur War, which erupted in the Fall of 1973, became a watershed moment for men like Starry. Although no American forces participated in the conflict, Donn was one of several observers who sought to glean lessons from the war in Galilee. For the third time in a century, the Israelis fought the Arabs (notably Syria and Egypt) on a two-front war. Just as they had done in 1948 and 1967, the Israelis won a decisive victory, but this 1973 iteration had come at a terrible cost. New weaponry and new tactics had made this the most destructive conflict in Arab–Israeli history. Indeed, Arab and Israeli armored units suffered 50 percent casualties during the first *two weeks* of combat. The worst offender had been the new antitank guided missiles (ATGMs), many of which were found aboard the first-generation BMP Infantry Fighting Vehicles. With the rise of the ATGM, many wondered aloud if tank warfare had become obsolete.

In many ways, it seemed that the 1973 Arab–Israeli War had ushered in a new era of lethality—high-intensity battles dominated by enormous firepower with higher rates of attrition. According to Starry, however, the 1973 Yom Kippur War was a fortuitous event because it validated what he and DePuy had envisioned for the battlefield of the future. Any conflict between NATO and the Warsaw Pact would surely mirror the fierce fighting that had occurred in the Middle East. Respectively, the Arabs and the Israelis had fought each other using Soviet and NATO equipment. Their tactics were likewise similar. A potential war against the Soviet Army Groups in Central Europe, Starry reasoned, would be just as bloody, with massive losses in manpower and materiel even below the nuclear threshold.

"I spent a considerable amount of time in Israel in 1974, 1975, and 1976, working with the IDF Armored Corps and with General Tal," Starry recalled, "who is the developer and father of the Merkava tank. Working those equations back and forth, we had help from both General Tal and General Musa Peled, then commanding the IDF Armored Corps, and General Bren Adan, who commanded in the Sinai during the Yom Kippur War. However, by this time, Bren was the attaché in Washington. He came to Fort Knox several times."

Taken together, these observations from the Yom Kippur War and the need for a revitalized doctrine, led to a revision of Field Manual 100-5 *Operations* (FM 100-5), which appeared in July 1976. Written mostly by DePuy and Starry, "it confronted the key problem for the US Army at the time: how to fight and win on an armor-dominated battlefield against an enemy who enjoyed vast quantitative superiority in both men and equipment." The manual was predicated on the concept of "Active

Defense" and emphasized the need to win the first battle of the next major conflict. According to the manual's introduction:

> Because the lethality of modern weapons continues to increase sharply, we can expect very high losses to occur in short periods of time. Entire forces could be destroyed quickly if they are improperly employed. Therefore, the first battle of our next war could well be its last battle … This circumstance is unprecedented: we are an army historically unprepared for its first battle. We are accustomed to victory wrought with the weight of materiel and population brought to bear after the onset of hostilities. Today, the US Army must above all else, *prepare to win the first battle of the next war.*

This revised version of FM 100–5 stated that the 1973 Yom Kippur War had been a defining moment in maneuver warfare, and that it foreshadowed the battlefield dynamics of a potential war against the Soviets. But because NATO was outnumbered, DePuy's version of FM 100–5 focused almost entirely on *defensive operations* and contained virtually nothing on maneuver. According to historian Robert Citino, "If they were to survive, US and NATO forces would have to exploit all the traditional advantages of the defense: skillfull use of cover and concealment; choosing the ground on which to fight; sighting weapons for maximum effectiveness; mines and obstacles; and the advantage of first fire. Maneuver was nowhere near as important to DePuy's scheme as was firepower."

Naturally, this meant that the commander had to rely on terrain and firepower instead of personnel. Using a highly mobile defensive scheme, FM 100–5 called for NATO forces to concentrate their firepower at key points along the Iron Curtain. "Given the high lethality of the new weaponry, particularly tank guns and antitank guided missiles, firing first had taken on an even greater importance … in fact, it was now absolutely essential. The defenders had to be ready to engage the assault force at ranges of up to 3,000 meters, forcing the enemy to reveal his intentions and beginning his destruction."[9]

Overall, the defensive nature of FM 100–5 stemmed from the Israeli experience in the 1973 war. "We learned an enormous amount from all of them," Starry admitted, "and we really owe them a great debt. With their experience and background, most recently in the Yom Kippur

War, they identified things about which we were unsure", such as how to fight a close-quarters battle.

> In the 1976 edition of FM 100-5, we did a reasonable job of describing doctrine for the close-in battle—what had to be done to be able to fight that tactical-level battle successfully. What we were not able to cope with, and I knew it at the time, was what to do about the follow-on echelons. I wrote most of the defense and offense parts of that 1976 manual, *and I knew that something was missing—what to do about the follow-on echelons.* You can stand on the Golan Heights—in the command post that northern command occupied during the Yom Kippur War, and you can see Damascus—only 40 or 50 kilometers away. There the Syrian Army deployed, row after row after row, 2,000 meters wide, rank after rank of tanks, fighting vehicles and artillery, marching from Damascus toward the battle line along the Golan Heights.
>
> The three brigades deployed along the Golan front had, in fact, stalled the Syrian offensive. *But what would those already badly-wounded brigades have done if those follow-on echelons had kept on coming?* About this time Musa Peled's (reserve) division began to arrive. Musa proposed to counterattack directly on a line toward Damascus, along the exposed left flank of the Syrian force. Debate ensued. The prime minister was called. She dispatched Bar-Lev to referee the debate. Bar-Lev sided with Musa's desire to seize the initiative with a counterattack. With no more than two-thirds of his division on site, Musa moved toward Damascus, whereupon the Syrian Army broke and ran. The front echelons on the Golan got up, got out of their T-62 tanks, leaving the engines running, and ran away *on foot.* It was that close. So, we were left with the questions: "What systems do we need to fight the follow-on echelon, and what tactics do we need to fight the follow-on echelon?" All of this occurred at the very time we were trying to determine how to fight the first-echelon battle—the battle at the FLOT [Forward Line of Own Troops]. By the time we wrote that [manual] in 1975, *I knew what the problem was, but I wasn't quite sure how to solve it.*

As it turned out, Starry, DePuy, and the other TRADOC leaders had limited time to compile their thoughts and data for FM 100-5:

> He was in a hurry, General DePuy was, because he realized that he didn't have a lot of time. He realized he had taken considerable time to produce that first draft, and if he went back and did it again, he was looking at another year or two of drafting. That being the case, the thing would never get done on his watch. As a result, the Army would continue to drag along in whatever shape it was in tactically. We couldn't wait that long. Anyway, we wrote it the way it was, for better or worse, because our judgment was that it was better to try to describe the tactical battle, get that settled first, then try to solve this operational-level problem.

Still, the new edition of FM 100-5 generated much controversy upon its release. Many field commanders derided it as a manual of "attrition warfare"—one that emphasized body counts over maneuver. The new field manual, they said, returned the Army to a World War I-style of warfare, defending along narrow fronts while hoping to bleed the enemy of his manpower. Much like Starry, others realized that the new doctrine had no plans for engaging the enemy's second, third, or fourth echelons. Even if NATO forces had won that first battle, there was no protocol for how to fight the *second* battle. According to one officer, after theoretically destroying that first echelon, Active Defense became "something of a Chinese fire drill." Another officer described Active Defense as "how slowly do you want me to lose?" These shortcomings, however, motivated Starry to find a solution.

On September 4, 1974, Starry was shocked to learn of Creighton Abrams's untimely death. A heavy cigar smoker, Abrams had developed lung cancer and died following complications from surgery to remove his cancerous lung. At the age of 59, he was the only Chief of Staff to have died in office. General Frederick Weyand, the Vice Chief of Staff, was named as his replacement.

Meanwhile, Donn and Letty Starry busied themselves improving soldiers' lives (and their families' lives) at Fort Knox. Straddled by massive budget cuts and a lukewarm Congress, a soldier's quality of life steadily declined throughout the 1970s. Because military pay and allowances had failed to keep pace with inflation, many soldiers found themselves living off food stamps. Also, for the first time in history, many junior enlisted men were having families of their own. This meant that, under the current pay scale, a corporal with a small family would be living below the poverty line.

Although the Starrys couldn't do anything about a soldier's pay, they could take great strides to ensure that he was well taken care of while in uniform. To that end, Donn and Letty devised a series of morale, welfare, and recreation programs that would eventually morph into the modern Army Community Services program. Aside from revitalizing the Fort Knox Welcome Center and establishing a "sponsor program" for newly arriving soldiers and officers, Starry took great strides to improve the quality of on-post housing.

Admittedly, he was bothered by the current condition of the Fort Knox community. "That's an important part of a soldier's life," he said, referring to the on-base community programs—"you need to pay some attention to how the soldier lives and how his family lives." Thus, on Letty's recommendation, Donn initiated the Community Life program at Fort Knox. "We started sprucing up the communities in terms of management as well as facilities," he said. "Fort Knox has about 4,000-and-some-odd sets of quarters. At the time we were there, they had more family quarters than any other post in the United States, and yet they spent less money on their family quarters than most posts in the United States. They showed it. There was a lot of dissatisfaction, unhappy wives and unhappy families, because of the way they were having to live."

To make matters worse, the facilities engineers were apathetic to the needs of the residents. And the lack of funding for on-post maintenance had further fueled their apathy. Starry then made his appeal to General DePuy:

"I've got to have some money." Something in the order of $10 million.

Sympathetic, DePuy agreed to release the funds on condition that Starry produce qualitative results within a year.

Starry accepted the challenge. Instead of relying on the reluctant engineers, however, he went directly to the families:

> As we talked about this one night, my wife recommended that we start a program whereby we involve the families in the improvement of their communities ... she said, "Those housing areas are geographically isolated at Fort Knox. What if we elected mayors in each one of those communities and had the mayors appoint town councils and let them establish the priorities as to what they want done to fix their place up? Can you do that?" And I said, "I don't see why not." So we did it. We had community elections and elected the mayors. In the first round they were all women, as a matter of fact. We allowed them to appoint their town councils, arranged however they wanted.
>
> I got the mayors together and I laid out the budget for them. I said, "First, you are going to establish the priorities in your housing area and determine what needs to be fixed. We're going to match that with the engineers' perception of what needs to be fixed, and then we'll [reconcile] the two somehow. Second, I'm going to make available to you some discretionary money.

In other words, Starry had set aside money for the "mayors" to use for any community project that fell beyond the purview of housing maintenance. One such project was an RV park on the Fort Knox reservation:

> The recreational vehicles were parked all over the streets. The kids were darting in and out, which was dangerous, and it looked cluttered. They couldn't get back and forth with their cars. So, the first thing that the community wanted was a recreational vehicle park. Well, that's pretty simple—put up some chain-link fence, put down a pad, put the RVs out there, and provide for some controlled access. So we did that. Well, the engineers resented it … but I made the mayors a part of my personal council on that. In the three budgets of Fort Knox, maybe four, over which I had any control, we spent about $40 million on family housing. That was more money than had been spent altogether in the preceding 20 years on family housing. It shows you how bad the neglect level was.
>
> One area, I remember, needed roofs—all the houses needed to be re-roofed. It was a big contract. As I recall, we engineered it at something like the $4.5 million level. Some guy bid $2.8 million and they gave it to him. When I looked at the difference between what we had engineered it at, and what he had bid—and won the award as the lowest bidder—I realized what he was going to try to do was make up, at my expense, the difference between $2.8 and $4.5 million. So we got the wives and the mayor of that particular area together, and I said, "Okay, prepare a briefing," which she and her staff gave. They got all the housewives together and said, "All right, here's what is going to be done. These guys are going to come and put in the roofs, and here's the schedule." I allowed them to make out a schedule to suit the traffic patterns, the schools, and everything else. They worked up the schedule of how the roofing was going to be replaced. We went down through the contract with them and showed them what the roofer was supposed to do … and what he was forbidden from doing. He's not going to slop tar all over the front of your house; he can't mash the bushes; he's got to leave in place all the things that were in the contract. If those things don't happen, you call the mayor, and the mayor will call me, the chief of staff, or a central office that we have established.

Starry admitted that his reason for involving the mayor and her council was that, after reviewing the size of the labor contract, he knew the contractor would try to rip off the command for a few million dollars. "I told the chief of staff that I wanted to hire some more quality-control guys. He told me that we didn't have the money to hire quality-control guys. The contractor was going to evaluate his own performance! I said, 'Okay, we are going to make these wives quality-control and quality-assurance people.'"

A few days later, the contractor came around to see Starry and said, "You've got to get these women off my back." When Starry asked the wayward contractor what the issues were, he began citing a litany of complaints that the wives had fielded. Starry quickly silenced him: "You make me a list of the complaints, then you and I will go over them one by one with the contract laid out beside us." If the complaints were bogus or exaggerated, Starry explained, he would be happy to assuage the complaining wives. "But if the wives' complaints are legitimate," he added, "then you and I are going to have to have a talk about why you're not performing according to contract."

Fortunately for Starry, there was not a single complaint on that list that was not validated by the contract. The contractor came back several days later with a confession: "General, let me tell you what's going on. I bought this contract, as you obviously have figured out, to try to keep my workforce alive. I'm waiting for this big project up in Louisville to develop. I've been doing work down here for 25 years and I suppose, by your terms, I've been ripping you off for 25 years. You're the first guy who caught me at it. I'll tell you what I'm going to do; I'm going to perform on that contract. It's going to cost me about $1.5 million to do it, but I'm going to do exactly like the contract says because I really admire what you're doing. Somebody should have done it a long time ago. I guess, all things considered, philosophically, I've made enough off of Fort Knox so that I can afford to do it." True to his word, the contractor performed the services at the $1.5 million mark.

Reflecting on the need to manage his contractors and engineers, Starry opined that "if you don't terrorize them, they'll slack off."

I used to ride around in a jeep and my aide [Sergeant Norman] would carry a bucket. We'd go around the post visiting the paving contractors, and I'd just scoop up a bucket of what they were using and send it to be analyzed. Nine times out of ten, they had a bunch of crap in the paving material that wasn't supposed to be there, which degraded the quality. Just driving down the street one day I stopped and picked up a bucket of paint from a painter. It was about half gone, and I said, "You've got a new bucket?" He said, "I've got one in my truck." And I said, "Well, give me the old bucket." We sent it away to be analyzed, and it had twice as much water in it as it was supposed to have. The guy was giving us watered down paint, half and half, and he was pocketing the other half. So, I threatened to take him to court. In any case, the painter came around and said, "What do you want me to do?" I said, "I want to you to paint all that stuff over again with paint that's certified, and you and I are going to inspect it." ... and we did.

In total, the Community Life program was a great success at Knox because it gave the residents a degree of ownership in the quality of on-post living. "They put up an RV park and got the RVs off the street," Starry reiterated. "People would look around and say, 'Hey, we did that!' It wasn't that I had done it; it was *we* did it. 'We said we wanted that and it got done.' You only have to do that once or twice and everybody becomes a believer."

But the success of the Community Life program, with its "mayors" and town councils, underscored the importance of having a supportive military spouse. Indeed, Community Life had been Letty Starry's idea. Her innovative and compassionate plan to revitalize the community spirit showed that the best military wives viewed themselves as partners in their husband's command. Ideally, while the commander oversaw the professional development of the troops, his wife would be the driving force behind keeping the families and community together. It was a delicate balance, though, and not all military wives could do it well—some tended to dominate the other wives and metaphorically "wore their husband's rank."

In fact, when selecting his subordinate commanders, Starry would often base his decision on the wife's personality:

> I believe that when you put a person in a responsible job, especially in command ... you're really putting a husband and wife team in command. I always selected my commanders based on the guy and his wife. And, as a matter of fact, I turned down several major generals and above for commands in my time because their wives were a disruptive element that we simply couldn't stand. Now some of those general officers were pretty good commanders ... [but] didn't get commands because I knew their wives very well and didn't want them out there screwing up my outfit. Command is a team effort. You can't go out there without a wife, or with a wife who is non-supportive. All you have to do is look around you at the posts where you're having difficulty, where the Army Community Services, the Red Cross ... are sort of going along but not getting the attention they ought to get. You look at what the CG's wife is doing and you'll discover that she's not interested.

There is no way that some guy is going to go out and take command of an installation or a command and be able to look at all of the aspects of it that are important. In today's world, so many of the young enlisted people are married. And so there's a whole world of work that needs to be done ... to build a community. And some of that is women's work. Guys can't do it. Guys are not smart enough to do that or sensitive enough to some of the problems to do it. So, it's a team effort. Most of the good ideas that I ever had about how to improve the communities we lived in were *her* ideas. She was sensitized to the things that were making people unhappy and causing unrest and to the opportunities for improving the situation, I guess because she saw it all from a totally different aspect than I did. She always gave pretty good advice. Where I couldn't pay for it, she'd organize volunteers.

I've said many times that, behind every successful guy, there's a bunch of kids and a wife, each of whom has paid some kind of price for daddy's success. They've had a lot of fun. They've lived in a lot of different places in the world. They've made a lot of good friends. But, in terms of what their peers have been doing in the civilian world, I think the kids have paid a price. Still, they've gained something that nobody else has. Most of them come away from that experience with a hell of a lot better sense of dedication to the country and to the values that the military system still espouses. At the same time, in terms of school, educational opportunities, and a lot of other things, they've all paid a price.

I spent almost three years in Vietnam, three years plus, and it was at a bad time in this country. We had kids in high school, and it was a bad time for daddy to be away. They've all recovered from it fairly well, but you always have to wonder what they would have been sooner than they were if you hadn't been gone. And there was the trauma. You know, the street we lived on in Springfield, Virginia, the guy who lived down the street—who was a federal employee, as a matter of fact, the head of the Federal Prison System—used to send his kids up the walk to throw eggs all over our car, particularly when the windows were open, because he was anti-Vietnam. The kids see that, and there's no way to explain that to them. So the family pays the price.

Realizing that military life could be tiresome and stressful for families, Starry took special care of the married soldiers (especially the young fathers) who served under his command. Melanie Starry recalled that "there were a couple of times in the middle of the night when a young dad would come up and knock on the door ... and wasn't sure if he should be in the Army or not. And Dad would sit there on the front porch with him at Fort Knox and talk to him for hours. And that happened multiple times, where he would just sit there and talk to a young soldier who was saying 'What am I getting myself into? What I am doing here?' And my Dad would sit there all night, talking to him and trying to help him through it." Such was the rapport that Starry had with his soldiers.

While improving the quality of life for his soldiers, however, Starry also tackled the problems of how to improve their training. During his command of the Armor Center and Fort Knox, Starry introduced television training simulators to help tank crews sharpen their gunnery and maneuver skills. These television simulators, while bulky and primitive by today's standards, were the most high-tech training tools available during an age when computer simulators were either impractical or nonexistent. Starry also implemented master gunnery courses as means to turn the highest-performing soldiers into "technical gurus" for their respective line units.

In the midst of it all, Starry also had to contend with the Army's ever-changing modernization program. Prior to Creighton Abrams's death, he had successfully laid the foundation for the "Big Five" weapons systems. The process of developing these weapons, however, had been beset by design flaws and bureaucratic friction.

"Shortly after I arrived at Fort Knox in 1973," Starry said, "the ARSV [Armored Reconnaissance Scout Vehicle] prototypes were delivered for testing." The ARSV had been on the drawing board since before Vietnam. Now that the war had ended, the Army decided to fully resurrect the ARSV program alongside the requirement for an infantry fighting vehicle to keep pace with the Soviet BMP-1. "There were two candidates" for the ARSV, "one full tracked and one wheeled."

Starry wasn't impressed by either vehicle.

Having been straddled by the M551 Sheridan airborne, "I was extremely reluctant to buy into another uncertain program," he said. "We tested the candidates at Fort Knox and recommended the program's termination." In retrospect, however, Starry admitted that he should have kept the program alive and made recommendations to "fix" the vehicle. The Army's long-term solution, however, was the Bradley Fighting Vehicle—a single platform whose M2 and M3 variants were respectively modified for mechanized infantry and cavalry operations.

Early prototypes of the M2/M3 Bradley (then called the MICV, Mechanized Infantry Fighting Vehicle) were delivered to Fort Knox where Starry and others evaluated them during field trials. "Just on observation it was worse than the ARSV. However, having just terminated ARSV, we feared cancellation of another major program would eliminate TRADOC as well. So, it was decided to 'fix' the MICV by redesigning the power train, adding armor, mounting the TOW ATGM system, finding a suitable cannon and fire-control system, and including firing ports for mounted infantry. Hence the Army eventually fielded two versions of the Bradley fighting vehicle, one for infantry and one for cavalry scouts. However, neither model met the requirements. Recognizing the Bradley's shortcomings for fighting the central battle alongside tanks, despite the serious upgrades just mentioned, the vehicle was inadequate for the task. We then considered revising the XM1 tank [the M1 Abrams prototype] design to provide space inside for an infantry fire team, a concept similar to that of the Merkava tank then being developed for the IDF. Design change of that magnitude would have severely delayed the XM1 program, a risk we decided not to accept." As a result, the M2/M3 Bradley went into production. Although the vehicle performed well during the Gulf War and during the opening stages of Operation *Iraqi Freedom*, the vehicle remains a source of derision among many cavalry troopers and mechanized infantrymen.

On a brighter note, however, the XM1 program continued unabated and it addressed the documented shortcomings of the current M60 Main Battle Tank. Essentially an upgraded version of the M48 Patton, the M60 was the US Army's last main battle tank fielded before the Vietnam War. Although it was a marked improvement over its M48 predecessor, the M60 still had a high silhouette and a relatively low field endurance. The forthcoming M1 Abrams, however (so-named in honor of the recently deceased Chief of Staff), would feature a low profile and turbine engine powered by jet fuel. But time was of the essence to get M1 fielded. Indeed, by the early 1970s, the Soviets had jumped a generation ahead of American armor, fielding the T-62, T-64, and T-72 Main Battle Tanks. Plus, the new T-80 was on the horizon. Although the first operational M1s weren't delivered until 1980, the Abrams outclassed nearly every tank in the Warsaw Pact inventory.

In January 1976, Starry recalled that "I was comfortably rocking in my swivel chair behind my desk at Fort Knox one rainy afternoon when the phone rang and my secretary came bouncing in and said,

'The Chief of Staff of the Army is on the telephone.' And sure enough, he was.

I said, 'You're kidding me!' and she responded, 'No, no. He's on the phone.'

You know, I'd been a major general for almost three years at that time. I didn't know what major generals had to do to get promoted. I wasn't worried very much about that at all. So it was a bolt out of the gray afternoon sky. I'm sure General DePuy had a big hand in it." On the other end of the phone, General Weyand wasted no time:

"I'm sending you to the V Corps in Europe."

CHAPTER 6

Freedom's Frontier

V Corps was one of two US Army corps then forward stationed in West Germany. Headquartered in Frankfurt, its subordinate units included the 8th Infantry Division, 3d Armored Division, and the 11th Armored Cavalry Regiment (which had relocated to Germany after the Vietnam War). As it turned out, the current V Corps commander had been relieved of duty for a host of reasons, ranging from dereliction of duty to toxic leadership.

Fresh from his command at Fort Knox, Donn Starry seemed just the man for the job. In fact, General DePuy had written of Starry in the latter's evaluation that: "General Starry is the best school commandant in TRADOC. He has been the strongest commandant on the tactical side and on the technical side and throughout the scope of combat development activities. He has dominated the Armor School with his strong, brilliant mind a very practical yet technical bent."

Arriving at V Corps Headquarters in Frankfurt, Donn realized just how poorly the outgoing commander had performed. "He was the kind of person who thought he had it made with every promotion," Starry recalled, "but being a lieutenant general blew his mind. He took his private car down to the motor pool and had them weld star plate brackets on the front and back of it. Then he put [3-star license plates] in those brackets. So, in his Buick or Oldsmobile or whatever it was, up the road he drives, visiting his friends along the way with his brackets and the star plates on his private car. He went to Frankfurt to command." However, upon his arrival, this commander decided that he didn't like the house he had been given for his commander's quarters, despite the fact that this house was a virtual *mansion*. "It was full of antique furniture," said Starry. "It had been the American High Commissioner's house for a long time in the early days [following World War II]. The corps commander had lived there ever since." Instead, the pompous commander chose a home in Bad Vilblel with a portico over its circular driveway. "Over the little portico," Starry continued, the commander "had erected this large red sign, and I mean a *large* red sign. It was six or eight feet across and two or three feet high—with three big white stars on it. It was illuminated at night. Now here we are on an American kaserne in the middle of the German community, where the Germans [and] here is this obscene American with this insignia of rank over his door, floodlit at night. In addition, there is a big corps patch, made out of plywood, about six feet tall, sitting beside the door. It, too, was floodlit at night. He signed a letter certifying that he had to have his own furniture over there because of his position. He had a house full of the most beautiful antique furniture in all of Germany, but he had to have his own private furniture over there because of 'his position.' He turned all that stuff in to the quartermaster, and I don't need to tell you what happened to it—it disappeared … all the generals' wives in Europe had come and raided it. I spent a year trying to recover it. When he left the house, there was nothing left in it."

Starry reported to V Corps Headquarters with his trusty aide, Sergeant Norman, in tow. "My wife and the girls were still living at home," Starry recalled. Melissa was in her second year of college while Melanie was a rising high-school senior. Melissa welcomed the move as it presented an opportunity to study abroad. Like her eldest brother, Mike (who had commissioned as a Field Artillery officer and was also stationed in Germany), Melissa had enrolled at the University of Kansas. "When they [Mom and Dad] called me to tell me that he had gotten orders to go to Germany, I was like, 'Well, I think this is an awesome education opportunity, Dad.' They agreed, so I packed up everything at school and I went over with them to Europe for his tour with the V Corps. And that was the experience of my life. I can't begin to explain all the wonderful opportunities I had." Indeed, as a young college co-ed, Melissa Starry had the opportunity to see West Berlin, Luxembourg, and several other destinations on the non-communist side of Europe. She and her sister Melanie recalled several parties and functions where their parents were guests of honor. "In Europe," said Melanie, "they treat their military officers on the same level as a countess or count … like royalty. It was incredible going to these gorgeous castles and having dinner in estate homes that were built in the 1600s and 1800s."

But as the girls prepared to meet him in Germany, Donn Starry was trying to come to grips with the empty house that the previous commander had left him. "So Sergeant Norman and I walked into the house, and there's not a goddamn thing in the house—nothing. We broke out some sleeping bags and air mattresses and slept on the floor for the first week until the quartermaster could find some furniture of any kind to put in there." Starry ultimately relieved that quartermaster. "He was a civilian whom I had to fire for incompetence. If public executions were allowed, there would have been one."

Regardless, Starry was aghast at how toxic and presumptuous the previous commander had been. "He just came unscrewed and behaved like a blithering idiot." But the housing situation was only the beginning. Midway through his first week in command, the Corps G-3 came in and said:

"Sir, it's time for you to go and see the 'cutting edge' room."

"What is the 'cutting edge' room?" Starry replied, confused.

"Well, that's where we keep track of the maintenance situation in the corps."

Starry followed the G-3 into the room, but what he found would shock him. Flanked by a major, three sergeants, and two captains, this "cutting edge room" contained a giant side-lighted Plexiglas that had been built to resemble a Form 2715—the Army's standard form for completing Unit Status Reports. To his surprise, Starry noticed that *every* company-sized unit in the corps had lines and the columns indicating the readiness of each of their vehicles. "The company, battery, and troop phone numbers are up there," Starry noted, and whenever the previous corps commander found that a particular vehicle was "Non-Mission Capable," he would phone the company commander demanding an explanation.

Starry was not impressed. This was micromanagement on the worst level.

"What is the purpose of this?" Starry asked the G-3.

"Well, it's how the corps commander keeps track of the maintenance in the corps."

"What are the brigade commanders … and the division commanders doing?"

"Oh, this is the corps commander's network," the G-3 replied. "The heat goes directly to the troop, battery, and company commanders." Starry was beginning to see why the previous commander had been ousted so quickly. "As I recall," Starry said, turning to his G-3, "the corps commander is not in the 2715 reporting chain."

"That's right, he's not," said the G-3, sheepishly.

"What's the purpose of this, then? The *division* commander is responsible for this, and he reports it through another channel. We monitor those reports, and if he needs help, we can give it to him, but he is responsible for it. There is no provision for me to be a part of this. Why was it necessary in the first place?"

"Well," they responded, "the OR (operational readiness) rate was down."

"How far down was it?"

"Well, it was about 80 percent."

"What is it now?"

"It's about 56 percent now," they said.

Starry was incredulous: "You mean under this system it's gotten *worse*, not better? I'll tell you what, men. You have exactly 24 hours to get rid of this whole mess—this room, these people, this stuff, this reporting system, and the whole thing. And Major, I want you to go back to wherever it was you were before—captains, sergeants, the same thing. Get this whole thing out of here."

Leaving the "cutting edge room," Starry called every division commander in V Corps and told them, "You guys and the regimental commanders are in charge of the 2715, the AR 220-1 Reporting System … I don't want to hear any more about it. If you have a problem, I expect you to call me. If you don't have a problem, I don't expect to hear about it. The OR rate should run about 98 percent or better, and that's all the guidance you're going to get from me." Starry's guidance was met with a chorus of applause, "thank you," and a few sighs of relief. He had just ended a culture of hostile micromanagement. Within a few weeks, the V Corps' readiness rate began to climb. "It hit 98 percent, and it stayed there or better for the whole time I was in command."

Another relic from the previous commander was the poorly conceived training system he had implemented throughout V Corps. He had come to Frankfurt after relinquishing command of the 2d Armored Division at Fort Hood, Texas. The training system he brought with him was the same he had used at Fort Hood, whereby the division's units would rotate through a "stand down" period for maintenance and administrative tasks. At any given time, roughly one-third of the division would be in this "stand down" reset period. Reflecting on his predecessor's flawed training program, Starry said that "at a post like Fort Hood, where the facilities are crowded and the training facilities are limited, and given the circumstances of units in the States at the time, that may have been appropriate. But it was a totally nonrelevant training program for V Corps or for any deploying corps for that matter. It was something you shouldn't and couldn't do, given the mission. He apparently arrived with that document, the 2d Armored Division document, handed it to the G-3, and said, 'Implement that in this corps,' without ever going around to look … to see what the training situation was, what the circumstances were, and what really needed to be done."

Thus, Starry had to overhaul the training system. One of the first things he did was take his division commanders to their assigned defensive areas along the Inner German Border. "I took them out on the ground and made them walk around and describe how we were going to accomplish our mission," he said. This technique was known as the "terrain walk" and its tactical bent made the commanders envision where and how they would array their forces to defend against an Eastern Bloc aggressor. "I got General DePuy to send me several hundred draft copies of the new FM 100-5," Starry said. "We passed them out and made people use them."

But several of Starry's subordinate commanders were leery of the new manual and the Active Defense doctrine that it espoused. "Just to show you how people reacted to that," he said, "I had one brigade commander who had done a very unsatisfactory job of describing what his brigade was to do out there. I told him, 'Look, I gave you a copy of this thing. You're supposed to read it and do what it says. Why aren't you doing that?'

'Well,' he said, 'General, that's not going to be approved, that manual.' And I said, 'What do you mean?'

And he said, 'Well, it's not approved. It doesn't have the Chief of Staff's signature in the front of it … and I've worked in the Chief of Staff's office a lot, and I can just tell you that that manual is never going to get approved. You're talking about something that's never going to happen.'" Starry tried to maintain his composure. As it turned out, the Chief of Staff *had* approved the manual only a week before, "which I knew he would all along," Starry added. "So, I said to this colonel, 'Now here I am, the corps commander, and you are the brigade commander in this division, right? You understand that, right?'" The colonel answered in the affirmative. "I am telling you as the corps commander," Starry continued, "that this is the way we're going to fight the war here until somebody tells us not to. But you're telling me that you're not going to do that." The wayward colonel simply replied: "That's right, because it's never going to get approved. It isn't signed by the Chief of Staff of the Army."

By this point, Starry had heard enough.

"Okay, Colonel, I thank you for your opinion. I would like you to turn your brigade over to your executive officer. Your successor will be on station as quickly as we can find somebody to succeed you." Indeed, Starry replaced him that afternoon. "I got the new guy in and I gave him some instructions and turned the battalion commanders around. It was a good brigade after that. But here is a colonel in the United States Army, saying to his corps commander, 'That's bullshit, General. That's never going to get approved. Therefore, I ain't gonna do it.' That's insubordination!"

But insubordinate colonels and half-baked field manuals didn't get to the heart of the problem. As he walked the terrain of V Corps' defensive area, Starry became more convinced that he had to address the lingering threat of the Soviet's follow-on echelons. "One of the underlying purposes," he said, "of doctrinal revision was to try to figure out how we could fight and win when outnumbered." Yet even if V Corps could defeat the enemy's first echelon, Starry realized that he did not have the time nor manpower to "reset the defense" before being overrun by the second echelon. Hence, the fatal flaw of Active Defense.

"If you can win the battle up at the FLOT [forward line of troops]," Starry recalled, "what are you going to do about the second-echelon? Do you have enough left to fight that fellow, or do you have to … turn to the nukes? Well, the answer is, if you can get the forces deployed there in time, you can fight the second echelon." At the time, there were four echelons of Soviet ground forces between the Inner German Border and the borders of Russia proper. Even in a conventional (non-nuclear) showdown, Starry knew he would have to fight at least *three* of the enemy's four echelons.

But the problem, according to Starry, was that V Corps and its NATO allies couldn't even defeat the first echelon unless they could simultaneously destroy the follow-on echelons before they arrived at the front. Hence, Starry found his solution: destroy the enemy's follow-on forces before he has a chance to mobilize them.

But the only question was how to accomplish this and remain below the nuclear threshold. For as Starry found out, NATO didn't have enough tactical nuclear weapons to destroy the enemy's first echelon. Thus, NATO's front-line nuclear deterrent had no teeth: "even if you use nukes, you're not going to achieve success," Starry concluded. "You've still got to do something with the follow-on echelons. And the question is, 'Can you do that conventionally?'" The answer could only come with a revision of the Army's tactical doctrine. One way or another, Active Defense had to go.

Starry reasoned that NATO forces could destroy (or severely disrupt) the enemy's follow-on echelons through a chorus of intelligence, surveillance, long-range artillery, and tactical air support. Essentially, Starry would have to "extend the battlefield" and "attack deep." Integrating intelligence and surveillance would be the most difficult part of the task, especially given the "stovepipe" nature of the competing intelligence agencies operating within the European Command's footprint. Integrating air–ground assets, however, would be easier, but there was virtually no doctrine on how to synchronize Army–Air Force operations at the theater-level. Although Starry recognized these shortcomings, and the potential solutions, he was in no position to change the Army's doctrine … yet.

For comparative analysis and inspiration, Starry looked to the defensive plans of the Korean peninsula. Since the end of the Korean War in

1953, the US military had set up defensive positions along the DMZ, a deterrent against any further aggression from North Korea:

> If you look at the Korean war plans and at the way that battle turns out, there aren't that many echelons, and that's the secret. They're not looking at four echelons; they're only looking at about two. And someday ... about the 10th or 12th day of the battle over there, if the scenario unfolds along the lines of central tendency, the Korean and US forces are going to win that battle, and the war—unless someone else intervenes, of course. But the problem in Europe is just echelon after echelon and the growing strength of the Soviet conventional forces.

In fact, Starry knew that over the past 20 years the Soviets had taken great strides to improve the vitality their conventional forces. From then-current Soviet literature, Starry learned that the Communists themselves were struggling with the same problem he had outlined following his visits to the Israeli battlefields—"how to fight the theater-level war and win it without having to resort to nuclear weapons." The Soviets, according to Starry, had done a much better job of conceptualizing the problem because they weren't pre-occupied with threat of tactical nukes. "They have always believed that you could fight successfully at the theater level and win," Starry said. "Their impetus toward conventional development, improving their conventional forces over the years ... I think has occurred in large measure, if you read their literature, because they just can't solve that nuclear dilemma. So, they said to themselves, 'Okay, guys, we need to build a conventional capability that is so impressive and so overwhelming ... that all we're going to have to say to him is, "Look, don't do that or we will do this."' Nuclear weapons are not part of that equation."

Conventional wisdom, however, said that if the Soviets overwhelmed NATO's front-line echelons, the US would retaliate with intercontinental missiles, leading to what some experts had dubbed "Mutual Assured Destruction." Starry's response to the geopolitical experts, however, was simple: "I think that's a risk they're willing to run. Don't forget, they didn't start the conventional development ... until after they thought they had nuclear parity. And nuclear parity, in their view, is that they are just a little bit better than we are." Looking at the situation from his post in V Corps, Starry found no cause to argue. The incoming intelligence reports indicated that the Soviets had a comfortable margin in both theater-level nuclear weapons and intercontinental ballistic missiles. "Because of that baseline," Starry said, "they were willing to proceed on an enormous conventional growth program against a backdrop of a nuclear force with which they were comfortable."

At times, however, it seemed that Starry had more reason to fear spies and saboteurs than the Soviet Army. Indeed, one of the more problematic adversaries of Donn Starry was the commander of the Soviet Military Liaison Mission (SMLM). Established in the late 1940s, SMLM was created through treaty agreements amongst the US, USSR, and West Germany. Under the terms of this agreement, select members of the Soviet military were granted access to monitor NATO activities. The US had a similar liaison mission in East Germany that likewise collected data on Communist troop operations. The SMLM, however, "were not authorized to go out while NATO forces were on exercises, but the SMLM commander decided he would do it anyway." While scanning their defensive sector near the Fulda Gap, Starry caught the SMLM commander spying on the 3d Armored Division's maneuvers. Jumping into his command jeep, Starry grabbed his driver and aide-de-camp, and barreled down the dirt road in the direction of the snooping Communist. Alerted by the telltale rumble of the jeep's engine, the SMLM commander made a run for it. Starry, however, finally cornered the Soviet officer in a town near the border, where he was quickly detained by the military police—"embarrassing the heck out of the Soviet mission."

On another occasion, Starry and his headquarters were targeted by the Baader-Meinhof Gang, also known as the Red Army Faction. A left-wing terrorist group, the Baader-Meinhof engaged in a series of bombings, assassinations, and kidnappings in West Germany throughout the 1970s and 1980s. As part of their ongoing terrorist campaign, the left-wing militants planted a bomb in the parking lot of V Corps headquarters. Luckily, the bomb did not cause significant damage, but even after the fall of Communism, the Baader-Meinhof continued to terrorize the unified German government well into the 1990s.

Another problem for Starry was tackling a culture of low morale – the leftover resentment from Vietnam and the impact it had on many a soldier's pride. Some commanders within V Corps had never even *seen* their designated fighting areas, much less walked them. Recalling the errant brigade commander who had defied FM 100-5, Starry indicated that the commander's attitude had infected his entire unit:

> He had a lousy brigade. That was also the brigade in which I found a battalion commander who had never been to a general defensive position [GDP] before. The colonel didn't think that was important. The colonel himself had never been out to his GDP until the division commander made him go out because he knew that I was going to come and talk with him about it. *The man had never gone out there to figure out how his brigade was going to fight the battle.* I asked him about that before we had this other conversation. "Well," he says, "this isn't important to me. What's important to me are the statistics—the AWOL rate, the number of phone calls to the Dial CINC system, the 2715s—and we're having trouble in the motor pool, as you know from reading the 2715s—and so on. The community affairs are in bad shape. I've got more important things to do than to be out here doing this." There was a lot of that.

This aversion to training and readiness had even infected the higher echelons of V Corps:

> One of my predecessors in V Corps was a gentleman whom I'm told never left his office except to go to official functions. Essentially, he didn't prowl around in the motor pools, the training areas, the tactical deployment areas, and whatnot. He did it all by reading reports and writing memorandums to people … but I respectfully submit that you can't command a corps that way. You can, but it won't be a very effective organization. There was no focus on what they were supposed to be doing.

Meanwhile, drug abuse, violent crime, and desertion were on the decline, but many of the American facilities had become blighted and fallen into various states of disrepair. As the Army stripped its European divisions to feed the war in Vietnam, "the cost was enormous in terms of facilities, troop housing, family housing, and training areas. We simply didn't do anything with them. We spent 10 years building that back up. I'll tell you what, in the six years from the time I left in 1964 to the time I returned in 1970 to look at it again, *everything* had gone to hell in a handcart. The training areas, the family housing, the troop housing, the accommodations, the places where the people had to live and work had just gone to hell. That's unconscionable!"

Starry was further dismayed that none of the local commanders had taken any initiative to improve the condition of their facilities:

> It's one thing to have the barracks run down, it's another thing to do something about it, even minimal things. And my impression of them in the early 1970s was that they were sitting there on their asses, waiting for someone to come and do something. There was no initiative being taken at any level.
>
> My oldest son [Mike Starry] was an artilleryman and was in a barracks over there, one of the old German barracks from way back. As you know, they are solid old buildings, but they tend to get dingy-looking very quickly. He was an FO [forward observer] and battery executive officer with a subsequent tour as a battery commander over there, and I said to him one time, "Mike, why don't you do something with these damn barracks?"
>
> "Well," he said, "somebody else is supposed to do that."
>
> "No, no," I said. "You don't have to let the plaster fall off of the walls and just leave it lying there. Somebody can clean the damn stuff up, and you could patch the plaster. You can get the stuff to do that. You can have a self-help program down here and at least make your battery area look decent." I said the same thing to his battalion commander, who said, "Oh, no, we've been told to stay away from that. They're going to do it for us." So they were all sitting there waiting for someone to come in and fix them.
>
> Let me tell you something—I was over there in 1949, 1950, and 1951, and there wasn't any money back then, either. I mean, there was no money in those days. I remember when I was a lieutenant I put—and lieutenants in those days could ill afford to do this—about $25 a month into a fund that Lieutenant Patton and the rest of us kept to buy paint to paint the barracks. We actually bought the paint and the ladders ... and we bought those big old German bamboo sticks they used to paint the high walls. We bought that stuff and painted the damn barracks ourselves because we couldn't get anybody else to do it. Now I'm not suggesting that everybody ought to do that, but having had that background, I can testify that a little initiative will do a lot to keep a place clean, neat, orderly, and looking like a soldierly enterprise—even though, in general, it isn't as well maintained as it ought to be. But, you know, the engineers come and do grand things to a barracks—big plumbing, big heating repairs, and whatnot. But the simple little housekeeping things that you need to do to keep a place looking nice, looking soldierly and orderly, they weren't doing. *It was a lack of initiative at all levels.* They were sitting there waiting for somebody to come and fix it up for them. It should have been obvious for a long time that nobody was going to come and fix it for them. That's the thing I really objected to, the lack of initiative, just as there was no initiative in the battle-fighting sense.

A plan to renovate the barracks and facilities had begun a few years prior to Starry's arrival. By 1976, however, the program had only upgraded about one-quarter of the American facilities in West Germany. Starry, however, took great strides to keep the maintenance program an ongoing affair. "The thing that concerned me, even then, was that it wasn't enough just to fix them once. There had to be a program because, by the time we were finished with the program, the ones that we had done first were going to need redoing. There has to be a continuing program, and somebody needed to program that out." But Starry's crowning achievement of the facilities renovation program was paving the 11th Cavalry's motor pool in the town of Fulda. Indeed, since Starry's first tour Germany in 1949, the Fulda motor pool had been nothing more than mud and rocks on the top of a hill. "Nobody had the brains to go out there and say, 'Let's spend a little money paving the motor pool.' We finally did it."

Starry would command V Corps for only 16 months. "I was so busy as the corps commander that I really hadn't bothered to give any thought to how long I was going to stay." As it turned out, General DePuy was retiring and had tapped Starry to be his successor as the TRADOC commander. Finally, Starry would have the opportunity and the clout to rectify the doctrinal shortcomings he had seen in Europe.

Reflecting on his command of the forward-stationed corps, however, Starry recalled that it was, "all things considered, the best job I ever had." As a corps commander, he had fewer administrative tasks than his post command of Fort Knox. "If you do what we did when I was there [in V Corps], and spend your time worrying about tactics and training, it's going to be a super job. There can't be any better. I really had no idea what was to come next, if anything."

Starry's command of TRADOC, however, almost wasn't. For in the summer of 1977, he found himself in the proverbial "cross-hairs" of an angry Stars & Stripes reporter:

> I was invited to make a speech, the graduation speech, at Frankfurt High School in June 1977. So I did. We [Donn, Letty, Melissa, and Melanie] were busy doing a lot of other things, and I have to admit that I delayed thinking much about what to say until it was really too late to sit down and dream up anything very substantive. My oldest daughter [Melissa], who was home from college at the time, suggested that I drag out a speech that I had given at Fort Knox when she

graduated from high school. I thought it was a good speech at the time. The kids thought it was a good speech. So, I got it out, changed it a little bit … and gave it.

I talked to the graduates about four things: peace, truth, God, and the Class of 1977. With regard to peace, I said that it was a noble goal … but it is an elusive one. I told them that it would be as elusive in their lifetime as it had been in mine, and that they ought to think about that. I encouraged them to form an intelligent opinion about that because, although peace is a noble goal, they had to recognize that it is probably not going to be achieved. Truth—a fragile commodity that some people don't tell much anymore, maybe because it always seems to be unpleasant. But one of the important things in life is to have some personal opinion about that, some personal stance about telling the truth and being honest and candid about things. God—although the press some years ago tried to bury the poor fellow, He still seems to be alive and well. Whatever your religion … an attitude, an opinion at least, a personal decision about God and how that relates to life in general, and to you in particular, is important. I commend that to your attention. Class of 1977—what is the future and so on?

In trying to illustrate the problems of peace, I mentioned the fact that, while the world was in an unsteady state of peace at the moment, there were a lot of places in the world where peace was likely not to persist and that war could break out almost overnight. I used the Middle East and the Yom Kippur War as an example. I pointed out the fact that there had been several wars since the end of World War II. I pointed out the Sino-Soviet confrontation … and the fact that it had been—although it doesn't get a lot of publicity—an open war off and on for about 15 years at that point and that it was probably likely to continue. If not an open war, then it was some kind of a standoff. If that were to break out, it was difficult to see how other major powers, including the United States, could avoid becoming somehow involved in it, although perhaps not as active participants. It would be difficult to see how we could avoid taking sides. I stayed away from Korea, because this graduation came just shortly after the period of time when General Jack Singlaub had been relieved as the Chief of Staff of Eighth Army because he had disagreed with the Carter administration's position on the redeployment of troops from Korea. He didn't really come out and say he was against that. Somebody asked him a question, you'll recall, about what the Koreans thought about it. He said what the Koreans thought about it, and the reporter then asked him what he thought about it, and he said, "I agree with the Koreans." That's all he said about it, but a great furor arose and he was fired. With that as background, I elected not to say anything about Korea.

Anyway, a person who, it turns out, had been fired by several wire services, but who was still selling to UPI [United Press International] as a freelance writer and who taught journalism in the American University night classes over there, heard the kids talking about the speech. He was not present and did not hear the speech. Apparently, the kids thought it was a good speech, and he heard them talking about it. So, he called the headquarters and asked for a copy of it. He called my secretary as a matter of fact. And the secretary, because he called her directly, assumed that he had been through the public affairs channel and that they had okayed it. So she gave him a copy. He came and picked it up, for what purpose I really don't know. Somebody said it was to be used in his journalism class as an example of a good speech or something like that.

Anyway, he took out of context the description that I had made of the Sino-Soviet border dispute and filed a story that said that I had predicted that there would be a war between the Chinese and Russians and that the United States was going to get involved. Following on the heels of the Singlaub incident, that just blew up all over the place. I read the UPI story before it had been made public and had been printed. I took the speech, made a message out of it, and sent it to the President [Carter], the Chief of Staff of the Army, the Chairman of the several of my friends in Congress, and anybody else I thought would be interested in reading it.

The message read, "Here's what was said, and I followed the script very carefully. I think that the speech speaks for itself. I have no apologies one way or the other. I didn't predict anything." That, I think, tended to diffuse it a little bit. Then the issue became whether I had cleared the speech. Well, there was a big investigation about that. As a result of the investigation, it was determined that I had the best track record of any general in the Army for clearing speeches. I was rather meticulous about it. In that particular case, I had not cleared it because I had given the speech before. The PAO [Public Affairs Officer] at Fort Knox had gone through the process and had it cleared. As far as I was concerned, it was in the public domain. In fact, the script from which I read, with notes on it, at the graduation had the clearance stamped still on the front page. As I said, I did it almost at the last minute anyway and so it just never struck me that it was going to be necessary to re-clear it. After all, when you talk to a high school graduating class, you're really not talking about national policy, and I wouldn't think that it would be an appropriate thing. But that became the issue.

We were coming home anyway to go to TRADOC. I'd been nominated a couple of days before the speech was made, and of course that made it a big turmoil. So, we all got on an airplane and started for home. It was kind of a dismal departure situation because I didn't know whether I was going to be fired, asked to retire, cashiered with my buttons cut off, or whatnot. When we got home and landed in New York, someone picked me up, put me on an airplane, and I flew down to the Pentagon to confront the Secretary of the Army and the Chief of Staff, General Rogers. I left my wife and the girls in New York. General Rogers was engaged in what he called a large damage-limiting operation in which he was very successful. But I had some friends in the Congress whom I contacted to see how much damage had been done. I couldn't find anybody who was all that excited about it. By that time, Walter Cronkite had come on either a TV or a radio show of his. I had sent a copy of the speech to him. I had heard a tape of it, and Cronkite, in effect, had said, "I don't agree with everything the general said, but he has every right to say it. There is nothing in here that is as alleged in the UPI news release. He is not criticizing national policy or taking exception to the President's views on anything." In fact, he said, "I don't know what the President's views are about peace, truth, God, and the Class of 1977, because he has never expressed them. Therefore, you can't accuse this general of having commented contrary to the President's wishes, because we don't know what the President's views are." That diffused the whole thing.

By the time I got to Washington on a cold, rainy afternoon, the only person pacing the corridors was the UPI bureau chief in Washington, who was waiting to pounce on me as I came out. So, the Chief of Staff and I went down the back stairs, got in his car, and went up to his quarters, where Mrs. Rogers was kind enough to feed me dinner.

Although the worst of the ordeal was behind him, Congress still hadn't acted on Starry's nomination to command TRADOC, and "there was some conversation about whether or not I was going to have to go and testify," he said.

The Chief said, "Go on leave," so I went on leave. I went home to Kansas. By this time General DePuy was handling it. He called and said, "Go ahead and start for Fort Monroe, but we don't know how this is going to turn out." So we packed everybody up in two cars, the girls driving one and my wife and I in the other one, and hit the road. We got to Fort Knox and thought we could make Fort Monroe with that entourage. They [DePuy and his staff] called from Monroe and said, "Well, we're not sure that confirmation is going to come this week, which means that the Fourth of July holiday will intervene, so it may be a couple of weeks. The Chief of Staff doesn't want you anywhere near Fort Monroe, lest it be presumed by the Congress that we are acting on the presumption that they're going to approve this when, in fact, they're not. So you can't go to Fort Monroe." So I said, "Okay, here we are at old Fort Knox." So we unpacked the cars, put one of them in the garage, and set out to drink friends out of booze and eat them out of house and home, up and down Fifth Avenue at Fort Knox.

Late the next afternoon they called again from Fort Monroe and said—I think this was a Wednesday afternoon—"You have to be in Fort Monroe Friday morning. Confirmation is going to take place tomorrow or Thursday. The Chief is going to be on a little overnight vacation down at Fort Story, and he wants to come in and promote you into office on Friday morning at 9 o'clock."

I said, "Okay, roger that."

So I looked at the logistics situation. One car was in the shop and two rooms in the guest house were piled full of stuff. So, I said, "All right, girls, pack up your overnight kits, because we're going to get on an airplane and go to Fort Monroe." We left all the cars and all the stuff right there and went to Fort Monroe and moved into the guest quarters. I was sworn in on Friday morning as the TRADOC commander. As I recall we finally got the cars and whatnot all back together after about six weeks. But there were about 10 days or more when we really weren't sure whether or not I was going to be on active duty or driving trucks for a living.

Throughout the ordeal, however, Starry had the backing of General DePuy, General Rogers, Secretary of the Army Cliff Alexander, and even President Carter himself. In fact, after reading the speech, Carter allegedly said: "I think I'll make him the Chief of Chaplains instead of the commander of TRADOC." The full text of the speech appears in Appendix B.

Emerging from the debacle relatively unscathed, Starry assumed command of TRADOC and was promoted to four-star general on July 1, 1977.

CHAPTER 7

AirLand Battle

Throughout his command tenure at TRADOC, Starry focused on two priorities: re-packaging FM 100-5 with a better doctrine, and developing the concepts for "Division 86." The idea for Division 86 began with the Division Restructuring Study (DRS) under General DePuy:

> He and I were convinced that we needed smaller divisions … our convictions were confirmed by the command and control problems that we saw in the lessons of the Yom Kippur War, problems that started at the platoon and worked up through the division and the corps. We started work when I went to Knox in 1973. We started an investigation of how many tanks there should be in a platoon, in a company, and in a battalion, and how you could command and control those. With my foreign liaison officers, the Germans, the French, and the British, we met for several weeks looking at that problem. Each of those countries, of course, had a different organization than we did at the platoon, company, and battalion levels. We started that work in the summer of 1973 and, in the fall, came the Yom Kippur War. When [DePuy] left TRADOC, DRS was still ongoing at Fort Hood.

When Starry took over TRADOC, he wanted to make doctrine a priority. He knew that he needed to change Active Defense and codify the concepts of "deep battle" beyond the first echelon. "So, we needed another cycle of [FM] 100-5," he said, "and if I could reasonably expect to stay at TRADOC for four years or so, we might get most of that done on my watch. But first we needed to finish what General DePuy had started. So I went to Fort Hood to look at how the DRS field trials were doing."

To his dismay, however, he saw the that DRS trials were not going well. The reason for these lackluster results, he said, was because the high-tech instrumentation for validating field trials was not very well developed in those days. For instance, Starry pointed out an instrumentation system in which there were rotating lights on a pole on each vehicle:

> If your vehicle got hit by a signal from an attacking vehicle, that light went on and you were "dead." That was an imperfect system for a lot of reasons. One, the soldiers clearly didn't want to have their vehicles destroyed, so they learned quickly that, if they put a field jacket over the sensor, it couldn't receive the signal from the firing tank and they wouldn't get "destroyed." They would finish the battle … but soldiers, as they will always do, managed to circumvent the system. So, what I saw there was a trial in which you could not tell whether you were looking at better organization, better tactics, a better commander … or some combination of those factors. You couldn't identify what determined the outcome of the trial. So, after a lot of conversation … we decided to stop DRS. We closed the test down, finished it out, paid our bills, and just said we thought we knew enough now to proceed with structuring our organizations.

Of course, the "rotating lights" system described by Starry was the earliest incarnation of the Multiple Integrated Laser Engagement System (MILES), whereby tanks essentially played "laser tag" to sharpen their tactical maneuvers. At the time of writing, MILES gear remains a staple of Army combat vehicle training.

After terminating DRS, however, Starry gathered the training center commanders and most of his TRADOC staff together at Fort Leavenworth. "We met there … at least once a month, sometimes more than that," he recalled. "The purpose of those meetings," he said, "through 1978, 1979, and 1980 was to take what we knew … from studies and from the field trial evaluations, put all that together, and arrive at some consensus about what we ought to do about organization."

By necessity, Starry had to make Division 86 a priority because,

> we had a whole lot of equipment developments underway … ranging all the way from tanks to field jackets … and that was going to happen to us whether we looked at organization tactics, doctrine, or anything else. The question is, if all that stuff comes to the divisions of the Army, *what should the divisions of the Army then look like?* You have to begin anything, any development, of a new organization, new tactics, force modernization—which is what I am talking about—with some

framework of operational concepts. *You must begin with a conceptual notion of what you want the organization to be able to do.* Then you should design the equipment, the tactics, the organization, and the training system toward that goal. So the first order of business is to lay down that conceptual framework—how is the battle to be fought? To do that requires some analysis of the threat.

Thus, Starry began his Division 86 overhaul by asking for a "threat analysis" validated by the intelligence community. "It didn't make any sense to me to start a reorganization without first identifying the problem we were trying to solve. For, absent a certified definition of the threat, we could proceed with the whole reorganization, only to have the threat community [the intelligence analysts] come along and say, 'Look, you've got it all wrong.'" Starry knew that any threat assessment would include the Warsaw Pact—that was a forgone conclusion—but the Army had to be prepared for other contingencies. "So I asked the intelligence community, specifically the DIA [Defense Intelligence Agency] for a validated threat projection 10 years hence. In other words, *what could we expect the world to look like 10 years from now?*" The DIA, however, was hesitant to comply with Starry's request. Historically, they preferred to overestimate the threat projections rather than underestimate them—essentially, prepare for the worst but hope for the best. "Their reputations were at stake," Starry said, but "I finally tied them down to an eight-year projection. So, eight years from 1978 was 1986"—hence Division 86.

> There was nothing magical about 1986. It just happens to be the furthest-out year in which we could get a validated threat estimate. We agreed also to review that estimate periodically. I wanted to do it every three years; they [the DIA] wanted to do it every five years. I guess we never did settle it except to say that, as time went on, we would see what happened on the other side and make our judgment to revise on the basis of whether or not there was something dramatically new. In other words, it might not be wise to just regularize it and say three years or five years, but to do it on the basis of some significant event on the other side.

Ironically, within a decade, the Cold War would begin to thaw and the Soviet Union would be on its deathbed. "So, I saw Division 86, from the beginning, as an interim exercise between where we *were* and where *we wanted to go* with the next organization. It was never designed to be something around which we wanted to pour a lot of concrete and let that be it forever." Division 86 soon became a nested concept within

"Corps 86" and "Army 86" as a means of optimizing the Army's lethality and mission command capabilities. Thus, with a new nomenclature, and a defined eight-year threat estimate, Starry began fleshing out the concepts for Division 86.

Starry's work on Division 86 focused on the heavy division (armor and mechanized infantry) as the critical combat element for the European theater. Because the 1986 threat assessment identified the Warsaw Pact as the most viable adversary, Starry organized Division 86 against the backdrop of his doctrinal notion to disrupt the enemy's follow-on echelons.

But, as Starry admitted, the final product was a compromise. "General DePuy and I," he said, "started with the belief that we needed more, smaller divisions. To us, that meant three tanks in a platoon, perhaps no more than 10 or 11 tanks in a company, maybe 30 or 35 tanks in a battalion, hopefully fewer than that." In other words, Starry envisioned an Army that had bigger *companies*, but smaller *battalions*. He had derived this concept from the Israeli command-and-control model, which had produced great results during the Yom Kippur War in 1973:

> We had to compromise with Division 86 for several reasons. One had to do with the tank itself. The tank, the XM1 at that time, was undergoing field trials in the desert at Fort Bliss. We were having a horrible time with the power train. We couldn't keep the dust out of various compartments in the turbine. We were spending a fortune on air filtration systems trying to get the dust under control. So, the reliability of the power train in the XM1 was a big question when we sat down to decide how to organize. That was unfortunate, because it drove us to a *four*-tank platoon … and a bigger battalion than we thought we wanted in the first place. As it turned out, we solved—at a considerable expense, it's true—the turbine problem in the power train.

In retrospect, Starry admitted that, had the XM1 not been so problematic, he would have taken a hard stance on keeping a three-tank platoon and a smaller battalion footprint.

"There were compromises in the cavalry," he continued. "One of them was the divisional cavalry squadron, which we decided to turn into a reconnaissance and surveillance organization … for a lot of reasons it was an acceptable compromise at the time. But, in the end, we produced an organization that was acceptable to the Army because the center commanders had had a part in it, every one of them. I forced *them* to make the compromises. I didn't make the compromises and then shove [it] down their throats. They participated! If it didn't turn out the way they wanted it, they knew exactly why not." Nevertheless, each of the TRADOC chiefs were satisfied that their arguments had been heard. "We evaluated it, and everybody had had a say. All the arguments were out on the table."

The Army ultimately adopted most of the Division 86 framework for its heavy divisions. For instance, under the Division 86 reorganization, each division had about 20,000 men. The armored divisions had six tank battalions and four mechanized infantry battalions. The mechanized infantry divisions had an even split: five tank battalions and five mechanized infantry battalions. Within these maneuver battalions, the number of line companies increased from three to four. Division 86 also increased the size and lethality of the aviation and division artillery brigades. The Army retained much of this divisional framework well into the 1990s.

Starry foresaw, however, that the Army's divisional structure would eventually look nothing like Division 86. He was correct. Division 86 (and its Corps 86/Army 86 counterparts) eventually morphed into the "Army of Excellence," followed by "Force XXI," and ultimately the brigade-centric "Modular Force." Reflecting on Division 86, Starry called it an "unhappy compromise." He further admitted that "we knew it at the time, but perceived ... that we would evolve from [Division 86] directly into the next cycle of organization."

Almost simultaneously, Starry began laying the foundations for his new doctrine. "I believe doctrine should drive everything else," he said. "In this case, operational-level doctrine [corps-level doctrine] drove everything else. Once I understood the need to attack deep ... the imperatives of smaller tactical units became more and more stark. The fact that we needed to fight the deep battle—not just with firepower, but by going deep with maneuver forces as well, starting with attack helicopters, followed up by ground maneuver forces, much on the order that the Israelis did on the Golan Heights in October 1973"—highlighted the need for deep surveillance, deep fires, and command and control. "What I saw as the operational need for the next edition of doctrine, which of course became the 1982 original version of AirLand Battle, drove the whole Division, Army, and Corps 86 reorganization."

First, Starry called the new doctrine "Modern Armor Battle," then "Corps Battle," then "Central Battle," and finally, "AirLand Battle", as it sought to synchronize air–ground assets as a means of destroying the enemy's follow-on echelons. But whatever form or name it took, the forthcoming doctrine would be codified in the next edition of FM 100-5.

The existing doctrine of Active Defense, meanwhile, had been much maligned throughout the Army for two reasons: First, none of the European-based commanders thought the concept was feasible. Second, General DePuy had written the doctrine *without* input from the Command and General Staff College (CGSC) at Fort Leavenworth. This bureaucratic snub had angered many of the stakeholders at Leavenworth because CGSC had been the traditional conduit for writing Army doctrine. Excluding CGSC from the process had, therefore, created an even stronger tide of resentment towards Active Defense. Thus, to avoid a repeat of the bureaucratic resistance, Starry integrated CGCS into the AirLand Battle planning process. At the same time, Starry also returned doctrinal writing, as a whole, to the TRADOC schools. After all, Starry was convinced that if the schools didn't write doctrine, they could not effectively teach it.

The team that Starry ultimately employed to write AirLand Battle came from the Department of Tactics at CGSC. This team included bright young officers such as Lieutenant Colonel Huba Wass de Czege[10] and Lieutenant Colonel Don Holder. A Hungarian immigrant, Wass de Czege served two tours in Vietnam, during which he earned *five* Bronze Stars and a Silver Star for gallantry. He later co-founded the School for Advanced Military Studies (SAMS) at Fort Leavenworth. Holder had also earned the Bronze Star in Vietnam and would go on command the 2d Armored Cavalry Regiment during Operation *Desert Storm*.

Starting with the basics, however, Starry realized that his new doctrine had to take into account (a) the enemy's follow-on echelons and (b) how to fight outnumbered and win. To this end, Starry and his team of doctrinal writers "identified leadership as an element of combat power equal to firepower and maneuver, and emphasized the validity of training, motivation, and boldness. Success depended on the basic tenets of initiative, depth, agility, and synchronization. AirLand Battle sought to defeat the Soviet second and third echelon forces deep within their own territory before they could attack while simultaneously defeating the first echelon. To accomplish these missions, the doctrine proposed using distant fires and electronic warfare to slow, damage, and confuse the enemy in a deep attack, thus creating gaps for a lightning-fast counterattack by mechanized forces, supported by tactical air power."

But tactics and equipment were only part of the equation. Per the tenets of Starry's new doctrine, striking deep into enemy territory and coordinating air assets required *adaptive leadership* and *initiative* at the small-unit level. According to Starry,

> the history of the small unit battle—battalion, brigade, perhaps division—tells you it's possible to fight and win outnumbered if you know what you're doing. It takes a mindset on the part of the officers, senior ones particularly, that sees the advantages of seizing the initiative—of being willing to move around on the battlefield. Tough to do—if you're defending, you would be sacrificing much of the advantage the defender could make of the terrain. But commanders must learn to strike in some new direction, move quickly, seek the flanks and the rear. That's the kind of battle that they've got to fight. They must disrupt the enemy so that his follow-on forces cannot load up on the battle at the forward line of troops. I don't think it takes officers, necessarily, or sergeants, who are any smarter than they have been before. I think it does take an early widespread and comprehensive understanding of the battle concept—what we're trying to do and have to do to fight and win outnumbered, particularly in Western Europe. History tells us not to despair. But history also tells us that, if we're going to win, we've got to do some things very well. We've got to disrupt the follow-on forces in the enemy rear, fight the battle at the forward line of troops, and at the same time figure out how to do something else to completely disrupt the enemy's battle plan.

To this end, Starry drew inspiration from classical German doctrine. One German concept that Starry pushed into the doctrinal development was *Auftragstaktik* (mission-type orders). "This is the idea that subordinate leaders can change the mission within the commander's intent without having to ask for permission in order to obtain the objective." Another German idea that influenced AirLand Battle was *Schwerpunkt*—"combined synergy, fragmentation, successive operations and momentum, deception and surprise, within systemic maneuver. It emphasized both the logical linkage between concentration of effort and accomplishment of the operational aim, and the principle of directing one's own main strike into the enemy's principal operational weakness."

Starry also predicted that the next war would occur within what he called the "Extended Battlefield." Starry's concept of the Extended Battlefield "dealt with areas of the world such as Central Europe, the Middle East, and Korea which have relatively large numbers of modern and well-equipped mechanized forces that use Soviet-style operational concepts and tactics." Thus, the Extended Battlefield became the geographical basis for AirLand Battle. "The battlefield was extended in depth, time, and inter-service cooperation. First, it was extended in depth, with engagement of enemy units not yet in contact in order to disrupt the enemy's timetable, complicate his command and control, and frustrate his plans. This wrestled the initiative away from the enemy. The battlefield was also extended forward in time to allow leaders to plan attacks on follow-on echelons. It was this coordination both in space and time that defined the extended battlefield."

Attacking deep into this extended battlefield, however, necessitated a close synchronization of Army and Air Force assets—primarily in the roles of air interdiction and suppression of enemy air defenses. The Army and Air Force had a long-standing debate over the jurisdiction of air support roles, capabilities, and their respective weapons systems. However, to diffuse the inter-service rivalry, Starry worked closely with Air Force General William L. Creech, commander of the Air Force's Tactical Air Command. Throughout much of the Air Force's history, its combat aircraft had been divided between two commands, Tactical Air Command (TAC) and Strategic Air Command (SAC). TAC maintained operational control of the Air Force's tactical fighters and ground attack aircraft. SAC, on the other hand, oversaw the Air Force's strategic bombers (the B-52, B-1, et al) and nuclear strike forces. Starry and Creech worked tirelessly to outline and clarify the inter-service responsibilities for suppressing enemy air defenses. "The main question," according to historian Martin D'Amato, "was jurisdiction over the suppression of enemy air defenses close to the forward line of troops. The big problem was convincing the Army and the Air Force to cooperate with each other."

That rivalry, however, largely subsided on April 3, 1981, when Starry and Creech signed a joint operational concept produced by the Joint Suppression of the Enemy Air Defense (J-SEAD) project. "Under this agreement, the Army assumed primary responsibility for the joint suppression from the forward line of troops (FLOT) to the limits of observed fire, but it authorized Air Force crews to attack independently surface air defense points as targets of opportunity inside the fire support coordination line in accordance with certain carefully designed rules of engagement when such attacks did not interfere with the mission objectives. This was the first time the Army and the Air Force agreed on jurisdiction for close air support and interdiction."

On May 23, 1981, the Air Force and Army Chiefs of Staff approved the TAC-TRADOC agreement on the comparative allocations and responsibilities for offensive air support. "This agreement adequately established the Army corps commander's role in prioritizing targets for Battlefield Air Interdiction (BAI). The Air Force component commander apportioned his tactical aircraft to various roles and missions based on the combined or joint force commander's decisions and guidance. The key feature in this agreement was the Army recognition of Air Force management of its deep attack capabilities, and Air Force recognition of the corps function of locating and prioritizing targets for battlefield air interdiction."

Part and parcel of this Army–Air Force synergy was the development of the Joint Surveillance Target Attack Radar System (JSTARS). The idea began as two parallel programs within the Army and the Air Force to develop a capability for detecting and locating enemy armor far beyond the forward line of friendly troops. In 1982, the Army and Air Force programs merged into one, with the Air Force taking the lead. The result was an airborne, ground surveillance and battle management platform known as the E-8 JSTARS (essentially, a modified and militarized Boeing 707). The E-8 has since become a remarkable asset for detecting enemy troops, tanks, and air defenses.

Another gamechanger in the evolution of AirLand Battle was the introduction of the Army Tactical Missile System (ATACMS). A surface-to-surface missile, ATACMS could reach distances in excess of 100 miles. ATACMS was then incorporated into the new M270 Multiple

Launch Rocket System (MLRS), a tracked behemoth that satisfied the Army's need for a mobile, surface-to-surface, rocket artillery platform. Equipped with 12 ATACMS, a single MRLS could reach farther, faster, and deliver more firepower than an entire battery of self-propelled tube artillery. Upon its delivery in 1983, the MLRS was parceled out to Division and Corps-level artillery units. Thus, the MLRS provided a corps commander another means by which to achieve the ultimate goal of AirLand Battle—attacking deep to disrupt the enemy's secondary echelons.

After assembling his team of doctrinal writers, and laying down the fighting concepts he wanted them to use, Starry gave them a wide latitude to craft the new FM 100-5. The doctrinal writers sent him the drafts, virtually chapter by chapter, and he would return it to them with edits and corrections via express mail.

Meanwhile, Starry found an ally in General Edward "Shy" Meyer, the new Army Chief of Staff. Although Meyer was not directly involved in the formulation of AirLand Battle, he nevertheless lobbied Congress and the Department of Defense to support the new doctrine. "He then used the support he gained from AirLand Battle to help gain support for weapons acquisitions and coherent research and development programs." Another champion of AirLand Battle was Brigadier General Don Morelli. In fact, it was Morelli who had suggested the name "AirLand Battle." As the Deputy Chief of Staff for Doctrine, Morelli had been recruited by Starry to work closely with the Congressional Reform Caucus and solidify support with the Armed Forces Committee of both houses. In fact, Starry recalled that Morelli's persuasion and salesmanship won the support of Congressman Newt Gingrich, who had previously opposed the concepts of AirLand Battle.

Finally, in 1981, as Starry prepared to relinquish his command of TRADOC, the principles of AirLand Battle were pieced together and codified in the new edition of FM 100-5, set for release in 1982. As Starry described it, this 1982 edition was,

> a mature conceptual notion of how the battle ought to be fought. It deals with all aspects of the battlefield: the assault echelons and the follow-on echelons; the balance between firepower and maneuver that's necessary for success on the battlefield; the chemical problem; nuclear problems; and it's a much more

mature battle-fighting framework than we had at the outset. One argument against the 1976 edition of [FM] 100-5 was that it was in too much detail. In the 1982 edition, we backed off detail at the tactical level but added the deep attack, assuming that most folks understood pretty well how the battle was to be fought at the FLOT. The 1982 edition was a better-balanced description and more in the genre of what an FM 100-5 ought to be.

The new FM 100-5, however, was not without its detractors. For according to Starry, "the 1982 version was criticized for being too aggressive. A lot of this came from [General Bernard Rogers's] comments in Europe." After relinquishing his duties as Army Chief of Staff, Rogers had become the Supreme Allied Commander in Europe.

> From his comments I concluded that he simply hadn't ta ken the time to try to understand what was said in the book, and he was deathly afraid of anything that suggested that we were going to cross the East German–West German border. He contended that doctrine suggesting such a course of action was too aggressive—too provocative. My contention was that, given Soviet responses to our initiatives, we needed to let them know from the beginning that if they started something in Western Europe, then what they started was going to be decided on the basis of ground rules yet to be announced.
>
> If you left it uncertain in their minds about what you were going to do, cross the border or not, that magnified your deterrent capability considerably. In fact, it did.

Some former Soviet officers later confided to Starry that "it was the uncertainty in their minds about what we might do that made AirLand Battle so threatening." Furthermore, according to Starry:

> General Rogers and some of his NATO-assigned Germans believed that the purpose of the NATO defense was simply to restore the Inner German Boundary. Well, you could restore the boundary in a lot of ways. The best way would be to go across the boundary *and destroy the enemy in his own territory so he understood clearly that the boundary was not his to cross.* In fact, even as these objections were being raised, I was in communication with Chancellor Kohl and his people. Helmut Kohl had been Minister President of Rheinland-Pfalz when I commanded V Corps, a large part of which was stationed in his Lander. He and I had discussed the matter off and on for several years. The German officers were saying, "It's against our government policy." Their Chancellor was saying, "It's not against my policy. We may not want to talk about it too openly, but the fact is we've got to do it about that way." So, I think that criticism of the 1982 edition was unfounded; the critics simply did not understand what we were trying to do and didn't understand the enemy all that well.

As it turned out, AirLand Battle caused an even greater stir on the opposite side of the Iron Curtain:

> My personal view is, having read a lot of what the Soviets have written and having watched changes in their organization, equipment, and tactics, that we had a significant impact on them, In the armor–antiarmor business, for example, when we laid down Active Defense they did several things. They changed the timelines they gave their forward commanders—how long they were to have to get to their objectives. They had a very set routine about that. First echelon was to go here, and that was as far as first echelon was to go. Second echelon would come along and go here, and so forth. They changed those timelines and speeded them up considerably.

Apparently, the Soviets feared that if they did not accelerate their own tactical timelines, NATO forces would gain more time to establish their deeper battle positions with long-range antitank weapons, thus eliminating the chance of a Soviet breakthrough. One Soviet officer later confided to Starry that the Warsaw Pact armies had accelerated their timelines on *three* separate occasions:

> That is, they changed the timelines three times to speed them up. Further, they simply could not afford to disperse in the rear as their doctrine prescribed. In order to make the new times, they took to closing up tight … so they could get started quickly and make the objectives, even though they recognized that by doing so, they made themselves more vulnerable, not only to nuclear weapons but to longer-range conventional weapons. In Active Defense, they didn't see that we could attack deep. When Active Defense gave way to AirLand Battle, they looked to AirLand Battle and said, "Oh, my god, they've figured how to target us deep."
>
> And in the experimentation we did in trying to decide what kind of sensors we needed on JSTARS and so forth, you could see it. We actually went so far as to measure the [enemy's] dwell times in areas where they stayed before they moved … in order to make their timelines. And we built the targeting system in JSTARS against that set of requirements. Once they looked at what we were developing in JSTARS, and they understood ATACMS, they really got nervous. We're talking about being able to "see" 200 or 300 kilometers, and target at those depths. Then here comes a missile system that has nearly that capability, deep in their territory, and here they are all clustered up back there in order to make their timelines. And they got very, very nervous about that whole thing.

In fact, the then-current Soviet doctrine had been tailored to counter the concepts of Active Defense. But now that AirLand Battle had replaced

Active Defense, the Soviets realized that their doctrine had become obsolete. And it seemed they didn't have an effective answer to the problem of being targeted in depth. According to Starry, the Soviets were also nervous about the capabilities of the M1 Abrams and the proliferation of NATO antitank weapons. Indeed, the more antitank missile that lay along the Inner German Border, the harder it would be for any of the Soviet tank divisions to break through the Fulda Gap. "They realized," Starry said, "that organizationally, we were putting more antitank guided missiles into the infantry. No question about that. Organizationally, when the M1 came along, they looked at the smaller organization. They figured we calculated that we had that much more capability and we didn't need five tanks any more in a platoon, we only needed four."

However, the true testament to AirLand Battle's success was the overwhelming victory of US forces in Operation *Desert Storm*. On August 2, 1990, Iraqi forces under the command of Saddam Hussein invaded the tiny emirate of Kuwait. In response, the US led a military coalition of 34 nations to eject the Iraqis from the oil-rich emirate. Following a 30-day air campaign, US forces launched a ground war that defeated the Iraqi army (the fourth-largest in the world) in less than 100 hours.

Reviewing the ground phase of the operation, nearly every facet of AirLand Battle was present. American forces had fought outnumbered and won; they had a technological edge that allowed them to see and shoot farther than the enemy; they had "attacked deep"—targeting the Iraqis' follow-on echelons with tactical air and artillery support. All the while, American forces operated within a culture of promoting small-unit initiative and decisive action at the lowest level. The Iraqis, meanwhile, had styled their tactics and organization after the latter-day Soviet Army. Thus, the potential match-up of NATO and Warsaw Pact forces had, in many respects, played itself out in the deserts of Iraq. According to Starry,

the proof was in the VII Corps attack around the flank. That is exactly what we told them to do. Proof is in the whole thing. You have to do something about the follow-on echelons. The Air Force was able to do more than we had anticipated in AirLand Battle. They did it extremely well, and thank God for Norman Schwarzkopf and the single-air tasking order. I think we still have to resolve the issue of where the fire support coordination line is, because there are some people who wanted to fire artillery out there who couldn't because Lieutenant General Charles E. Horner [commander of coalition air forces] had closed them down. It was a mistake. Otherwise they did exactly what the doctrine said we were going to do.

We had to do something about the follow-on echelon so they couldn't come out and screw up the front-line battle. We avoided his strength. We took the initiative … at a time and place of our own choosing. We went deep enough in his formations. He was pointed the wrong way. Mike Starry [Donn Starry's eldest son, who served in the 1st Cavalry Division during the Gulf War] tells stories about driving up to these positions, and he said, "The guns were all pointed south. They were looking for the 1st Cavalry Division to come out the Wadi Al Battin [an intermittent river bed tracing the border between Iraq and Kuwait], and here we come on their right flank." He continued, "It is more fun to fire at the right flanks of the T-72s because they blow up easier." It was just masterfully done! Norman Schwarzkopf deserves enormous credit and so, especially, does Frederick Franks, the VII Corps commander. It always helps to have a corps commander during an operation who was present at the [birth] of the doctrine. Don't forget he was my exec when we were putting the deep attack [concept] together. One of his tasks was to find some of the technology to make deep attack possible; JSTARS was one such technology. So, he knew as much about that as anybody on the battlefield, and he did it superbly. Not because I had anything to do with it, but it worked! We got it done without killing a whole bunch of our own people. I don't think we could have done it any quicker.

[The Gulf War] all matched the little list of rules I used to use as CINCRED [Commander in Chief of Readiness Command]. What are you trying to do? What is the political objective? The President blocked that out very specifically, thanks to Brent Scowcroft. Do you have the force to do it? Can you get them there in time?—a little risky in this case. Can you sustain them once they are there? We did it. If you have a coalition, can you hold it together long enough to pull it off and keep the coalition members from wandering off on their own? The President did a superb job with that. Can you sustain public support in the United States long enough to get it done? And the best solution to that is to just do it quickly and get it done with. That is a lesson that we learned from the Israelis. I think the whole force just did a super job. I am just [sorry] I couldn't participate in it.

Starry was also quick to point out that American technology saved many soldiers' lives. Because the US equipment could see and shoot farther than any of its Soviet-made counterparts, the US suffered fewer casualties in the long run. "One of the driving ideas behind AirLand Battle," Starry said, "was the notion that General Abrams used to put forth all the time … that it is just damn foolishness on our part to send soldiers out there to do things that we should be sending technology to accomplish, instead of getting soldiers killed unnecessarily in the process. One of the great things that Norman Schwarzkopf did for us in the desert was to make the concept work, and we didn't have the casualties that we could have had. There is a great line from Shakespeare's *Much Ado About Nothing* that says, 'A victory is twice itself when the achiever brings home full numbers.'"

Battlefield victories aside, however, Starry saw a *greater* victory in the professional conduct of American soldiers. His son, Mike, having earned his commission in 1971, marveled at the professionalism and vitality shown by American soldiers during the Gulf War. Indeed, the younger Starry had been a junior leader during a time when apathetic, uneducated, and drug-addled soldiers had been the norm. Calling his father from the Gulf, Mike reported that "I was out watching a bunch of gun crews today … and I looked at those guys and thought, 'We are about as good as we are going to get.' I really hope the war starts very soon, because these guys have been together day after day for the last five months, the same guys doing the same job over and over. We've had a lot of ammunition to shoot … and these crews are really good. This is the best artillery organization I have ever seen. This is the first time I have really understood what you have been saying [about unit synergy, consistency of personnel, and railing against the replacement system in Vietnam]."

Reflecting on his son's remarks, the elder Starry opined that "I think one reason we did so well is because those troops had been over there for so long training together … and it obviously paid off. So, you have the case for unit rotation", as opposed to the individual rotation system that plagued Vietnam. Thus, both Starrys saw just how well the Army had transformed itself from the post-Vietnam rabble to the high-tech professional fighting force of the 1990s.

Starry relinquished his command of TRADOC in the summer of 1981, with no clear picture of where he would go next. At this point, he had been in uniform for more than 30 years, and he had begun to consider the prospect of retirement. "As commander of TRADOC," Starry said, "General Meyer thought I was a logical candidate to succeed him as Chief of Staff. But, in order to do that, I needed more joint visibility.

So, he persuaded me that I ought to take REDCOM [US Readiness Command]." Headquartered at MacDill Air Force Base in Tampa, Florida, REDCOM was a unified combatant command "whose primary responsibility had been deployment planning." Originally established in 1961 as US Strike Command (STRICOM), its assets included the Strategic Army Corps and the Air Force's Tactical Air Command. At the time, it also had geographic responsibility for operations in the Middle East and southern Asia. However, STRICOM was divested of these regional responsibilities when it was re-designated as the US Readiness Command in 1972.

Starry accepted the REDCOM position, but not without great reluctance. "At the time, I had several job offers, to include three or four college presidencies or chancellorships, which had been discussed or offered." A few European officers asked Starry if he would be willing to be the Supreme Allied Commander in Europe. "But," as Starry admitted, "they were not willing to go to the administration and say, 'We don't like General Rogers. We'd like for him to go away. We want you because you have done an awful lot of work with the Germans and the Brits over the years, particularly in TRADOC, V Corps, and at Knox as well.' I personally, and the organizations that I commanded, had a super rapport with the British and the Germans and also with the French. Because I had spent so much time over there and really looked on Germany as kind of a second home, I had a particularly good relationship with the Germans." To boot, General Rogers had long-standing reputation as a toxic leader.

> I would have welcomed the opportunity to be the Supreme Allied Commander. I thought there were some things I could do for Europe and for the Alliance. Same thing with the Chief of Staff job. I thought there were still some things that the Army needed to have done for it. The SACEUR [Supreme Allied Commander Europe] decision was made because General Rogers kept coming back and getting himself reappointed. Nobody ever raised a voice against that. The Chief of Staff decision was made by the Secretary of the Army without consulting with his Chief of Staff or with anybody else. Apparently, he never asked General Meyer or anybody else for a recommendation.

Starry assumed command of REDCOM in August 1981. At the time of his arrival, however, REDCOM had been the focal point of an ongoing debate concerning the evolution of the Rapid Deployment Joint Task Force (RDJTF). Conceived by President Jimmy Carter, RDJTF was to be an inter-service contingency task force. Ideally, RDJTF could deploy worldwide and conduct sustained operations without diverting forces from NATO or Korea. By 1980, RDJTF had grown to include the US Army's XVIII Airborne Corps, the 1st Marine Division, three carrier battle groups, and numerous tactical fighter wings. In light of the Iranian Revolution and the Soviet invasion of Afghanistan, RDJTF was given a regional "area of responsibility" that included the entire Middle East and North Africa.

At the onset of the Reagan Administration, however, Secretary of Defense Caspar Weinberger advocated turning RDJTF into its own unified combatant command. "When I went down to take REDCOM, my predecessor [General Volney Warner] had been very vocal about his disagreement with the decision to make a unified command out of the RDJTF." In fact, Warner had resigned and retired in protest:

> When I [Starry] was asked if I would take the job, I went to see the Secretary of Defense. He said to me that he could not understand why General Warner had been so vocal in his opinion about the unified command and that he couldn't understand why he wanted to retire in protest. They had offered him another job but he wouldn't take it, and Mr. Weinberger couldn't understand that. I said, "Your intent is to create another unified command down there, whether we need it or not?"
>
> "Well, yes," said Weinberger, "we're too far along … we can't back away from it."
>
> "I don't think it's a wise idea [Starry replied]. I don't think you need that other command. I also happen to believe that there are some things at Readiness Command you should be doing and can be doing quite apart from the RDJTF, missions that are useful and necessary in the joint area. If that's what you want done, I'll be willing to go do that for you, but I tell you that, in my opinion, you're making a mistake."

Starry thought the creation of a new unified command would be a needless expense. "If they'd looked at it carefully, they would have seen that all they were doing was recreating the Strike Command mission. [REDCOM] was perfectly capable of absorbing a little bit of an increase in manpower and recreating that other joint task force that Strike Command used to have for that very purpose—deployment to the Middle East. But, oh, no, they've got to have a unified command, with all the expense of officers, overhead, and the whole damn thing." After

being transformed into its own unified command, RDJTF became US
Central Command (CENTCOM) in 1983. Having forfeited its primary
mission to CENTCOM, Readiness Command was abolished in 1987.

Starry commanded REDCOM for only two years. During his relatively
brief tenure, however, he worked tirelessly to refine joint doctrine that
dovetailed into AirLand Battle. By the summer of 1983, however, Starry
had reached his 35th year of service and was revisiting the option of
retirement.

Although there had been muffled talk of Starry becoming the next
Army Chief of Staff, or perhaps the Supreme Allied Commander in
Europe, he elected instead to hang up the uniform. By now, he was 58
years old, had put four children through college, and was ready to enjoy
the "golden years" with Letty, his lifelong sweetheart. Donn Starry retired
on June 30, 1983, ending 35 years of active military service.

Epilogue

Even in retirement, Starry refused to remain idle. Upon relinquishing his command of REDCOM, Donn Starry joined the ranks of Ford Aerospace, first as the Vice President and General Manager of Ford's Space Missions Group, then as the company's Executive Vice President. During his tenure at Ford Aerospace, Starry was instrumental in developing command-and-control systems for manned/unmanned space operations for NASA and the Department of Defense. He remained at Ford Aerospace until the company's dissolution in 1990. Starry then served as Chairman of the Board for Maxwell Technologies and Universal Voltronics.

Although he retired for good in the early 2000s, Starry remained an active member of several nonprofit organizations, including the Eisenhower Foundation, the US Cavalry Association, the Army Historical Foundation, and the Washington Institute of Foreign Affairs. All the while, he and Letty enjoyed the company of their seven grandchildren. Donn and Letty were married for nearly 60 years until her death on January 4, 2008.

After his wife's passing, Donn Starry withdrew from public life as his own health began to deteriorate. Indeed, by the fall of 2010, he was fighting both the onset of dementia and a rare form of cancer. He passed away quietly on August 26, 2011 at the age of 86. He was buried with full military honors at Arlington National Cemetery on January 11, 2012.

Donn Albert Starry left behind an incredible legacy. From the throes of the Great Depression, he joined the Army as a young private, anxious to rid the world of Nazism and the tyranny of fascist dictators. He instead found himself on the front lines of the Cold War, staring down the Red Menace across the Fulda Gap and fighting Communism in the jungles of Southeast Asia. In a war where counterinsurgency, hearts and minds, and airmobile infantry ruled the day, Donn Starry was a champion for the often-shunned voices of armored warfare. Commanding the 11th Armored Cavalry, he showed what a highly trained mounted force could accomplish in the jungles of Vietnam. His was a command that showcased the classical tenets of maneuver warfare (and demonstrated their effectiveness) against an enemy who refused to abide by the so-called "rules of war." In so doing, he was instrumental in disrupting the enemy's supply system in Cambodia and showed the North Vietnamese that cross-border sanctuaries were not so safe.

Emerging from Vietnam, Starry fought alongside his fellow stalwarts as they rebuilt the US Army from its postwar nadir into the high-tech, professional fighting force of the 1980s and 1990s. Whether fighting to maintain the Army's end-strength, or improving the quality of life at Fort Knox, Starry always put his soldiers first. As the US began shifting its focus away from counterinsurgency and back towards the defense of Western Europe, Starry once again found himself in a position to influence positive change. Taking lessons learned from the battlefields of the Golan Heights, Starry channeled his intellect into creating a doctrine that could defeat the Soviet Army, or any other peer threat, while staying below the nuclear threshold. The resulting AirLand Battle doctrine solved the problem of fighting a numerically superior enemy by targeting his secondary echelons before the he could mobilize them. This ushered in a new era of joint Army–Air Force cooperation and, in many respects, set the conditions for the US Army's victory during the Gulf War of 1991. For these reasons, Donn Albert Starry will forever be a visionary leader and an innovator of modern maneuver warfare.

Appendix A

Starry on Leadership

By General Donn A. Starry (USA, ret.)

This appendix comes from Starry's leadership speech to the Corps of Cadets at Georgia Military College, delivered in August 1980. Within its passages are the principles and philosophies that guide an officer and his working relationship with the units he or she leads.

A famous American historian once observed that leadership is likely the most observed, frequently commented on, and least understood phenomenon on Earth. Leadership is many things to many people. There is a seemingly endless debate about whether it is an art or a science, whether it is inherited, or can be learned; whether it is the same in business and industry as it is in the military. There is little if any comprehensive understanding of why some people are so much better at it than others; of why, after so much study, writing and teaching about it, there are so many daily examples of failed leadership.

Military leadership is a particularly intriguing study, for, among other challenges, it must cope with one of humanity's most pervasive problems—the conquest of fear. Fear—apprehension in the face of the unknown—is a phenomenon which we all experience: fear of being wounded, or of dying in battle, is manifestly its [fear's] most difficult and ultimate form. Therefore, all of leadership's most difficult problems are elevated to new heights in the tasks leaders must accomplish in the profession of arms. That is why the military profession lays such by the study of leadership, by the training and developing of leaders. That is why we have schools to train leaders. For the leadership of men in battle is foremost among essential professional skills; its study, practice, refinement and improvement are closely woven into the very fabric of military behavior.

Unfortunately, it is all too often true that not every good leader rises to the top; nor do the less competent fall by the wayside as soon and as often as they should. The effort to understand all these apparent inconsistencies and contradictions has fueled the fires of debate about leadership since the beginning of recorded history, and probably before that as well. Therefore, it would be presumptive of me to try to have some last, or even more profound words on the subject. Rather, it might be useful to try to distill some observations drawn from a lifetime of service in the Army, and in industry, into a few useful thoughts.

One of the most successful infantry battalion commanders in the Korean War was then-Lieutenant Colonel Gordon Murch, commanding the Second Battalion of the Wolfhounds [27th Infantry Regiment]. He once described the infantry small unit commander's leadership problem as follows: On any given day, in any given infantry rifle platoon in combat, the platoon leader should consider himself lucky if he has as many as twenty soldiers present and fit for duty. Of that number, he can expect that some three or four will act if something starts. Not that they will do precisely what is set forth in the field manual, or the unit Standing Operating Procedures, but they will do something in a situation in which action is clearly required. As the elder George Patton once remarked, it is far better to do something "about right" and do it now, than to do something precisely correct, only too late. So, of about twenty stalwart souls, three or four are what Murch called "doers." Another half-dozen or more of the twenty can be expected to do nothing—go to the ground, not fire their weapons, be passively protective of themselves, virtually mesmerized by the action unfolding around them. Murch called them the "non-doers."

The remaining dozen or so of the twenty can be expected to follow along with whatever is going on around them. If one of this group is nearby and observes a "doer" in action, he too will become a "doer." If, on the other hand, he observes a "non-doer" in inaction, he too will likely become a passive non-participant. The most important task of the leader of this platoon, this microcosm of the entire establishment, is to somehow train up a platoon of "doers," or at least figure out how to get the "go-alongers" in the middle of the group to become "doers" in the first place. All this in the most difficult, confusing, frightening and complex set of circumstances imaginable. It would indeed be difficult to cast a more challenging situation. Yet leaders cope with it, get the job done.

How do they do it?

Guts, common sense, understanding soldiers, professional skill with soldiers and weapons, a sensing of the enemy, a certain feel for the ground, a little imagination, and some luck ... all these together in some combination, a combination which will vary with circumstances of the battle and the people involved; all these together lead to success. It is the ability to put these ingredients, and others, together in successful combinations that makes the successful leaders.

It has been interesting, for me at least, to observe that the percentages in each category—"doers," "non-doers," and "go-alongers," is about the same at almost every level of military command, and in industry as well. Indeed, the phenomenon is repetitive to the point of being virtually universal. One can ask then, if the challenge is nearly universal, then why don't we train our leaders against its surety? For ultimately success will reflect how well we have been able to teach people how to cope with that leader challenge.

Now it's also true that leader styles vary with personalities, and to some extent with the circumstances in which the leadership must be exercised—some differences from war to war, from enemy to enemy, even from battle to battle. But when all is said and done, battles are really won by the courage of soldiers, the quality of leadership they have been provided, and the excellence of the training soldiers and their leaders have been afforded before the battle begins. Therein is the total leadership equation: leadership of people by other people; by leaders who have trained themselves to overcome their own fear, and who know almost instinctively how to help soldiers overcome fear.

If one certainty remains with me after a lifetime of service to our country, it's that the faith is a true faith which brings soldiers to risk and sacrifice their lives in a duty they acknowledge. Having tasted battle, these warriors know only too well the cynic forces with which reason assails the human mind in time of such stress. They also know too well the conflicting vicissitudes of terror, victory, death, and even humor in battle. After fighting in Vietnam, I have also come to believe that war's message be more divine than profane. For war's ultimate lesson is that it demands soldiers, and their leaders, to bring their full powers to bear, stretched beyond any reasonable limit, to solve life's most perplexing problem—the conquest of fear. And war leaves the warriors and their leaders with the indelible conviction that man has an unspeakable something that makes him capable of a miracle, able to lift himself above the commonplace by sheer might of his own will; able to face annihilation, based solely on faith in his God, faith in himself … and undying faith in his leaders and his comrades in arms. The ultimate challenge of his leadership is to harness the strength of that warrior faith in the desperate business of battle.

On the battlefield, there are only four important values: candor, commitment, courage, and competence. These aren't in any particular order of rank, so let's just take them as I listed them. *Candor* is not a very strong word. In fact, it's not used very often. Too bad, for it means more than just "honesty"—it's also openness and simplicity. It is the primary rule governing battlefield communication between soldiers. The stakes are too high and time is too short on the battlefield to deal with anything less than truth, honesty, openness, and simplicity. It is no place to deal with "I'm OK; you're OK" status games, hidden meanings, subtle overtones, and conducting "What did he mean?" type of analysis.

Communication between soldiers concerns facts and effects. They must be clean, whole, and accurate. Candor is what causes units to become great units. The candor of the battlefield is why lies there are punished not with gossip, but with action. Make no mistake about it, the battlefield is the most honest place in the world.

Commitment is another word not used very often. In fact, we seem to be moving towards a society that is more and more reluctant to make a commitment. It means a sharing; an exchange of your beliefs for someone else's and vice versa. Soldiers make only a few commitments because their world is small—first to their buddies, then to their crew or squad and then maybe a little to their platoon. After that, their commitment to big units and to their nation is much less. There's nothing wrong with that; that's how it's always been. Their buddy and their squad or crew, that's what's important.

How does commitment start and grow? With candor, honesty, simplicity, and openness. That's what all soldiers look for in a buddy and in a leader. When they find it, they make a commitment. This builds trust, which in turn builds security. Isn't security what soldiering is about? Commitment is what's written all through the citations for the Congressional Medal of Honor. Throughout our lives, we are all asked for commitments, but the strongest commitment is made on the battlefield to buddies, to crews, to squads. The commitment there is backed by a life—there is no higher sacrifice.

Courage is a very much talked about value. So let's get something clear about courage … it's not the absence of fear. Everyone has fears, all the time, every day. On the battlefield they become right sharp. Courage is the controlling of your fear and taking a risk. Risk is the daily environment of soldiers, yet they alone decide how much risk they can endure. When they make that choice, they control their fear even to the point of total risk. Now why do they do that? Because they've made a commitment based on candor. Courage grows because of the growth of the other two values. Courage makes things happen and courage sees the actions through to the finish. Courage is the most simple display of candor and commitment. Courage is contagious and spreads rapidly. That's why soldiers will follow leaders into impossible situations. They recognize the courage of their leaders and it awakens their own courage—built on candor and commitment.

The last value—*competence*—is the oldest value on the battlefield. It's a central value that anchors all the others. In simple terms, it means the ability to do your job. On the battlefield, candor serves to explain the soldier's changing degree of competence. Courage flows from the trust and belief in your own competence, your buddies, and your leaders. That courage built on competence, makes a commitment.

The funny thing about competence on the battlefield is that you can't just talk about it. You've got to show it. On the battlefield, actions speak louder than words. Competence establishes who the leaders and who the phonies are. On the battlefield, the leaders and the led respect competence more than any other value except courage.

Now, having said all that, what does it mean to us? Well, if we agree that these are the prime values of a soldier on the battlefield, why do we change these values in peacetime? In times of peace, all these values lost their clarity and importance among all the other so-called "important" values. We agree that our Army must prepare in peace to do what we must in war. Doesn't it follow that we ought to use the same values?

How do we make a shift in war to these values? What button do we push? What program do we start? What book do we read? The answer is plain: Unless we practice and live these values today, they won't be in operation on the battlefield. If you think about these values, don't they make sense for all of us? In peacetime, we practice tactics, strategy, and weapons firing. We must do the same with our values. We must develop the candor to display the courage to make a commitment to real competence, now, today. We can afford to do no less, for the time is short and the stakes are high.

I thought I'd reminisce and share some thoughts on the Army from a perspective of a new lieutenant. Perhaps the following story will give you a hint of what I mean. Some newly-minted lieutenants were undergoing an oral examination from a hard-bitten colonel. Up and down the line he went, saying to each one in turn, "You are going to have to pitch a tent. What is your first order?" Under the colonel's frosty eye, lieutenant after lieutenant shriveled and fell mute. One attempted to answer, "Break out tent equipment," but was cut off at once. And then the colonel reached the class goof-off and low scorer in all things military, "Well, Lieutenant," said the colonel, "if you were going to pitch a tent, what would be your first order?" The lieutenant snapped to rigid attention and barked, "Sir, my first order would be my only order. It'd be: Sergeant, pitch a tent."

Now that young officer understood much more about the Army than he realized, and it focuses on the problem that faces every new officer when he enters the Army—how do you lead, deal with, handle, get along with your subordinate noncommissioned officers and enlisted men? When I joined the Army and reported to my first unit as a second lieutenant ... I was young, fresh, and slightly apprehensive. Most of all, I was bothered by the problem of acceptance by some very grizzled veterans of World War II, my noncommissioned officers.

The first platoon sergeant I ever owned, or to whom I belonged, was an old gent named Leonard Lucas. Let me tell you that the raw officer material I provided Sergeant Lucas to work with was not the best. Somehow or other, Sergeant Lucas got me started, and as my closest noncommissioned advisor, he exemplified the sergeants that we call the backbone of the Army. That statement is still true today; the sergeants are still the backbone of the Army, just as the officers are the heart of the Army. But the relationship has changed a little. The noncommissioned officers of today are more often than not young, skilled, persons, both men and women, with a specialized knowledge of their jobs. More than ever before, they are going to look to [young lieutenants] to provide a complementary knowledge. The sergeants provide the framework, the continuity in the unit—but they look to [the lieutenants] to provide the heart—the high ideals, the central direction. Don't misunderstand. The sergeants have these things too, but they look for them *especially* in the officers.

Now what does that mean? It means that, first of all, you've got to be very knowledgeable about your job when you join your unit. You can't afford to sit back and wait for professional skills to come to you by osmosis. It won't happen. Oh, the sergeants will be glad to brush you up on some fine details, but they expect you to have learned most of the skills before you arrive. Not only those [skills] that are equipment-oriented—gunnery, maintenance, tactics, and procedures—but also the important skills that provide the heart I spoke about—loyalty, integrity, honesty, judgement. These latter ones are what you must bring with you from the start. It's too late to learn them when you join your first unit.

The thing that can make a 30-year-old platoon sergeant and a 38-year-old first sergeant and a 45-year-old sergeant major—grizzled, tough, and strong—look up to, receive instructions from, and obey the orders of a young 21-year-old, sometimes fuzzy-cheeked second lieutenant is not altogether what the lieutenant is, but what he stands for. Call those things duty, honor, country; call them intestinal fortitude; describe them as intangibles. No matter how you label them, they are the heart of the Army. In the final analysis, they are what separate the army from a lot of other jobs and occupations and, in fact, make being an officer more than just a job.

When those sergeants see you coming, they see beyond the fresh young officer to the potential company, battalion, and brigade commander, and maybe even to a potential Chief of Staff of the Army. If the young officer has those intangible qualities I described and the tangible ones of professional skill, the noncommissioned officer is eager and proud to help him prepare for higher levels. It may surprise you to know that those sergeants keep on watching you throughout your service, whether you serve for a career, or just during your required obligation. They are proud, sometimes jealously so, of your achievements, and if you are successful, you'll hear from them, whether to wish you well or to remonstrate when they think you're wrong.

It may be unnerving at first, when you join the Army, to see your sergeants doing some things you haven't learned yet. "How on Earth can I learn as much as them so they'll respect me?" Even more unnerving is when your sergeant slips up behind you and says, "If I was the Lieutenant, I'd ..." Now there you are in a dilemma. Your ears are flapping, waiting for his guidance, and at the same time you're wondering who is running this lash-up.

Well, the best advice I can give you is to listen, but listen carefully, to what the sergeant says. Weigh it, temper it with what you've been taught, then make a decision. You learn from experience, both your own and those who have been that way before—your sergeants. You're foolish to ignore it. As General of the Army Omar Bradley said, "Good judgment is based on experience, and experience is based on bad judgement."

Remember your job as an officer is to command a unit. Your sergeants run it. The distinction is a fine line. You make the decisions—that's your job. The sergeants carry them out—that's their job. You decide—he runs. Don't overdo it, don't take the sergeant's responsibilities away from him, and above all, don't try to run the whole show yourself. It can't be done; a lot of fine but unsuccessful officers have tried and failed.

There is an angle to this business of command that you should know from the start. There is a corner of the Army called "Sergeants' Business," and officers have to help guard that corner—mostly from officers—to make sure that only the sergeants do it. It is all too easy to get into sergeants' business and lash around like a bull in a china shop. Ultimately, it's you, the unit, and the officers. The sergeants' business I'm talking about is the care, maintenance, and training of the individual soldier. That's the noncommissioned officers' primary responsibility, and your job as an officer is to support him in that effort, not to supplant him.

Now how do you do that? Well, the most important preparation is to be professionally skilled—know your job, whether weapons or office procedures … so well that you can teach him, support him, and answer his questions. You can't wait, like I did, for him to train you too. There isn't enough time and you'll detract from his primary responsibility—the training of the men.

Your job is to train the trainer to train the men. If that means acting as a problem-solver or front man to see that he has the tools or time or resource to do it, then that's what you do. You decide the standards and conditions and check to make sure his training measures up. But in between, you are to be supportive. Does that mean you're "second fiddle" on the team? Of course not. He'll know you aren't, you'll know you aren't, and most of all the men will know you aren't. Your role as a training leader is primarily at the unit or collective training level, getting the squads, crews, and sections to act together as a team. The reason is obvious. The sergeants are the first-line supervisors, and they're with the men most of the time. There are more of them. There is only one of you, and you can't be everywhere. So you must rely on them to do the individual training. You concentrate on the unit tasks.

Now let me tell you something that we've learned from studies that backs this up. Our studies indicate that technology—improved weapons, systems, etc.—add about 3 percent to winning a battle. We found that well-trained crews … add about 15 percent. That's fine, but the real shocker is that well-trained crews in well-trained units—the lieutenant's job—adds up to 25 percent. Some hypothesize even greater than that.

That last is officers' business, and that's what comes from making sure that sergeants do sergeants' business and officers do theirs. That's what will get you the quickest respect from your noncommissioned officers, when they see you recognize where the fine line is between their business and yours. Remember, be supportive of their efforts, prescribe standards, and check to make sure they achieve them, but give them the responsibility and the backing to achieve standards in their own way.

One note of caution: recognizing where the line is does not mean abdication of command of unit into two separate fiefdoms. You are still the commander, and if you approach the sergeants as I noted previously, they will understand it. Most of all, remember that the administration of discipline is in your hands and *must* remain there if you want to command. If you give up any of it, then you lose command. I'm not talking about the sergeant correcting a recruit or chiding a man for some uniform violation or weapon misuse. That's part of the sergeant's responsibility as a noncommissioned officer. What is real discipline is deciding who is restricted or if extra hikes are needed. The man who makes those decisions is commanding, and it must be you. If you don't, the men will quickly realize who is deciding and, when they do, you'll be left in the cold. Discipline is indivisible from command and you must administer it. It's part of the lore of the Army, and when you get to where I am, you'll see how easy it is to look back and say, "Yes, that's right. That's how it's done." Unfortunately ... some will have to learn the hard way through experience and bad judgements that will prove General Bradley was right.

Appendix B

Fifty Years at the Business End of the Bomb

By General Donn A. Starry (USA, ret.)

Starry wrote this unpublished article in the Fall of 2003—on the heels of the Iraqi invasion and Bush Doctrine of preemption. Throughout his career, Donn Starry saw nuclear weapons as both an asset and a liability. For instance, he saw tactical nukes as a force multiplier to conventional ground forces, especially following the demonstration at the Nevada test range in 1953. By the same token, however, Starry feared that an over-reliance on strategic nukes would erode the military's conventional capabilities—as was the case during the late 1950s and early 1960s. Following the end of the Cold War, Starry feared that nuclear proliferation from the Third World and non-state actors would destabilize the international balance of power. Furthermore, we wondered aloud how nuclear weapons would factor into policies of preemption.

The second great war of the twentieth century ended with a great bang—two great bangs in fact: one at Hiroshima, the other at Nagasaki. Those two great bangs heralded the onset of the nuclear age. It was to be an age of seeking answers to complexities of international affairs and warfare between nations that we imperfectly understood as we stood on its threshold. It was a world that became significantly more complex and lethal at new levels, reflecting militarized technologies unleashed in both "Great Wars" of the century. As is ever the case, new threats and new technologies demand/produce new capabilities, new strategic goals and doctrines, new and generally more lethal weapons systems, new force structures … and an accompanying requirement for training new generations of soldiers.

In the early 1950s, reflection on the two great bangs led to a scramble among the nation's armed services to understand what nuclear weapons meant to warfare in general. Thereupon, it was decided to conduct a series of tests; with troops on the ground, troops who would be exposed to the effects of nuclear weapons detonations … to better understand and cope with battlefield nuclear matters and remain effective.

In pursuit of that aim, in one of the early tests in a longer series, several thousand Army troops gathered at the Nevada Test Site on March 17, 1953 where, with troops hunkered down in trenches scraped in the desert floor, test personnel detonated a "nominal" yield nuclear weapon [20 kilotons]. It was mounted on a tower 91.5 meters above the desert floor, a height of burst which guaranteed with high certainty that the fireball would not touch the surface [and thus infect the soil with radiation]. For reasons unknown, the front trench had been dug at the precise distance from ground zero at which one could expect two blast waves—one in the air and one a precursor along the ground, to reinforce one another producing a much-reinforced blast wave at and beyond the trench—further outbound from ground zero.

In the trenches, troops crouched down waiting, listened to the countdown to zero … then, as the two blast waves merged, the front-line trench collapsed on its occupants. I was the aide-de-camp to an Army general who dutifully took station in the front trench. Having been present beforehand at two days of briefings on weapons effects, uncertainties of yield and other matters, and being quite junior in rank, it occurred to me that a rear trench would be a more appropriate site from which I might observe the proceedings. My general ruled otherwise, so I joined him in the front trench.

Once the blast wave passed, junior persons present devoted prompt attention to extricating senior persons from the near burial of the front trench. No serious injuries, lots of spitting sand and dust, bruised egos, but no casualties. Senior folk and enlisted aides were then invited to walk to ground zero to view vehicles, equipment, buildings … that had been arrayed around ground zero itself. There were found trucks and other light equipment badly scattered and damaged by translation impact with other objects, buildings exploded or imploded … equipment damaged or blown away depending on weight and volume, tanks crouching on the desert floor undamaged. Thereupon I congratulated myself on my branch of choice; for despite dire predictions to the contrary, tanks appeared to be quite safe places to be. In fact, I got in one, fired it up and drove it about—it worked just fine! From the perspective of that tactical walk, I concluded that nuclear weapons, at least those of the size we had encountered, would be quite useful at the tactical level of war.

En route to the home station at Fort Knox, my general and I compared impressions. Finally, he said to me: "We have just watched the beginning of a second revolution in warfare in my lifetime. In 1914–18, industrial revolution weapons, especially machine guns and artillery, drove horse cavalry off Western Front battlefields. This weapon [the nuclear bomb] will change everything we do—strategy, tactics, weapon systems, organization, training, education—everything." He was a horse cavalryman ... commanded a troop of horse cavalry in the 2d Cavalry in the part of the regiment that deployed to France, rode horses borrowed from the French, and in a brief skirmish was driven from the field by machine gun and indirect artillery fire. Between wars, he was a member of the US Olympic Equestrian Team and a distinguished dressage rider. He commanded the 2d Cavalry Regiment pre-World War II, presided over the disbanding of his horse regiment, became a Combat Command commander in the 5th Armored Division, and fought the war with great distinction. "You will be at the business end of this nuclear matter for the rest of your career," he said. "Think carefully about what you learned today; think hard about it, for there are some very tough problems here." His name was John Tupper Cole; he was a wise man—how right he was!

Once the in-theater Soviet political and military threat to NATO collapsed in 1989, there remained the Russian thermonuclear threat resident in the Strategic Rocket Forces. However, the Soviet collapse peeled back the barely hidden inner layers of the onion: increasing numbers of nations developing or seeking to develop nuclear weapons; growing militarization of the Third World, perhaps represented by the Arab–Israeli wars; and the growing threat of terrorism.

With or without acknowledging these substrata, it was considered in the United States that, since the major Cold War threat had changed ... perhaps there was also a need for revision of the nation's nuclear strategy, which in turn would call for changes in nuclear force doctrine, weapons systems, structure and organization, training, and education. So it was that a Nuclear Posture Review, reporting in 1994, set forth guidelines for revision of nuclear policy, strategy, doctrine, and elements of the supporting nuclear infrastructure. All this without defining a new national strategy for the changed world: thus leaving the open question—do nuclear weapons continue to be an essential part of the national strategy? If so, for what purposes are they to be used? Given those purposes, what weapon systems are required? From past experience, is there a requirement for a stockpile? If a stockpile, then is a test program necessary for insurance—for security, safety, reliability?

Since the 1994 Nuclear Posture Review, the national security strategy has changed once again … [calling] for preemptive operations against global terrorism. The US-sponsored attack on Iraq [in 2003] and presidential declarations that the US would undertake such operations unilaterally if necessary, has given rise to considerable uncertainty about what is meant by preemption. Noted by some is the fact that preemption has always been an option; counter to that is the embarrassing truth that we have never organized specifically to provide a viable preemption capability. Information collection capabilities and ensuing analysis … have been reactive rather than proactive. Lured by the siren song of modern technology aboard sensors in the skies, a long-ago Director of Central Intelligence opted to de-emphasize HUMINT, the human intelligence collection capability, in favor of heavy investment in and reliance on satellite-borne sensors. There is now more than ample evidence that not everything needing to be known can be learned from aerial platforms, space or otherwise.

So the questions of the day are: What are the operational implications of a preemption strategy? What are the requirements for information-gathering analysis? What weapons do we need? How should we organize forces? What role, if any, do nuclear weapons play in the new strategy? Are we obliged to consider the threat of the use of nuclear weapons, either as a deterrent (threat) or as an operational capability seeking to avoid the need to employ large conventional forces?

We are indeed a long way from the statesman-like goals of President Eisenhower's 1953 "Atoms for Peace" initiative. He was of course firmly in the tradition of what had become our successful Cold War strategy—a combination of containment and deterrence largely put in place and sustained by multi-national agencies: the United Nations, NATO, SEATO. Initiated by President Truman, that strategy subsequently was confirmed as bipartisan policy by presidents from Eisenhower, Kennedy, Johnson,

Nixon (with modifications), Carter, Reagan (with deviations), the elder George Bush to Bill Clinton. In that long span of years, preventative war and certainly preemptive war was virtually unthinkable. President Truman publicly rebuked a Navy Secretary for proposing what amounted to a preemptive war against the Soviets in order to compel them to peaceful cooperation. In his own autobiographical memoir, Truman wrote: "I have always been opposed even to the thought of such a (preemptive) war." President Eisenhower, once asked by James Reston, then of the *New York Times*, what he (Ike) though of preemptive war, responded "I don't believe there is such a thing." When the Joint Chiefs of Staff proposed to JFK a preemptive attack against Soviet missile sites in Cuba in 1962, Robert Kennedy, JFK's closest political advisor, called the idea, "Pearl Harbor in reverse ... for 175 years we had not been that kind of country and we were not to start now."

Now, we not only do not have a tangible Atoms for Peace Program ... but we possess a considerable arsenal of nuclear weapons designed as a hedge against the failure of deterrence and containment in the Cold War and against a massive attack on NATO Europe employing the operational concepts first set forth by Mikhail Tuchachevsky and his "deep attack" compatriots. Tuchachevsky et al would, conceptually at least, become the source of operational doctrine for war against NATO ... using Operational Maneuver Groups against NATO's defenders—preferably without nuclear weapons, but with them if necessary.

Today's nuclear perspective must inevitably account the reality that nuclear weapons (or other mass destruction devices) are the poor man's entrée into the rich man's war. Example: with proliferation of nuclear energy sources and the availability of fissile materials from reduction of superpower stockpiles, the means for achieving nuclear status are today neither as technically challenging nor as expensive as in times past. If financially less well-endowed Third World nations want nuclear or other mass destruction capabilities, they can have them at a reasonable price. If there cannot be found terrorists willing to deliver weapons or devices, delivery means are available on the open market, either in the form of ballistic missiles, or in scenarios like that in Tom Clancy's popular book *The Sum of All Fears*—now regarded as far less bizarre than when it was published a dozen years ago.

So, while President Eisenhower's Atoms for Peace vision remains a most attractive goal … it remains elusive at best. For it is now overshadowed by the need to consider the role of nuclear weapons in contingency operations, absent the thermonuclear standoff between superpowers which tended to de facto regulation of regional conflict against the fear of intrusion and subsequent confrontation between superpowers. Several years ago, before the Nuclear Posture Review, a Defense Science Board Summer Study addressed itself to the issue of "Weapons of Mass Destruction in Contingency Operations." I co-chaired that study. When we reported, several officials who had been party to the requesting process invited us out of their offices. For the study examined worldwide threats, available technologies, [in-stock] mass destruction capabilities, potential delivery capabilities, acquisition economics, and likely proliferation projections. Then the study turned to countermeasures: what is required, what is available, what programs are in place to provide what is required, and how long will it be before we can have a reasonable capability to counter a most likely threat? The study played requirements against extant Service Program Objective Memorandums [POMs], scoring where each service [i.e. branch of the military] stood at the time of the study and how it might stand at the end of the POMs five years hence. All services scored low, some so low that there was no score at all, a fact that ensured a non-hospitable reception. It was nonetheless a good, if frightening, study.

A half-century after meeting my first nuclear weapon head-on from the vantage point of the front trench … I remain, perhaps more than ever, a believer in the utility of nuclear weapons—especially in contingency operations. However, I am as well seized with the need to find a rational solution to the dilemma of how to contain nuclear proliferation … thereby avoiding a civilization-destroying, out-of-control consequence.

It is in pursuit of that latter goal that we have spent a shah's ransom making delivery systems more accurate, weapons fusing more precise … all in order to either reduce the yield required to destroy a target or to lift the nuclear threshold completely. But proliferation will proceed, rogue states will continue to acquire more destructive means to satiate the fires of their hate. Consider the 29-year-old Palestinian lady lawyer who quickly changed from business clothes to Levi's [jeans] and, in that costume, detonated 22 pounds of explosives in a belt around her waist in a market place, killing herself and 19–20 others, wounding scores; that misguided lady would have loved a nuclear device with which to vaporize herself and hundreds, perhaps even thousands of others, especially Americans. [Starry was referring to Hanadi Jaradat, a member of the Al-Aqsa Intifada who detonated a suicide bomb in Haifa, Israel, on October 4, 2003.]

Dredging the foregoing from the memory sump, I am reminded of the agonies that arose in the scientific community once the nuclear scientists acknowledged the destructive potential of what they had created. In the opening pages of the third edition of *A World Destroyed: Hiroshima and Its Legacies*, author Martin Sherwin reprints his own introduction to the 1987 edition of that book. It's called *Reflections on the First Nuclear War*. Reading that earlier first edition at the time, and given my own experiences from the "business end," I long ago concluded it highly unlikely that the nuclear cat could be walked back. Nuclear weapons *are*, and will continue to *be*. We therefore must contrive ways to somehow prevent modern civilization from destroying itself, leaving whomever might survive in circumstances akin to those speculated on in Walter M. Miller's fascinating 1959 novel *A Canticle for Leibowitz*.

We have lived, and continue to live, in a world of unintended consequences.

Given that, what to do?

1. There is an urgent need for definition of what is meant and required operationally by a national security strategy of preemption. There are at least two preeminent reasons for this. First, our information collection capabilities, despite modern surveillance technologies, are not yet demonstrably good enough to ensure that the truly important targets can be accurately identified. Second, and perhaps more importantly, given the growth of armed conflict in Third World contingencies, accompanied by growth in the number of countries who have access to nuclear weapons, it would be foolhardy of the United States to elect not to possess a viable nuclear option for contingency operations, be they preemptive or otherwise.

2. From that definition, there is a need to define a spectrum of nuclear weapons effects requirements and for weapons designed to produce

those desired effects in contingency operations—at the operational level of war.

3. Weapons systems—weapons and delivery means requirements for employment of those weapons in operational-level contingencies must be defined, followed by design, development, and deployment of new weapons systems.

4. There will be a need for verification testing of new weapons designs, and post-manufacture testing of weapons in stockpile.

5. There will be a need for definition of force structure and organization needed to field the new weapons systems.

6. Training of troops and education of officers for nuclear operations must be written into training programs and school curricula.

7. There is an obvious need to revitalize the existing stockpile—it was designed for a different strategy; it employed technology and engineering processes now possibly out of date; it is old and needs safety verification if nothing else.

8. Meantime, and by no means last in priority, an Atoms for Peace program must be pursued. For sooner or later we must learn to use nuclear energy for peaceful purposes instead of just blowing up the world. Indeed, particularly in the energy market, such a program may be our only hope for adequate energy as supplies of fossil and other fuels deplete at an increasing rate.

Graduation Speech: Frankfurt American High School, Class of 1977

By General Donn A. Starry (USA, ret.)

This was the so-called "controversial" speech that earned Starry a summons to see the Secretary of Defense and President Carter. Although a wayward American reporter had characterized the speech as inciteful and postulating a war with China and the Soviet Union, the Department of Defense concluded that Starry had made no such statements or suggestions. Starry was cleared of any wrongdoing, but the immediate publicity surrounding the speech nearly cost him his four-star rank, his command of TRADOC, and nearly forced him into retirement.

I thought perhaps we could spend these few minutes considering several things that seem to me to trouble your generation. You might not put them in the order that I do, you might not label them the way I do; but I think you'll recognize them for what they are—I'd call them peace, truth, God, and you.

Peace because a lot is being said about it. A lot of things are being done in its name, but it is and will remain an elusive vision through your lifetime, and so a perspective about peace is important to you. *Truth* because no one seems to be telling it much anymore. There is loss of confidence in the truthfulness of our government, in the integrity of elected officials, which is having an effect on our society; it will continue to do so through your lifetime. So a perspective on the truth is important to you. *God* because although the liberals have tried to bury God several years ago, the basic values of our society are still those of our Christian heritage. You will live the problem of the decline of these values through your lifetime, and so the perspective of God is important to you. And *you*, because this is your day. A day to pause a moment to consider who you are, where you are heading, and what you might carry along with you.

So here we go.

Peace is an illusion. The absence of peace on the world is, and always will be a fact of life. Conflict of some kind is a natural state of man—not so much in war, as competition, competitiveness—in economics, foreign affairs, in the quest by governments for goals for the governed. Conflict reflects the imperfectness of man in this world, and the perfectness of God in his universe. There will probably be war in your lifetime. The Soviets will continue to encourage and help their Arab friends try to eliminate Israel. Our country may not be willing to go to war over this, but to turn our backs on Israel would be very difficult, and preventing Soviet control of the oil resources of the Middle East would be almost impossible. The more critical the situation becomes, the more likely we are to respond with violence. In your lifetime, the Soviets will fight the Chinese, possibly simply continuing their ten-year-old border conflict, but more possibly in a major war. Difficult as it may be to see the United States becoming involved in such a war, it is likely we would do so once it became apparent that one or the other of the antagonists was about to win and gain absolute control of the bulk of the Eurasian land mass. On the other side of the conflict spectrum, intra-national war—that is, war within the borders of a country—will be more likely, as both the Soviets and the Chinese continue to export their brand of revolution. The question of how to intervene in such situations without violating the national sovereignty of smaller states, when and how to meddle in what is essentially someone else's business, is not easy to answer.

More nations will have nuclear weapons—just as India has recently. This just increases the chance that a deliberate or irresponsible act by some small nation could trigger a war between larger nations. Could a nuclear attack on Los Angeles arranged by the Communist government of Ethiopia be distinguished from a Soviet attack in time to prevent the United States from launching a retaliatory strike on the Soviet Union? No one knows.

And so peace will not come in your time. The only peace you can expect and the only peace of any value is peace of mind; peace that comes with understanding the imperfections of mankind and of having figured out how to cope with imperfectness. It is a peace that puts you as much at ease as you can expect to be with your fellow man and the imperfections of the world you live in. Ultimately the price of that peace of mind is a willingness to sacrifice something for it; for it is still true that nothing worth having can be had for nothing.

Truth is a fragile commodity. The true state of things is frequently unpleasant. That's why we don't tell the truth more often—to ourselves or to others. It's more convenient not to. Instead we rationalize our own imperfections and those of the world around us. If we work hard enough at those rationalizations, we soon believe them ourselves, and when we do, our grasp of the truth is a little less sure than before. Like peace, truth is an imperfection; its distortion in our world is a measure of the imperfectness of that world, and of the perfectness of God. For us there is no absolute truth; there are versions of what it is, bound up in the bias of those who observe and report. In your lifetime the truth will be harder to learn than ever before. The liberal press has adopted the adversary doctrine. They are not interested in the truth, only in the five percent or so of the news that deviates from the norm, which in an imperfect world is the only truth there is. Presumably they would be willing to muckrake around over every public administration just to see it fail, without concern for the consequences to the country. By someone's standards we are all less than perfect. If one wants to make an issue of imperfections, some reason can be made to attack every man who has held or could hold public office. The ensuing turmoil simply feeds into the hands of those who claim that our form of government is not viable anyway, and has not the right or hope for survival. Being objective is important, being skeptical is necessary, seeking after all the facts you can get is essential, in order to make reasonable judgements about what's going on around you, and what you should do about it. The price of truth is a willingness to ask difficult questions, knowing all the while that if the truth really comes in response, the answers will be equally difficult.

Several years ago, the liberals buried God. He wasn't important to them. They found their God in a liturgy which denies that anything—peace, truth, God, even life, is worthy of reverence. And because the Christian ethic is the very basis of our culture, Western civilization has been stricken with the cancer of declining morality. Just over a month ago, I stood in the Garden of Gethsemane, then walked across the Valley of the Dead to Golgotha, over the land where seething masses of people have struggled so many thousand years. It struck me that in the time of Christ, they had a problem not unlike ours. They found peace and destroyed it with war; they found truth and destroyed it with lies; they found God and hung him on a cross. The denial of God will continue in your lifetime. You will be called upon to decide about him, who he is, who you are in relation to him. Perhaps it's not all that important; many people live their whole lives without solving this problem, but I suggest that your life takes on meaning, that the greatest value of a life is to spend it for something that lives after it, that in the end you become what you are through a cause you have made your own. And if you follow that line of reasoning, deciding about the part God plays in your world is important.

And now what about you? This is your life. I've recited some unpleasant realities simply to challenge you to think realistically about some hard questions that face you. Thinking seriously about what I've said could make you want to drop out of society. You can't drop out of society and remain a part of it. Three hundred years ago, the *Bounty* mutineers did that and the society they created to replace the one they left came to be filled with all the disillusionments from which they had fled in the first place.

You are young and full of dreams. Your elders say you'll get older pretty soon, more mature, and then you'll be all right. Well, that's not quite right. Youth is important. It's important that you stay young. Youth is not a time of life, it is a state of mind. Nobody grows old by living years. People grow old by deserting their dreams. Youth is a quality of the imagination, a vigor of emotions, a predominance of courage over timidity, and an appetite for adventure opposed to the love of ease. Whatever your years, keep in your heart the dreams, the urge to challenge events, the unfailing child-like appetite for what's next, and the knowledge that the joy of life is in the living; that when you fail to live life to its fullest, you miss all the joy of it. You are as young as your faith, as old as your despair. So long as your heart holds dreams of hope, beauty, courage; so long are you young.

And so tonight you pass this turn in the road of your life, full of hope, full of dreams, full of anticipation for what comes next. I hope you will strive for and achieve great things. But remember, in many ways it's a far higher ideal to live an ordinary life in an extraordinary way, to serve an ideal amid the drab, humdrum surroundings of everyday life, and still retain a vision of the common man as a shadow of God.

And so your world goes out on every side, no wider than your heart is wide, and up above the world, your sky no higher than your soul is high. May the road ahead rise with you to new heights, may the wind be ever at your back, and may God carry you always in the palm of his hand.

West Point Founder's Day Speech: March 25, 1974

By General Donn A. Starry (USA, ret.)

Starry was often critical of his alma mater. He rarely attended any reunions and frequently opined about the Academy's relevance to the Army. Many of his critiques were vocalized in this Founder's Day speech. The speech, however, did not put him in the good graces of his classmates nor the old guard of West Point graduates present at the Founder's Day celebration.

Several important personages were invited to address this distinguished gathering tonight. I was not among them. All declined. In a moment of weakness early on, I casually said that if all came to naught, I would leap into the breach. So as a result of my casual promise, I appear before you tonight acutely aware of the surrogate nature of my appearance, and my relative position in the pecking order of those whom you would prefer to hear.

I'm also more than a little humble. I really don't know much about West Point today. A year ago, I was there as a member of the group making the annual Army general staff visit. Some things impressed me favorably and some not so favorably. Talking to cadets, I found their attitudes not unlike yours or mine as cadets. Indeed, not unlike the attitudes of their peers in ROTC units on campuses over the country.

And I suppose, too, I should be a little embarrassed appearing here to talk about West Point—for I've often taken the view that young men from colleges with sound ROTC programs were by and large better equipped to take their place in the society into which they graduated than were their West Point contemporaries. So, it would be kind of inconsistent for me to recite some conjured-up list of virtues that you and I could claim as alumni. And I promise I won't do that. And I won't talk about the institution today. Instead what I can do is offer some reflections on my years as an alumnus, one who has observed and served with other alumni, and what I have come to believe the whole thing might mean to us all.

Last year, I heard a distinguished speaker refer to West Point as the conscience of the nation. Now the facts really don't support anything quite that pretentious. West Point is not and cannot be the conscience of the nation; for it does not affect the nation strongly, consistently, and pervasively enough to be its conscience. The nation provides its own conscience—for better or worse—and one of West Point's perennial problems is how to cope with that changing conscience in the attitudes of its young men.

Some would argue that West Point has done a lot for our country; no question about that. Winfield Scott observed that but for its graduated cadets, the war with Mexico might have been a more prolonged affair. Samuel Huntington wrote that at one point, the institution had produced more railroad presidents than it had generals. However, others would say that there are mixed blessings here. During that war between the States, some [able] and inept graduates perpetrated both deeds of towering heroism as well as some acts of singularly monumental stupidity, and in the end, they all managed to be key actors in a drama that killed more Americans than any single event before or since.

One could argue that the 1898 war in Cuba provided the stage for some members of the Long Gray Line to demonstrate their ineptitude for organization and staff work. Engineers they may have been—organizers and [mobilizers] of armies they were not. And it was a civilian lawyer, the Secretary of War, who finally forced upon the reluctant martial dragons, West Pointers all, the [tasks] in education and staff organization that finally made a professional outfit out of the United States Army.

There are some who point with pride to the great names in our great wars as being the names of West Point graduates. Others would argue that fundamentally it was Leavenworth [Command and General Staff College] and the War College, not West Point, that produced the victors. And their ability to do the things that made for greatness, especially in

World War II, came not from their West Point upbringing, but from the disciplined academic excellence of Leavenworth and the War College. And to a large extent, that is probably true.

Now one would hope that all these accomplishments are within the scope of the need perceived by the Revolutionary founders when they heeded the course of their experience and created a military academy, and that blame for the shortcomings could be laid at the feet of something other than the products of our alma mater. But in any event, the great deeds of the country stand as kind of a mixed bag, and one would be hard put to find consistency in the argument that through some gray magic, West Point has done more for the country than say John Hopkins, MIT, Cal Tech, or even Slippery Rock State.

So what strange mystique have we gathered to salute here tonight? The comradeship of an evening gathered around the old school tie, hung from the neck of some favorite graying monument? To sing the old school song loudly, and to drink again from the cup of Duty, Honor, Country, and so go forth refreshed by the familiar comforting things we've clung to all these years? I'd like to suggest there's possibly more than that for us to think about tonight. And let me see if I can articulate it.

Someone has said that West Point succeeds only so long as it continues to graduate men of character capable of leading other men in battle. Now, like the earlier list of anachronisms, I'd have to observe that there are many characters in the Long Gray Line, but not all members of the Long Gray Line have character. And I need not expand on that for this audience.

But it is important to recall that while its engineer graduates were building railroads, tunnels and canals, and others were forming successful businesses, some men of character—names famous and not so famous—were doing the thing which is the vital center of the institution—leading other men to victory in battle.

And so it is this essential character that shines through; through our individual and collective mediocrity and human frailties … strong enough to make it worth noting, and worth seeking after. And it is because we have been involved individually and collectively in the process that has as its goal the building of this essential character, that we gathered here together tonight. What are the ingredients of this character—the larger legacy left us by these men and all the others? They are several:

> DISCIPLINE: Discipline of regimented action and the sure knowledge of the synergism of strength that flows from disciplined action.
> LOYALTY: Loyalty to a group dedicated to goals larger than the group.
> INTEGRITY: Integrity of men responsible for other men's lives in an undertaking vital to them all, to their Army, and to their country.
> COMRADESHIP: Comradeship of human beings involved in an endeavor in which their own lives are at stake, and ultimately the life of their country is at issue.

Now I know war is out of fashion; and so what's the use of all this talk of men of character who lead other men to victory in battle? Call them by what names you will—I submit to you that discipline, loyalty, integrity, and comradeship, which I have suggested to you as essential character ingredients, are our larger heritage from the past, and at the same time our bulwark of faith for the future.

Our country and our profession have always needed these ingredients. In the days when no other institution existed to provide leaders of character, West Point did. And so it does today; even though we have other institutions which can also lay legitimate claim to graduating men of character capable of leading other men to victory in battle. But the essential ingredients are still the same, and we need them today as we have in times gone by. We need them to remind ourselves that our relatively comfortable routine is but a little space of calm in an otherwise tempestuous world, and being so reminded, we may therefore be a little more ready for danger when danger calls.

We need them in this time of individualist negation, of cynicism, of seeking after personal wellbeing at any cost, of denying that anything is worthy of reverence. We need them to remind us of all the things the buffoons would have us forget.

I don't pretend to know what's true any more than I pretend to know the meaning of the universe. For truth is in the eye of the beholder, and the universe in the eye of the God. But in the collapse of beliefs, in the denial of the virtues of duty, honor, and country, there are two things I do not doubt. The first is that faith is a true faith that brings the soldier to sacrifice his life in an accepted duty, in a cause he imperfectly understands, in a battle whose plan of campaign is to him at least vague. The second is that character is essential to lead the soldier. That is built on the ingredients of discipline, loyalty, integrity and comradeship...based on his faith in the disciplines of his profession; based on his fundamental loyalty to the institutions he serves; based on his confidence in the integrity of his leadership; and based on the character of the men who are his comrades in arms.

Notes

1. All quotations in this book are cited from Starry's writings, oral histories, and government documents unless otherwise noted.
2. A "brace" was an exaggerated position of attention which required a cadet to push his shoulders back and recoil his neck to the point where his chin was nearly touching the base of his throat.
3. "Horsemen" signifies mounted soldiers who fought while mounted; dragoons were mounted infantrymen who rode into battle but fought dismounted. In today's context, a dragoon is analogous to a dismounted cavalry scout or a mechanized infantryman.
4. From the German word meaning "barracks," a *kaserne* was the typical term used to describe a US Army garrison in West Germany.
5. Sobel, Brian. *The Fighting Pattons.* Bloomington: Indiana University Press, 2004; Pg. 63.
6. ibid.
7. Pronounced "mack-vee."
8. Phillips, Donald V. *Across the Border: The Successes and Failures of Operation ROCKCRUSHER.* Master's Thesis for the US Army Command and General Staff College. For Leavenworth: CGSC, 1999. Pg. 2.
9. Citino, Robert. *Blitzkrieg to Desert Storm: The Evolution of Operational Warfare.* Lawrence: University Press of Kansas, 2003. Pg. 257.
10. Pronounced "vosh-de-say-guh"

Bibliography

Primary Resources

Interviews

Interview with Melissa Starry, February 2, 2014
Interview with Melissa and Melanie Starry, April 27, 2015
Interview with Mike Starry, October 17, 2013
Interview with Mike Starry, February 2, 2014
Interview with Mike Starry, March 2, 2014
Interview with Mike Starry, May 9, 2014
Interview with Mike Starry, March 28, 2015
Interview with Mike Starry, April 12, 2015
Interview with Sara Starry Rogers, March 14, 2014
Interview with Sara Starry Rogers, March 28, 2014

Archival Material

US Army Military History Institute, Carlisle Barracks, Pennsylvania
The Donn A. Starry Papers, 1939–1983. Archival collection consisting of 38 boxes. Contents include correspondence, organizational documents, clippings, articles published, speeches, office files. Topics include the Vietnam War, Vietnamization, 11th Armored Cavalry, V Corps, Training and Doctrine Command, AirLand Battle, joint doctrine, and Readiness Command.
The Donn A. Starry Photograph Collection. One box consisting of 314 photographs covering Starry's tenure as TRADOC commander. Many of these photos came from Dr. Brooks Kleeber, who was the TRADOC historian at the time. Many of these photos feature General Starry during his visits to West Germany, touring various German facilities and demonstrations. Others show various social affairs held by or in honor of General Starry both in the continental United States and in Europe.
Spruill, Matthias A. and Edwin T. Vernon. "An Oral History of General Donn A. Starry." *Senior Officer Oral History Program* (US Army War College: Carlisle Barracks, 1986). Spruill and Vernon, both lieutenant colonels, interviewed Donn Starry as

part of the Senior Officer Oral History Program. The interview was a graduation requirement for the 1986 academic year.

Publications and Government Documents

Sorley, Lewis, *Press On! Selected Works of General Donn A. Starry*. 2 vols (Combat Studies Institute: Fort Leavenworth, 2009). This is an edited collection of Starry's papers gleaned from the collections at the Military History Institute. This two-volume set also includes a photographic section and digital copy of Starry's book, *Mounted Combat in Vietnam*

Starry, Donn A. "Aviation—Part of the Armor Family," *US Army Aviation Digest* (June 1974), pp. 24–28

Starry, Donn A. "Combined Arms," *Armor* (September/October 1978), pp. 21–22

Starry, Donn A. "Extending the Battlefield." *Military Review* (March 1981), pp. 31–50

Starry, Donn A. *I Remember Them! USMA Twenty-Year Book: 1948–1968* (Minneapolis: Jostens, 1968)

Starry, Donn A. *Mounted Combat in Vietnam* (Washington, DC: US Army Center of Military History, 1979)

Starry, Donn A. "On Making Our Smaller Army a Better One," *Field Artillery* (February 1991), pp. 20–24

Starry, Donn A. "A Perspective on American Military Thought," *Military Review* (July 1989), pp. 2–11

Starry, Donn A. "Principles of War," *Military Review* (September 1981), pp. 2–12

Starry, Donn A. "Putting It All Together at TRADOC," *Army* (October 1977), pp. 17–19

Starry, Donn A. *Senior Officer Debriefing Report, 11th ACR, 7 Dec 69 to June 70* (Washington DC: Government Printing Office, 1970)

Starry, Donn A. "Sergeants' Business," *Military Review* (May 1978), pp. 2–9

Starry, Donn A. "A Tactical Evolution—FM 100-5," *Military Review* (August 1972), pp. 2–11

Starry, Donn A. "To Change an Army," *Military Review* (March 1983), pp. 21–27

Starry, Donn A. "Training Key to Success of Force Modernization," *Army* (October 1979), pp. 30–34

Starry, Donn A. *USMA Forty Year Book: 1948–1988* (Minneapolis: Jostens, 1988)

Starry, Donn A. and George F. Hoffman. *From Camp Colt to Desert Storm: The History of US Armored Forces* (Lexington: University Press of Kentucky, 1999)

Secondary Resources

Citino, Robert. *Blitzkrieg to Desert Storm: The Evolution of Operational Warfare* (Lawrence: University Press of Kansas, 2004)

Cosmas, Graham A. *MACV: The Joint Command in The Years of Withdrawal, 1968–1973* (Washington DC: US Army Center for Military History, 2007)

D'Amato, Martin J. "Vigilant Warrior: General Donn A. Starry's AirLand Battle and How it Changed the Army," *Armor* (May/June 2000), pp.18–22, 45–46

Doughty, Robert A. *The Evolution of U.S. Army Tactical Doctrine, 1946–76* (Leavenworth Paper Number 1) (Fort Leavenworth: U.S. Army Command and General Staff College Press, 1979)

Fehrenbach, T.R. *This Kind of War* (Sterling: Potomac Books, 2001)

Guardia, Mike. *The Fires of Babylon: Eagle Troop and the Battle of 73 Easting* (Havertown: Casemate Publishers, 2015)

Hoffman, George F. *Through Mobility We Conquer: The Mechanization of US Cavalry* (Lexington: University Press of Kentucky, 2006)

Jarymowycz, Roman J. *Cavalry: From Hoof to Track* (Westport: Praeger, 2008)

Kaufman, Aaron J. *Continuity and Evolution: General Donn A. Starry and Doctrinal Change in the U.S. Army, 1974–1982*. Graduation Thesis, Advanced School of Military Studies (US Army Command and General Staff College, 2012)

Kitfield, James. *Prodigal Soldiers* (New York: Simon & Schuster, 1995)

Leonhard, Robert. *The Art of Maneuver: Maneuver-Warfare Theory and AirLand Battle* (Novato: Presidio Press, 2009)

Phillips, Donald V. *Across the Border: The Successes and Failures of Operation Rockcrusher*. Graduation Thesis (US Army Command and General Staff College, 1999)

Romjue, John L. *From Active Defense to AirLand Battle: The Development of Army Doctrine 1973–1982* (TRADOC Historical Monograph Series) (Fort Monroe: US Army Training and Doctrine Command, 1984)

Scales, Robert. *Certain Victory: The U.S. Army in the Gulf War* (Fort Leavenworth: US Army Command and General Staff College Press, 1994)

Shaw, John M. *The Cambodian Campaign: The 1970 Offensive and America's Vietnam War* (Lawrence: University Press of Kansas, 2005)

Sobel, Brian M. *The Fighting Pattons* (Bloomington: Indiana University Press, 2013)

Index